To my wife, Amanda;
and to my girls, Nina and Marie.

And to my dad, my earliest source of inspiration:
I know you'd be proud of me.

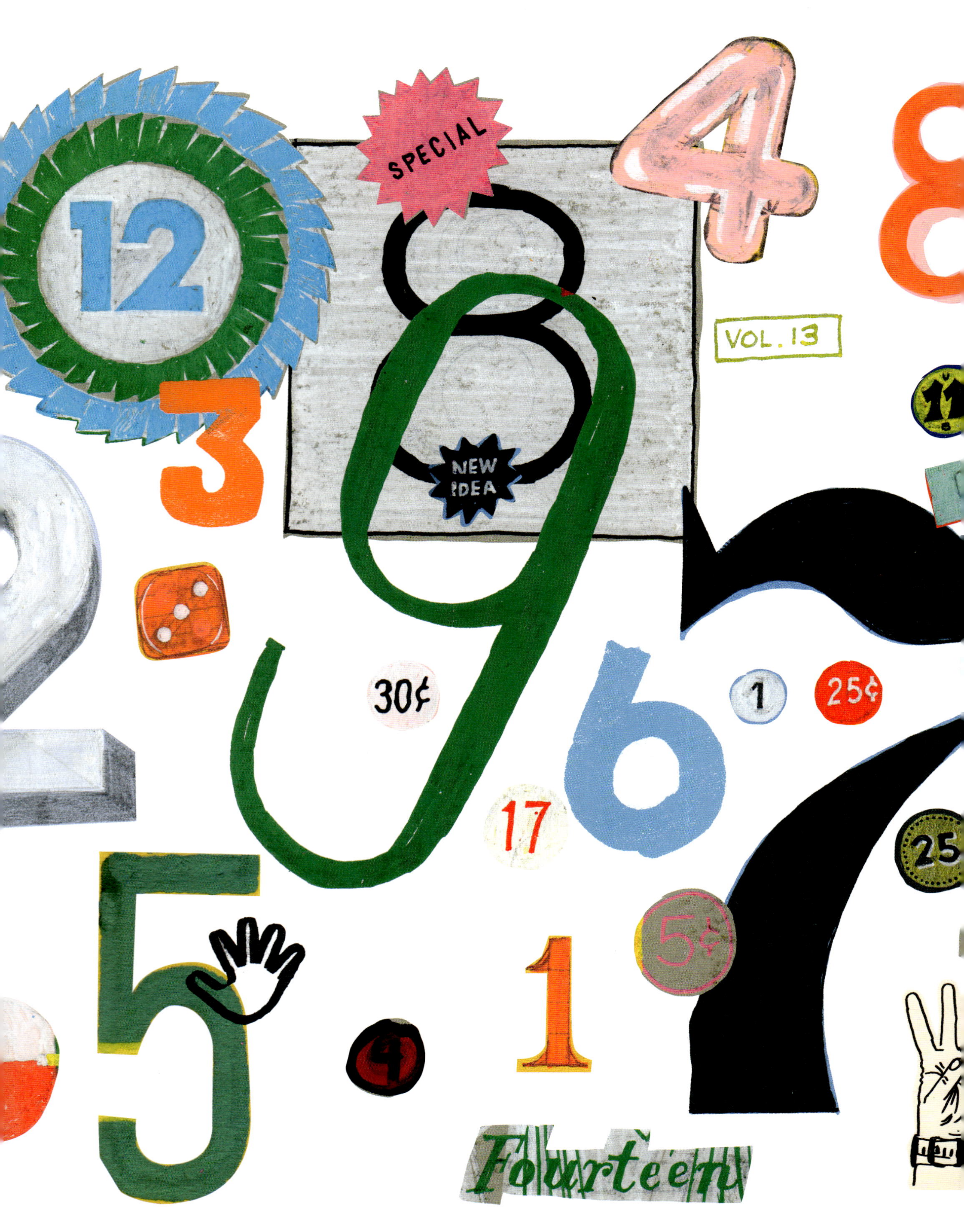

12
SPECIAL
4
8
VOL. 13
3
NEW IDEA
30¢
6
1
25¢
17
25
5¢
5
1
Fourteen

DRAW-ING IS IMPOR-TANT

How to Start a Lifelong Daily Drawing Practice

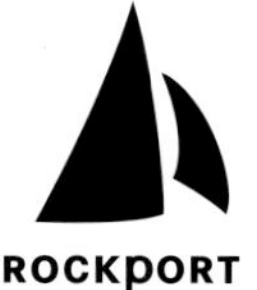

Tom Froese

Quarto.com

First published in 2026 by Rockport Publishers,
an imprint of The Quarto Group,
100 Cummings Center, Suite 265-D,
Beverly, MA 01915, USA.
T (978) 282-9590 F (978) 283-2742

EEA Representation, WTS Tax d.o.o.,
Žanova ulica 3, 4000 Kranj, Slovenia.
www.wts-tax.si

10 9 8 7 6 5 4 3 2 1

ISBN: 978-0-7603-9946-0

Digital edition published in 2026
eISBN: 978-0-7603-9947-7

Library of Congress Cataloging-in-Publication Data available

Printed in Guangdong, China TT122025

Design and Page Layout: Jolin Masson
Photography and Illustrations: Tom Froese except for the following: Mike Lowery: page 15; Sha'an d'Anthes: page 16; Lauren Nassef: page 25 (top right); Kate O'Connor: page 25 (middle right); Ray Fenwick: page 25 (bottom right); Bob Froese: page 29; Lauren Nassef: pages 30 -31; Brandon Campbell: page 32 (illustrations); Nicole Meyers: page 32 (photo); Gosia Herba: page 35 (illustrations); REI (trail guide): page 39; Tad Carpenter: page 41; Marcus Oakley: page 43; Nicola Thwaite: page 53 (bottom right); Ohn Mar Win: page 55 (top right); Mariah Knight: page 55 (bottom right); Jeanne McGee: page 57 (top right); Adam Ming: page 57 (bottom right); Flóra Gábor: page 67; Ez Pudewa: page 69; Janice Law: page 73; Adam Ming: page 79; Gosia Herba: page 81 (illustrations); Kasia Kaleta: page 81 (photo); Andy J. Pizza: page 89; Lisa Bardot: page 91; Lauren Hom: page 93; Tasha Goddard: page 95; Laura Fuller: page 96; Kimberly Carpenter: page 97; Ohn Mar Win: page 122; Chris Piascik: page 123; Tom Haugomat: page 124

CONTENTS

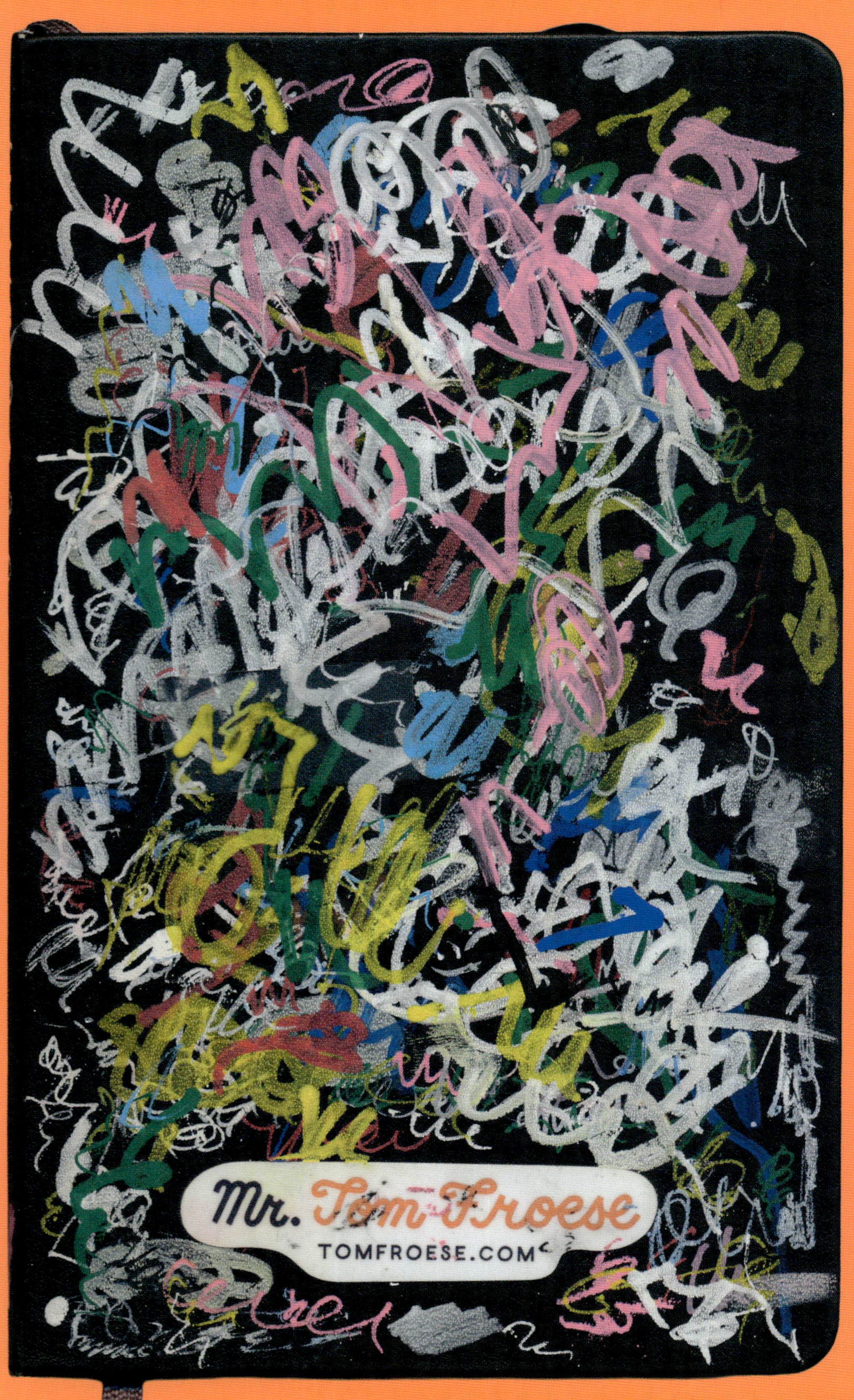
Mr. Tom Froese
TOMFROESE.COM

PREFACE

This isn't my first time writing a book, but it is the first time I succeeded. My first book was going to be about a totally different subject, but the harder I tried to write it, the less confident I felt that it was going to happen. I knew writing a book would be hard, but I didn't think it should be that hard. After much effort and deliberation, I decided to call it: If I were going to write a book, if a book were even a necessary endeavor for me at all, the process had to come at least a little more naturally.

Fast-forward a few years to when the vision for this book came to me in a flash. I was writing a small educational piece on daily drawing when I suddenly realized this was the book I was waiting for. If there's any topic I am passionate about, it's keeping a Daily Drawing Practice. Routine drawing and sharing has been consistent in my life since I started dreaming of a career in the creative industry. I believe it has been the one thing that has made any of my success possible. Drawing and sharing regularly has truly been the foundation of my success—first as a designer, then as an illustrator and teacher, and now, as a writer.

As someone who's struggled at times to keep a daily drawing habit, I knew there were many others out there who, like me, wanted to draw more but couldn't for various reasons. But after a very motivating incident in my own life, I found a reason to start daily drawing again (*see Interlude III: The New Year's Resolution, page 82*)—and sharing on a little Instagram account called @drawingisimportant. Not only am I still going, but since then, I've seen so much creative growth and so many new opportunities that otherwise would not have been possible.

Within a few weeks of the New Year's Resolution, a fledgling sketchbook company called Uglybooks reached out to me about trying out their new product—little pocket-size sketchbooks with deeply colored pages. I mention this because of how this changed my Daily Drawing Practice forever. The pages aren't great for traditional pencil drawing, but they're perfect for bolder media like paint pens and Sharpies. Discovering this as I tested out my first Uglybooks sketchbook opened me up to a whole new world of drawing beyond the pencil—which in turn has profoundly influenced my personal and professional work. I fell so much in love with daily drawing that I knew I had to make a class about it, which then became the namesake for this book. Since then, thousands of students have been able to pick up their pencils and their Daily Drawing Practices—some after years on the sidelines, and many for the first time.

Looking back, it's hard to believe I overlooked this topic in my first book attempt. Then again, my approach to drawing as a well-defined practice didn't shape up until more recently. Hindsight is 20/20, as they say, and so many of the ideas I'm sharing in this book would not be possible without the ensuing few years of my Daily Drawing Practice, especially since teaching a class on it. Now, I said earlier that the idea for this book came to me in a flash, but that's not exactly true. Like most creative endeavors, the aha moment is really just the result of a much longer history of effort and serendipity. This is a huge reason I am such a proponent of daily drawing, and this is exactly how it works: slowly and steadily, with long-term results after a sustained, intentional effort.

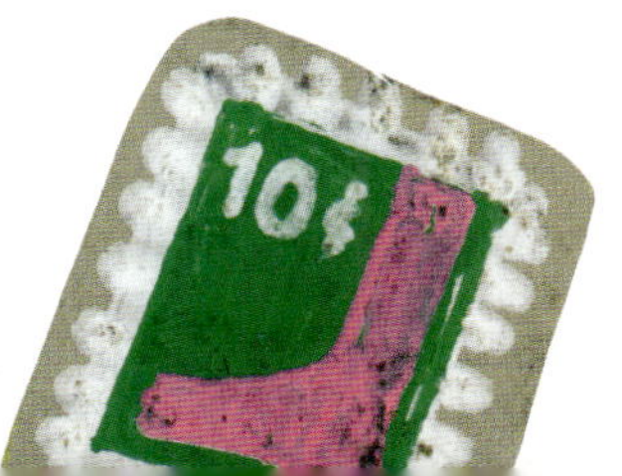

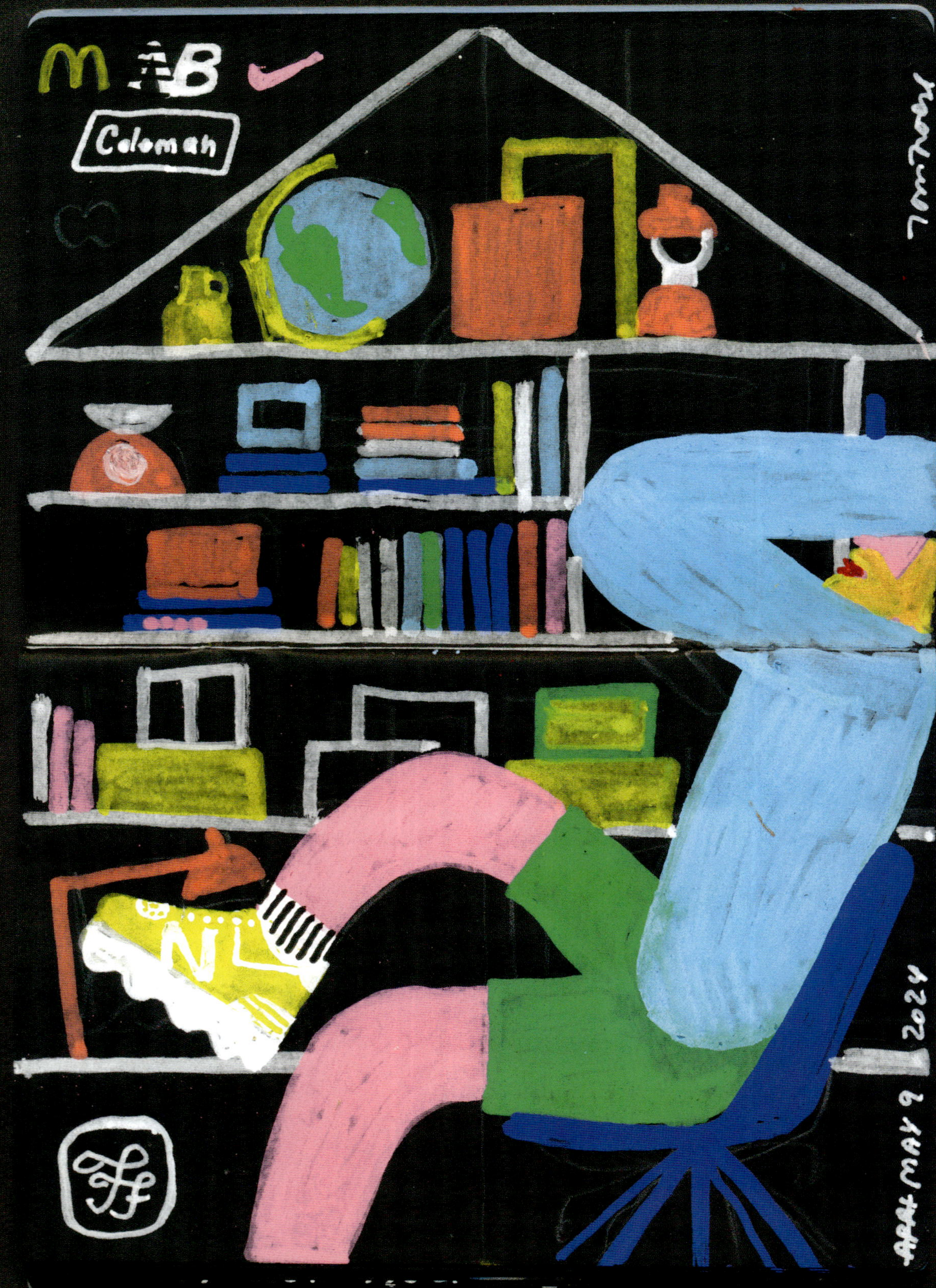
Coleman
MAY 9 2024

INTRODUCTION

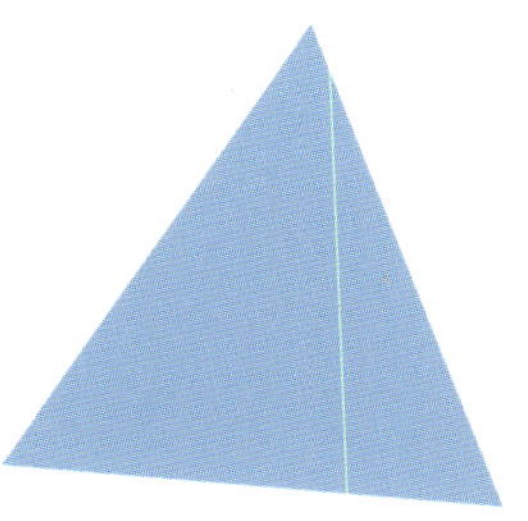

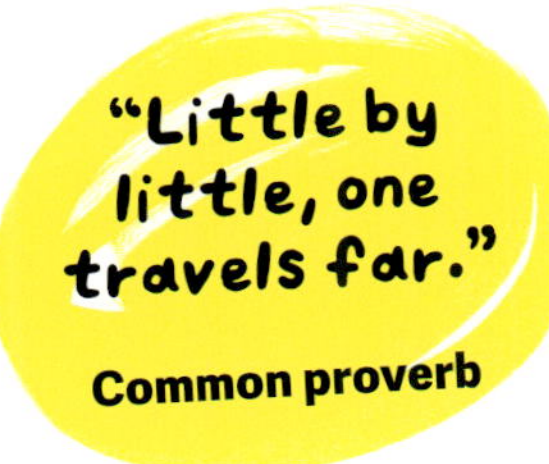

A Daily Drawing Practice is exactly what it sounds like: It's the practice of drawing every day. All three words here are key: "Daily" means that you're doing it every day, or at least regularly. "Drawing" means you're actually putting pencil (or whichever tool you prefer) to paper. And "Practice" means you're doing it with the intention of growth and development of some sort. Perhaps one of these words scares you most: Perhaps the idea of daily drawing excites you, but the thought of actually doing it seems impossible—and calling it a practice seems too serious. Or perhaps you'd love to have a Daily Creative Practice, but it's the drawing part that you're not so sure of.

This is just a wild guess, but I imagine you'd like to draw more, or you feel like you should be drawing more—but something you can't put your finger on is getting in your way. Ironically, we all drew as kids, and nobody had to tell us to do it, nor did we feel guilty about not doing it. We just did it. While some of us are lucky enough to naturally "just want to draw," many lose this instinct and find it harder to get back into the habit later in life, even if the desire to draw grows stronger. Sometimes wanting to do something isn't enough to get us to go and do it—we grown-ups often need more convincing. In this book, I aim to help you find the best reasons—your reasons—for drawing more regularly and drawing more on purpose.

In spite of this book's title, I'm not going to spend much time convincing you that drawing is important. I assume you already know that, and that's why you're here! Instead, I want this book to prove your own hunch right, and to give you enough inspiration and guidance to act on it—to begin and keep up your own Daily Drawing Practice.

I've aimed to keep this book as practical as possible, and to that end, I've included lots of actionable tips and exercises to help you build a strong foundation for a lifelong Daily Drawing Practice, plus many examples of what one could look like from some of my favorite artists.

The book follows a fairly straightforward structure: The main chapters lead you through the journey of starting and keeping a Daily Drawing Practice in a logical progression. You don't have to go through these chapters in order, but I can't imagine a more appropriate way to organize them. To mix things up a bit, I've broken up the chapters with Interludes, where I share key moments from my own growth as a Daily Drawing Practitioner.

There are perhaps hundreds of books available on the subject of a Daily Creative Practice, and thousands more on the subject of drawing. I don't claim to bring you anything brand-new in either of these fields. My unique angle is illuminating how a daily practice of drawing toward a specific goal, and sharing part of that process, can help you achieve that goal. The method I teach in this book has been helpful for many thousands of students in my Skillshare class, Drawing Is Important, and I'm excited to bring it to a larger audience in the form of this book.

You already know that drawing is important! If you are serious about growing your creativity or even getting into a creative career, then it's worth the effort to make it a daily practice—and I am happy to be your guide in doing just that.

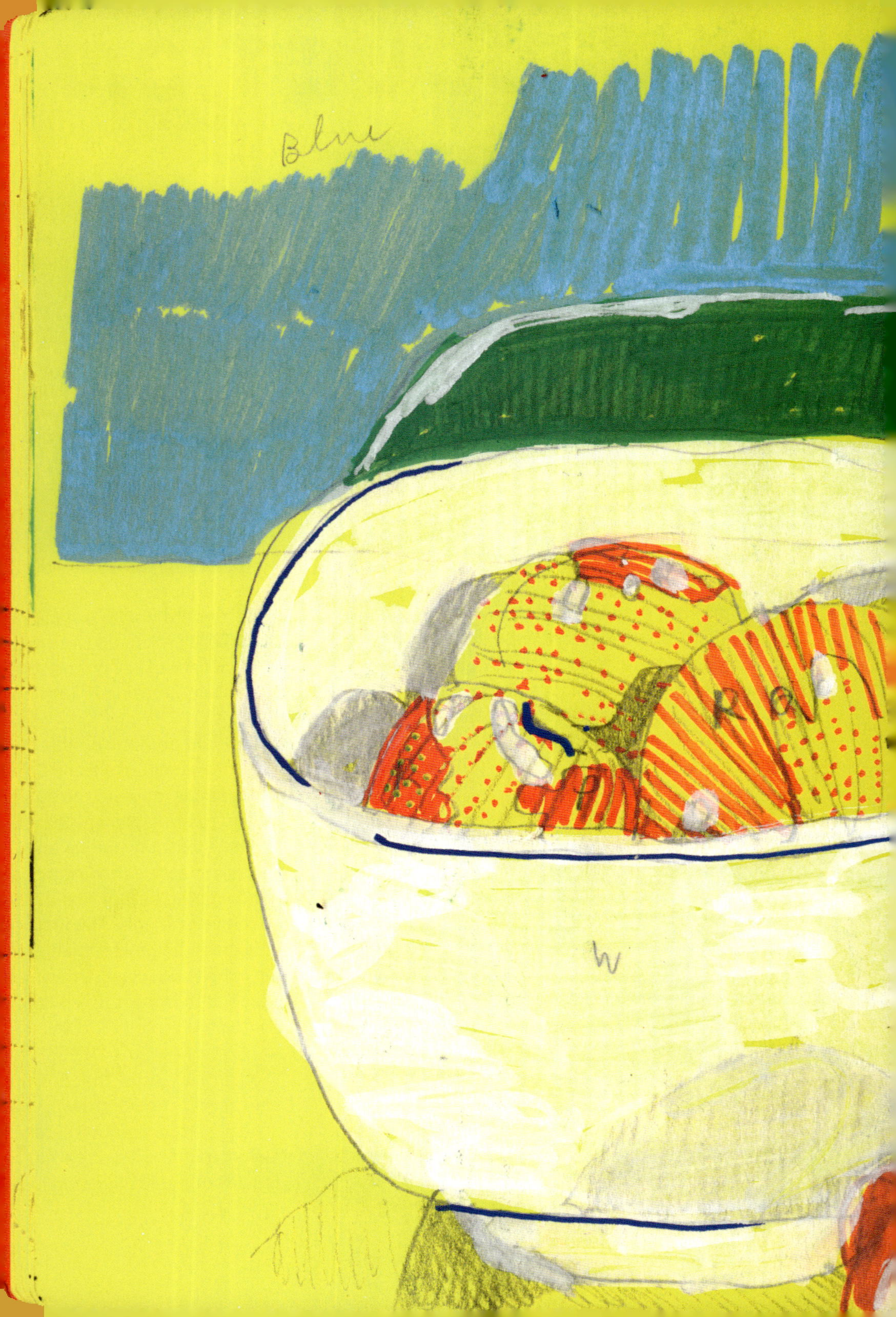
Blue
W

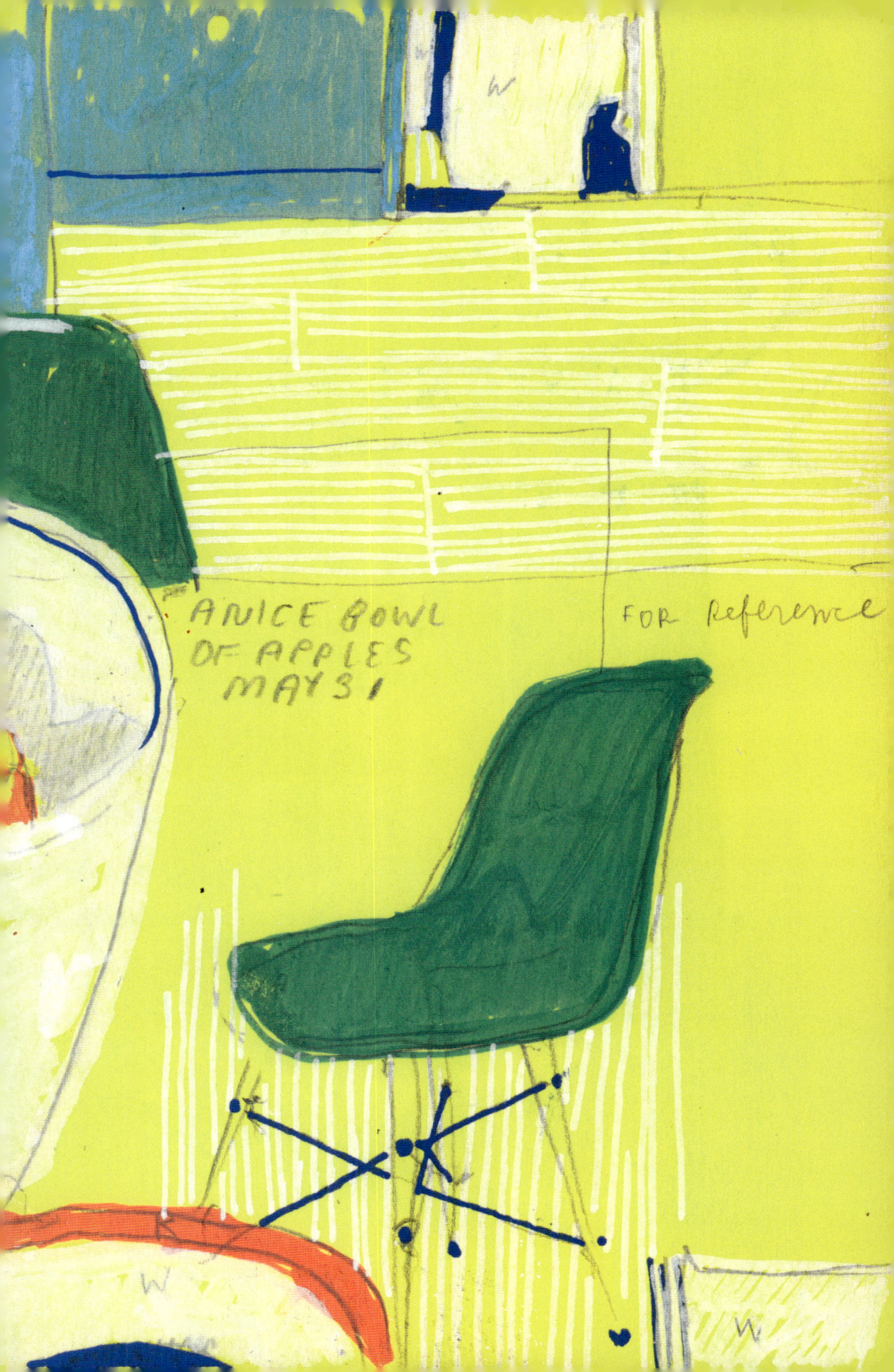
A NICE BOWL
OF APPLES
MAY 31
FOR Reference

SHOW UP
MAKE A PLAN
START WHERE YOU ARE
DO WHAT YOU CAN

START

Chapter

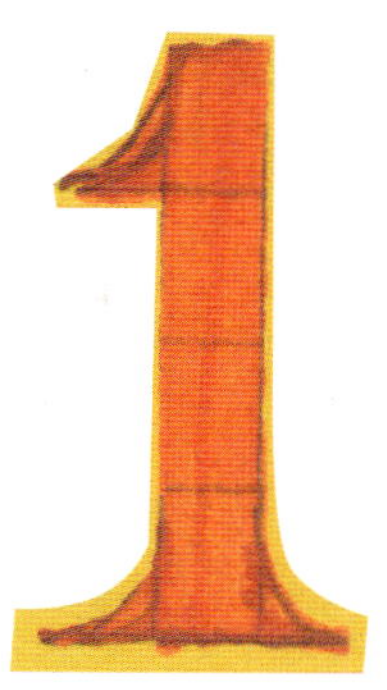

THE DAILY DRAWING PRACTICE

> "... forget about decades, forget about years, and forget about months. Focus on days."
>
> **Austin Kleon, *Show Your Work!***

What makes daily drawing worth committing to? In this chapter, we'll start by defining what a Daily Drawing Practice actually is—and why it matters. You'll learn about the key qualities that shape this kind of practice and the powerful benefits that come from drawing regularly. We'll also take a look at the most common obstacles that stop people from getting started, even when they want to. Most importantly, you'll reflect on your own motivations so you can begin your practice with purpose and clarity.

What Is a Daily Drawing Practice?

A Daily Drawing Practice is the habit of drawing every day, or at least regularly. But it's more than just drawing all the time; to me, it's an intentional, consistent effort to work out ideas on the page and, to some extent, on the public stage. Now, few people besides readers of this book would have such a specific understanding of this term. But I do think it's worth being as specific as possible so you can use your practice to achieve your specific creative goals. What I'm calling a Daily Drawing Practice is really just my way of describing any drawing or creative practice that has the following qualities:

1. A Daily Drawing Practice is intentional.
There is a purpose to it, and you show up with purpose each session, knowing that it counts.

2. A Daily Drawing Practice is regular.
Because it is a daily practice, you commit to showing up on a regular schedule to do it.

3. A Daily Drawing Practice is repetitive.
Each time you sit down to draw, you're working out the same kind of thing in order to get better at it. That could be technique, or drawing a certain subject, or exploring how you express something inside yourself in a visible way.

4. A Daily Drawing Practice is imperfect.
The purpose of daily drawing is about practice, not perfection. Also, because you do it so often, there is less pressure on each day's drawing to be "good." If you don't like it, there's always tomorrow!

5. A Daily Drawing Practice is shared.
While what and how often you share is up to you, in order to see the fullest benefit of your practice, you must share your work! It's only by sharing your art that it will see its fullest potential.

There are no formulas or strict rules here. There is no Daily Drawing Practice club, but if there were, it would be open to everybody. I've simply observed that these five qualities, together, seem to **1** result in a cohesive body of work that is created over a longer period of time, and **2** deeply inform other areas of their creativity and careers. What you call it really doesn't matter. Don't worry if you do or don't have a Daily Drawing Practice, or if you're doing it right. All of that will figure itself out if you draw with intention every day.

"Make sure you have a creative habit . . . The essential part of a creative habit is that habits are things you do without thinking. Should I make something today, should I not? You should do it. That it's your habit. Just keep doing that."
—Andy J. Pizza

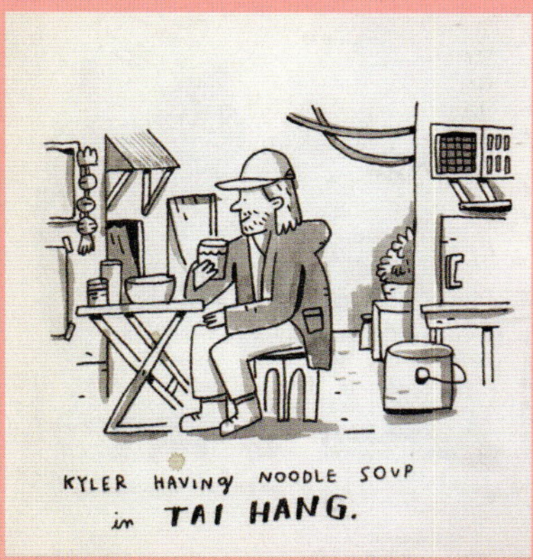

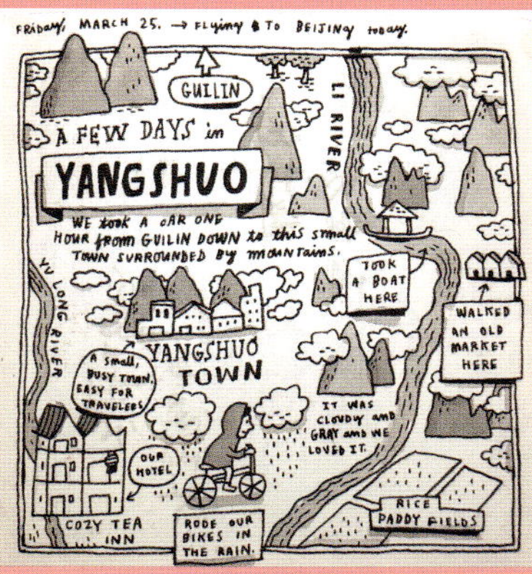

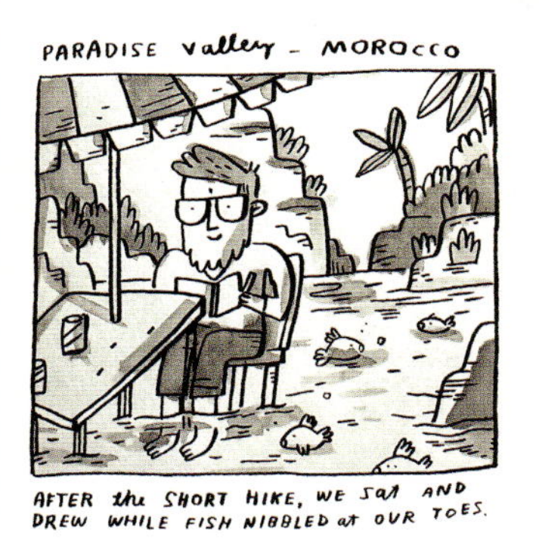

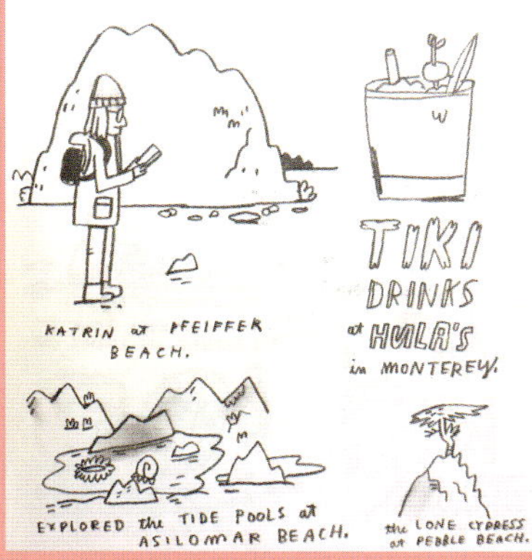

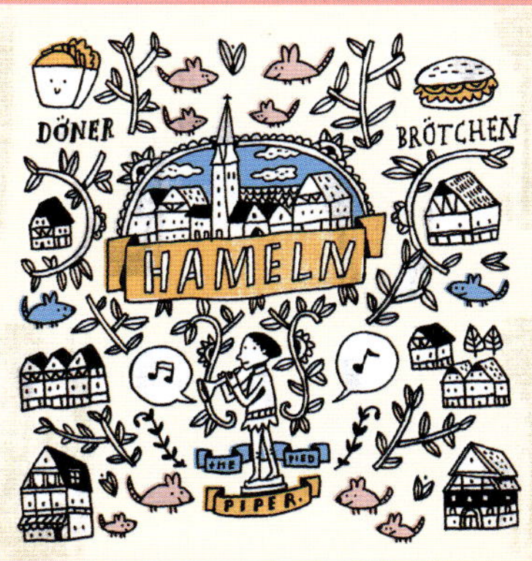

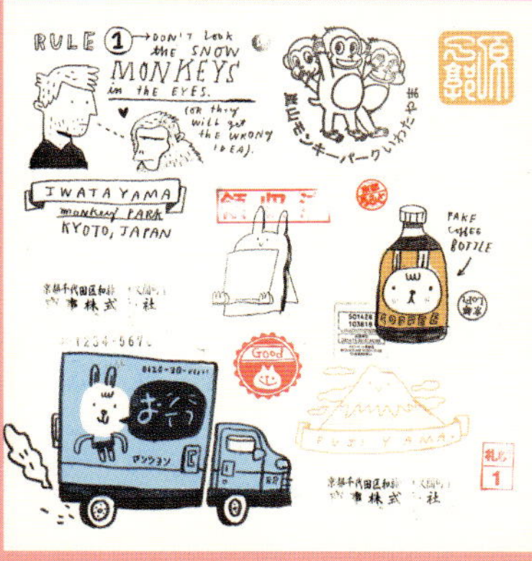

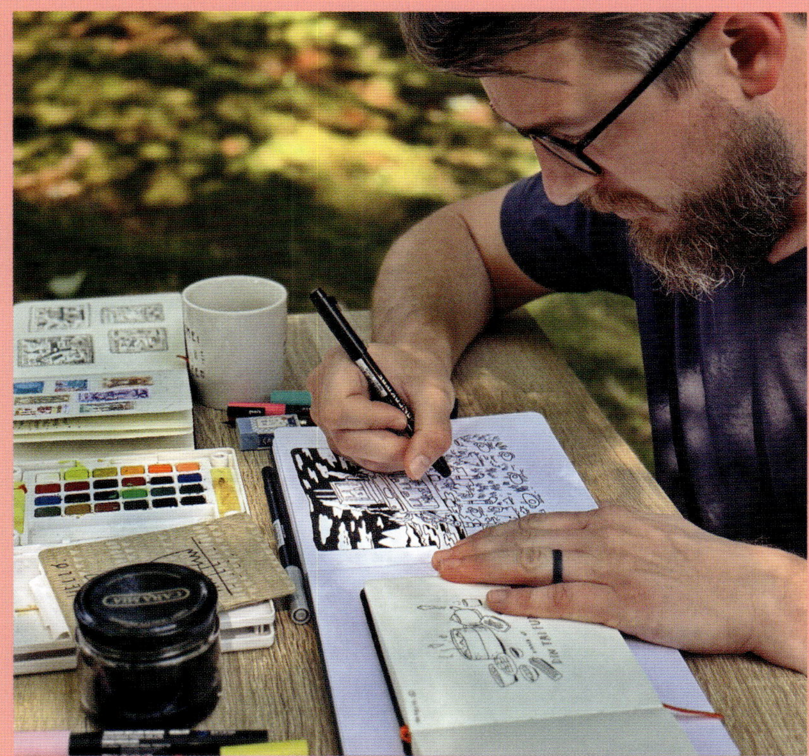

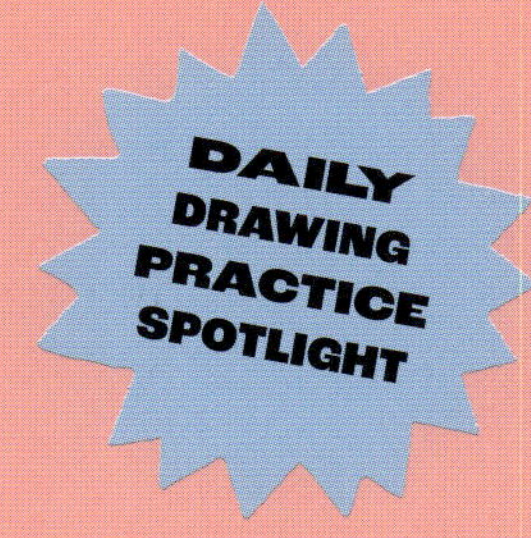

Mike Lowery

mikelowery.com
Mike Lowery is an illustrator, author, speaker, and collector of weird facts. He also happens to be a lifelong Daily Drawing Practitioner. As teachers who advocate for keeping a regular sketchbook, we have a lot in common!

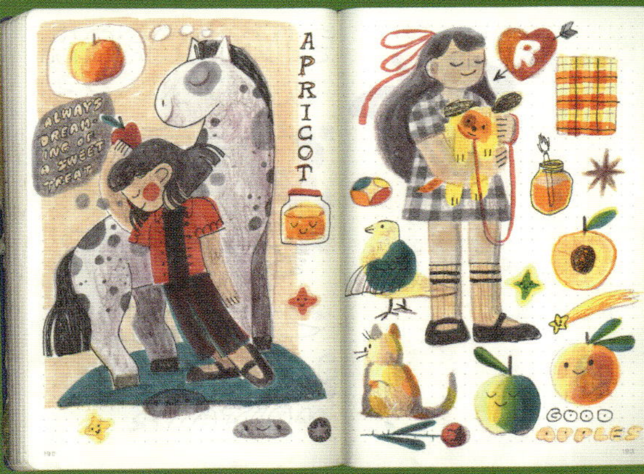

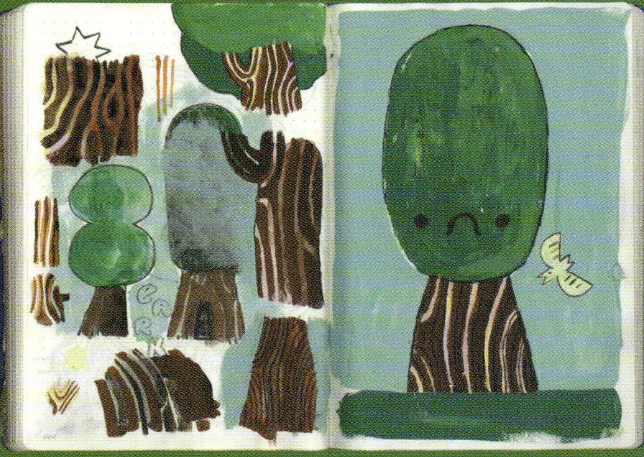

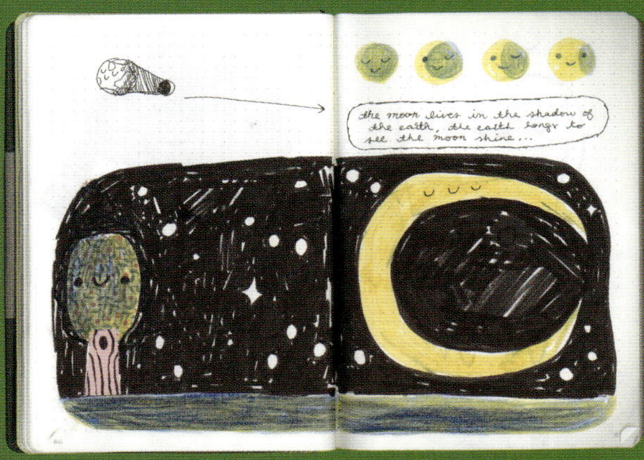

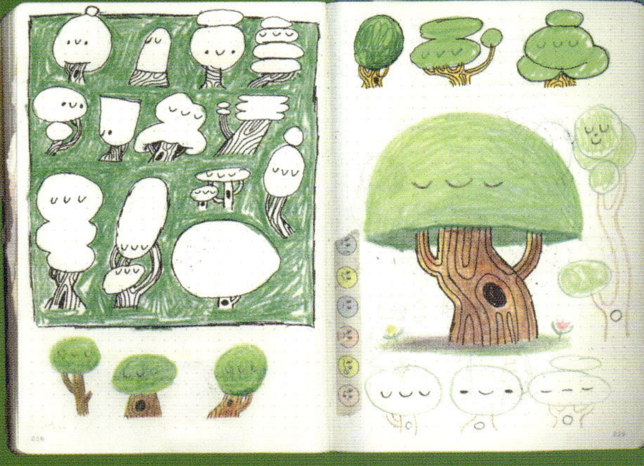

DAILY DRAWING PRACTICE SPOTLIGHT

Sha'an d'Anthes

furrylittlepeach.com
Also known as "furrylittlepeach," this Sydney-based illustrator, artist, and author is known for her brilliantly colorful, charming work. She's built a loyal following by sharing her creative journey online. In her own words: "I consider the documentation of my process a part of my practice, and it has been a pleasure to be able to share my journey as it happens on Instagram . . . and on Youtube."

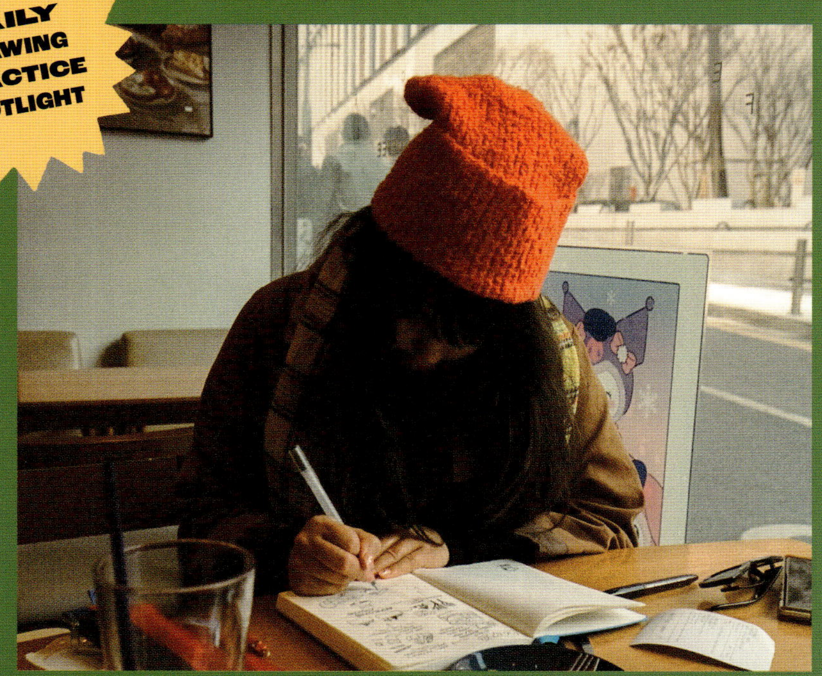

Why Have a Daily Drawing Practice?

Whatever your specific reasons for wanting to draw more (we'll get to that later in this chapter), there are four purposes for keeping a Daily Drawing Practice. You may find you identify with some of these more than others. As you read, pay attention to the reasons that speak to you most.

Reason 1: You'll draw more!
So, you'd like to draw more. A Daily Drawing Practice is first and foremost a method for helping you do just that! The more you do something, the easier it becomes to keep doing it, and the more it becomes a part of who you are. In his *New York Times* best-selling book, *Atomic Habits*, James Clear writes, "Every action you take is a vote for the type of person you wish to become." Each time you show up to draw is a vote for your identity as someone who draws, and future drawing sessions become more likely.

Reason 2: You'll grow creatively.
Creative growth is a huge benefit of regular drawing, and the structure of a Daily Drawing Practice is built for this purpose! How would you like to grow creatively? Would you like to get better at drawing hands? Loosen up in your drawing or illustration style? Whatever your goal, the more you practice something, the better you'll get. The power of a Daily Drawing Practice is that it gives you structure for focusing on one specific kind of growth at a time.

Reason 3: You'll discover your voice.
Learning how to draw, on its own, can be a wonderfully gratifying pursuit. But there may come a time when you want to do something more with it. It's one thing to master basic art skills, but what do you want to do with them? It could be as simple as learning to express yourself more confidently. Or, perhaps you'd like to develop a more unique style. In either case, you need to spend some time working out your creative voice. That is, what does your art look like? What makes a piece by you uniquely yours? The only way to find out is by working it out, repeatedly, over time. I can't think of a better way to do this than through a Daily Drawing Practice.

Reason 4: You'll become discoverable.
Drawing is expressive—and for many of us, there's a deep desire to be seen through our art. It's hard to think of a better way for that to happen than by drawing and sharing regularly. When I started sharing my drawings online, long before I had any sense of where it would take me, I instinctively knew it was about being seen by others. If you're hoping to draw more, chances are you feel this too. Of course, it's scary to share your work when you're not confident. But to be seen, you have to share. Many artists who found success started sharing before they were "ready." Their early work was unpolished, but over time, it grew more confident and unmistakably theirs. Sharing makes you vulnerable—but it's the best way to grow. Whether online or in a class project, stepping up and putting your work out there is where real discovery happens.

Why don't we draw more?

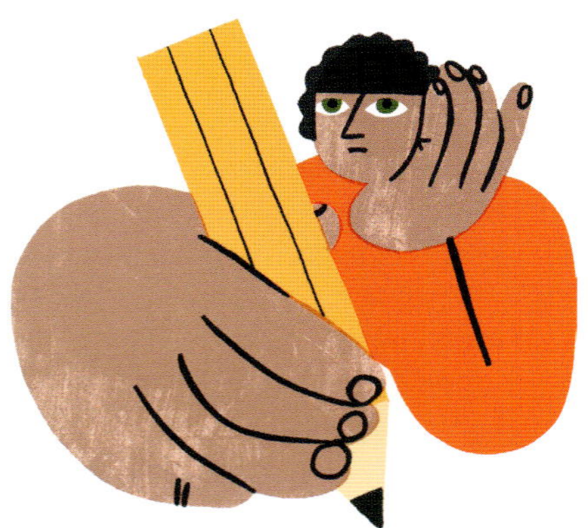

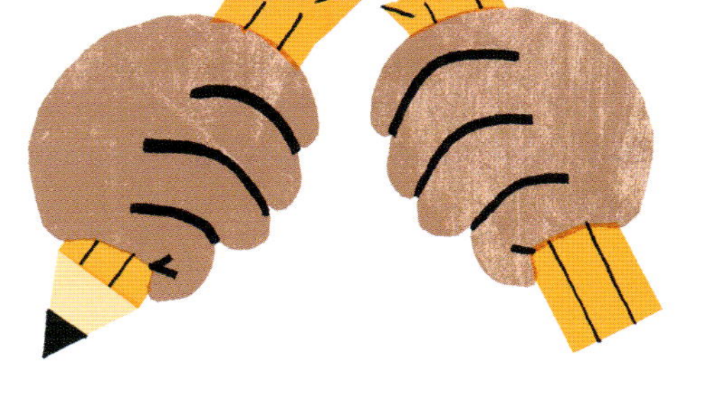

No one had to pressure us to draw when we were kids—we just did it, naturally and with reckless abandon! But as adults, picking up a pencil can feel strangely difficult. How did something so fun start to feel like a chore? In this section, I'll share the top four pain points that make it hard to draw regularly—and how to get past them.

Pain Point 1: Not knowing what to draw.
Have you ever felt a huge surge of creative inspiration, but when you sit down to actually make something, you realize you have no idea what to draw? This experience is what I call "the inspiration gap," where the urge to create meets a total lack of direction.

Antidote: Plan ahead.
The fix here is to plan your drawing subject in advance. As part of your Daily Drawing Plan (*see chapter 3*), you'll choose a topic or source for each day—maybe a themed prompt list or a go-to source of inspiration. Sometimes the problem isn't too few ideas but too many. When you know what to draw before you sit down, you'll spend less time worrying and more time actually drawing.

Pain Point 2: Not liking how you draw.
This one strikes at the heart of our artistic confidence. Many of us feel insecure about our ability to draw and make images that we think others will like to look at. Of course, daily drawing is a great way to start overcoming this lack of confidence (we get better through practice), but along the way, it can still feel more frustrating than fun.

Antidote: Set quantity-based goals.
Shift your focus away from quality and toward quantity. Instead of aiming to make a "good" drawing, set a goal you can measure objectively: five minutes of drawing, one object, half a page. Once you meet your target, you're done. It might sound like a trick, but it works! As a perfectionist myself, I know how much pressure can land on one drawing when you haven't made anything in weeks. But when drawing becomes a regular habit, you always know there's another chance tomorrow.

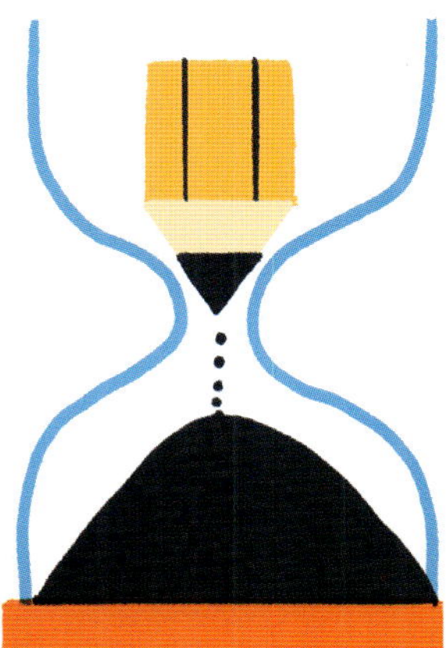

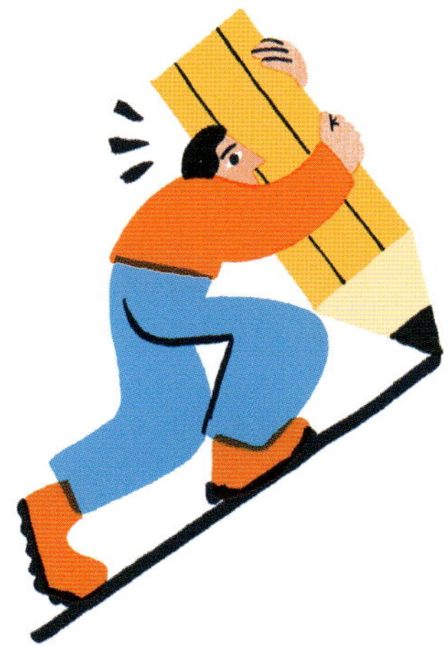

Pain Point 3: Not having enough time.
It's true, we're often so busy that it's hard to imagine making time for one more thing, especially if it's optional or competes with other things we'd like to do with the little free time we have!

Antidote: Set a sustainable schedule.
The trick here is to create a realistic, sustainable schedule. Drawing doesn't need to take long—even five minutes a day or a few days a week can make a difference. In chapter 3, you'll learn how to build a plan that fits your life: how often, how long, and when you'll draw. By setting a realistic schedule for how much you'll draw and how often, you'll be more likely to keep going, even when the rest of life gets crazy.

Pain Point 4: Losing motivation.
Motivation comes easy at first but fades over time. Even with the best intentions, it's hard to start drawing more if it's not a habit. We begin with much excitement and inspiration, but this quickly fades as the practice starts to feel like work. Without quick wins or visible progress, the spark can fade. Drawing naturally falls by the wayside.

Antidote 1: Have a bigger purpose.
Anchor your habit to a bigger purpose. Why do you want to draw? What's the goal it's helping you reach? At the end of this chapter, you'll reflect on that purpose—and in chapter 3, you'll use it to shape your long-term plan.

Antidote 2: Include sharing as part of your practice.
Sharing helps with accountability. As Austin Kleon puts it in *Show Your Work!*, you need to "make a commitment to learning . . . in front of others." While everyone has different comfort levels with sharing, I've always found it motivating to imagine that someone is waiting to see what I'll draw next. When I post my work online, that audience feels a little less imaginary—and a little more encouraging.

What's Your Purpose?

Soon, you'll get to write a full Daily Drawing Plan, but first, I encourage you to consider simply why drawing is important to you.

A Daily Drawing Practice can be the most exciting and rewarding part of your day, but sometimes you're just not going to feel like it. In order to work through those more challenging days, it's helpful to have a purpose that drives you forward.

Reflection Questions

1. Why is drawing important to you? Why would you like to draw more regularly?

2. Can you name any specific goals that a Daily Drawing Practice could help you achieve?

3. Which of the four reasons for having a Daily Drawing Practice matters most to you?
   a. Just drawing more regularly
   b. Creative growth
   c. Finding your voice
   d. Becoming discoverable

4. Which of the four pain points have been real in your life?
   a. Not knowing what to draw (creative block)
   b. Not liking how you draw (creative confidence)
   c. Not having enough time
   d. Losing motivation (it's hard to get started, or keep going)

I believe that you can have a lifelong Daily Drawing Practice! What gives you hope that I'm right about this? (Go ahead and write that down too!)

Instructions

Plan to spend at least ten minutes reflecting on these questions. The more you put into this exercise, the more you'll get out of it.

Write your answers down in your sketchbook or on the opposite page. This is a great way to break in a new sketchbook and overcome the blank page.

Don't worry about having the right answers! There is only what you know, right now.

Don't worry about the quality of your writing! You can write your answers in point form or full sentences. All you need to do to get something from this exercise is to be thoughtful and honest in your responses!

TIP

Drawing takes patience! If you want to get good at it, you need to slow down and focus on the moment. Writing is very similar. Set aside at least ten minutes to reflect on these questions. Assure yourself that this is going to be time well spent, and the more patient you are in responding, the more you will get out of the exercise. Tune out distractions, set a timer, take a breath, and begin.

Write Your Reflections Here

Interlude I

The Early Days

It's hard to pinpoint when my Daily Drawing Practice truly began. Beginnings often take shape before we realize them, only becoming clear in hindsight. Rather than a single moment of intention, my practice gradually came together over time. I've drawn all my life, but the habit of focused, regular drawing and sharing took years to develop—helped along by blogging and social media.

Looking back at my journals, I see a burst of activity around 2007, during art school. I had always drawn a lot and regularly blogged, but this was when I began merging drawing, writing, and sharing with a more focused purpose. I was exploring my creative voice, experimenting visually, and making my work more discoverable online.

Three key influences shaped this shift. My typography instructors, Kate O'Connor and Ray Fenwick, later took me on as an intern at their Halifax studio, Co. & Co. I loved Kate's loose, often hilarious drawing style, while Ray's diary-like, typographic illustrations and offbeat humor deeply inspired me. They also introduced me to Flickr, a major image-sharing platform before Instagram. My biggest influence, though, was Lauren Nassef, whose daily drawing blog showed me the power of consistent, intentional practice.

By this point, all the elements were in place: I was drawing regularly, focusing on themes and media, and sharing my imperfect experiments with a global audience. If there was ever a time when my Daily Drawing Practice truly emerged, this was it.

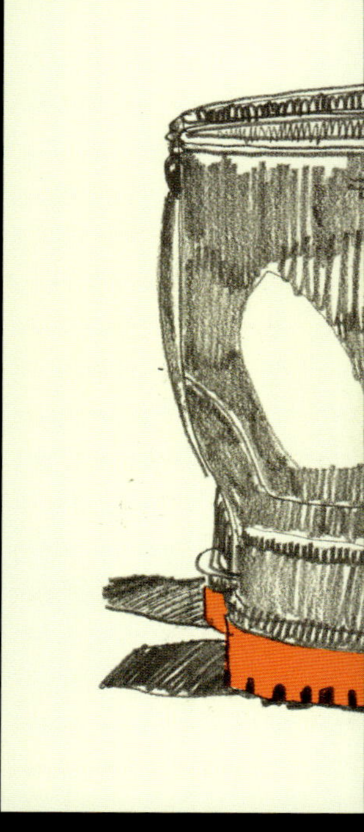

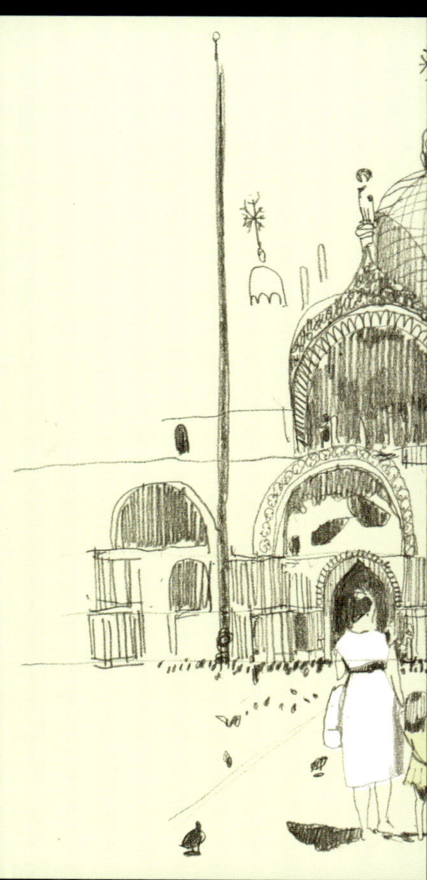

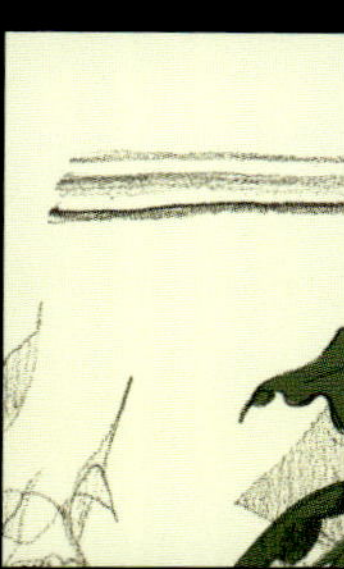

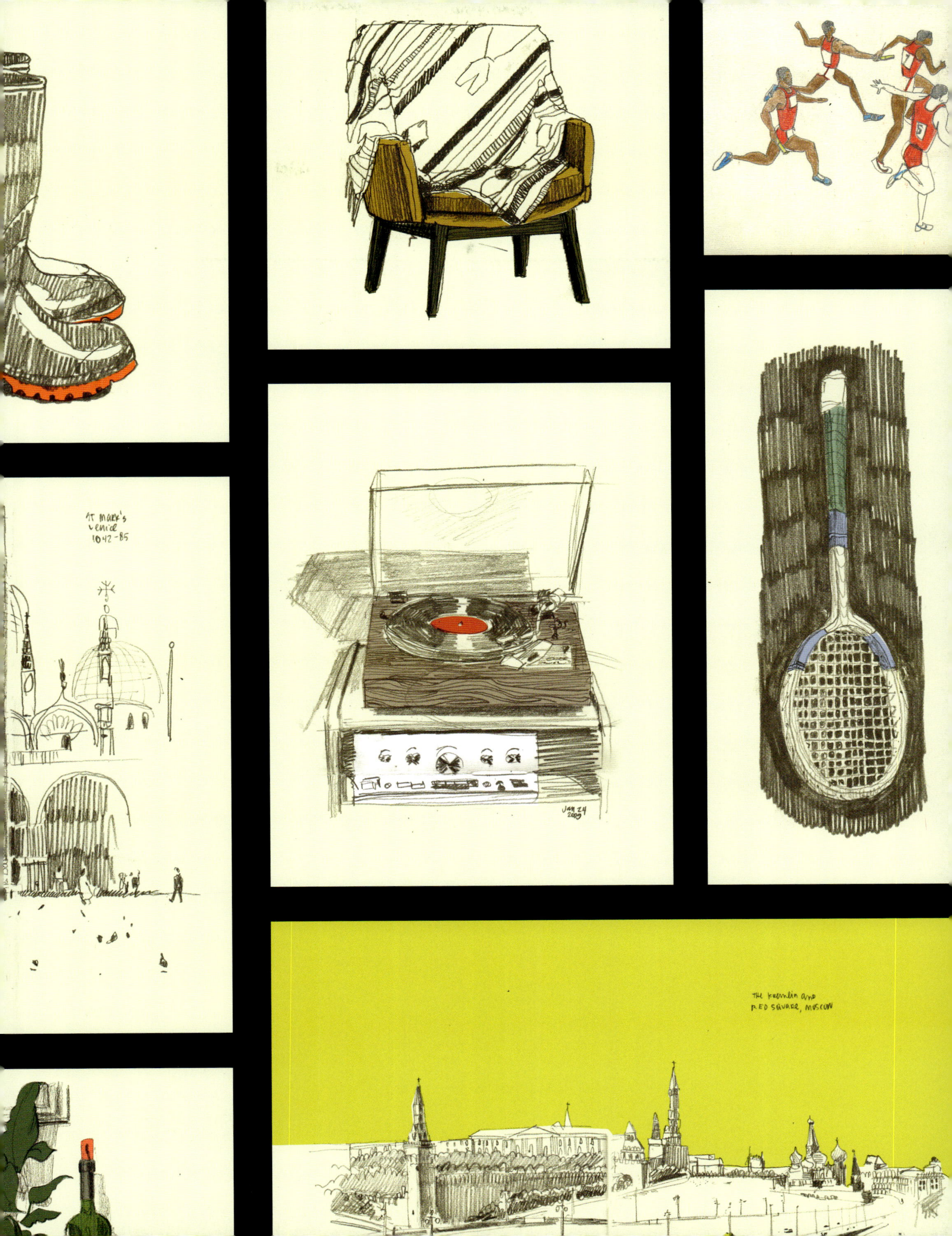
ST MARK'S
VENICE
1042-85
JAN 24
2009
THE KREMLIN AND
RED SQUARE, MOSCOW

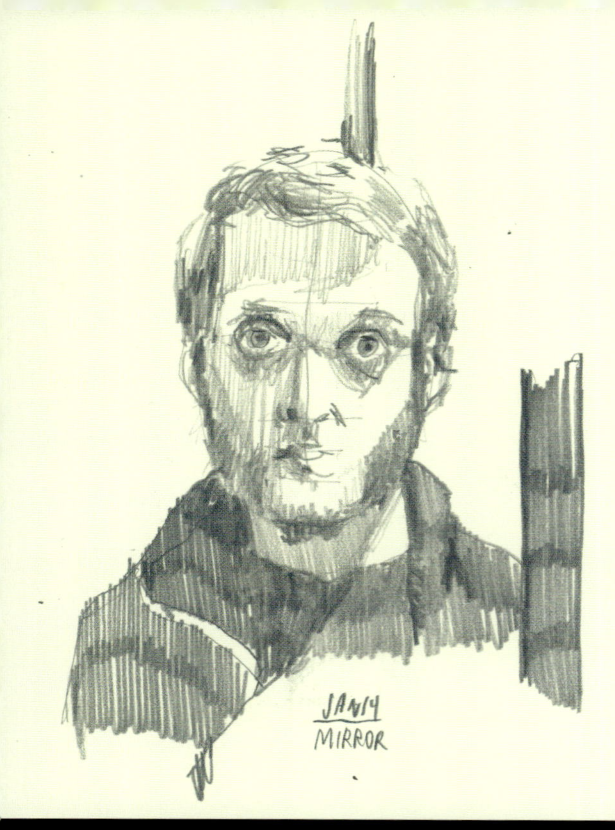
JAN14
MIRROR

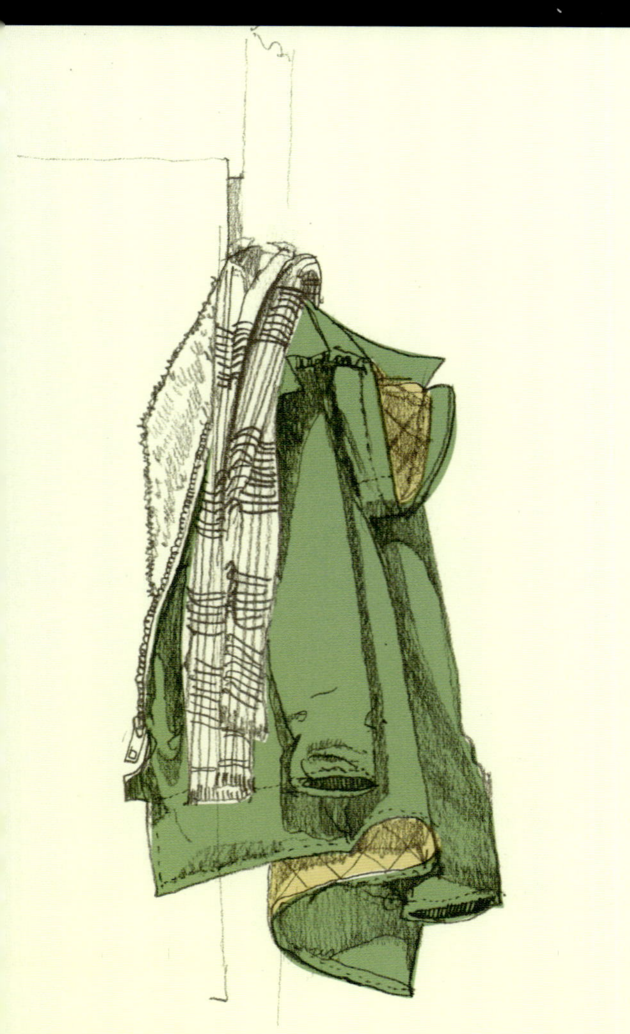

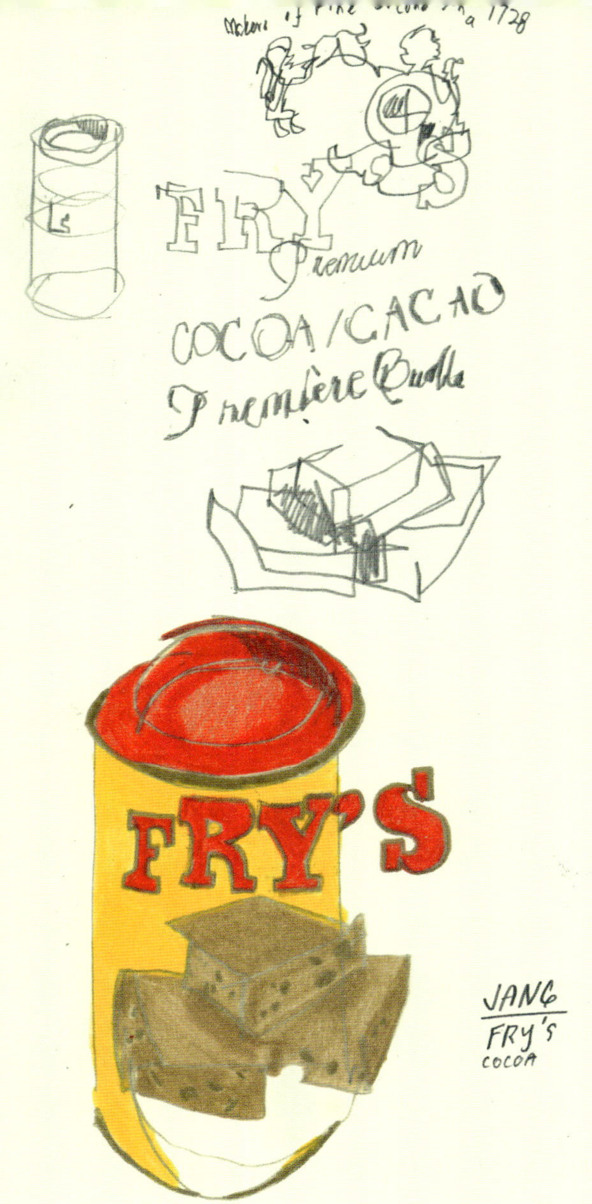
FRY
Premium
COCOA/CACAO
FRY'S
JAN6
FRY'S
COCOA

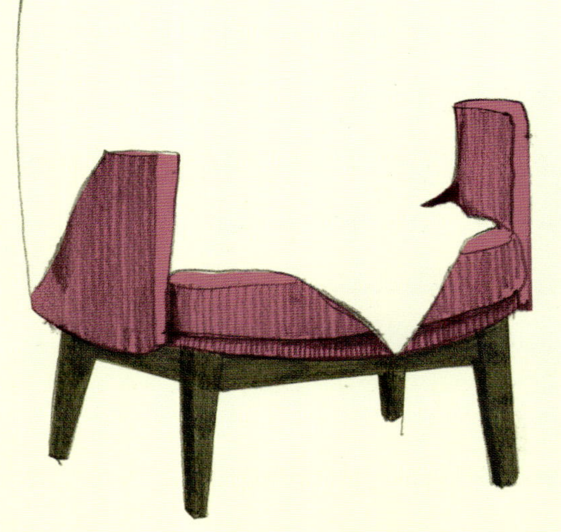

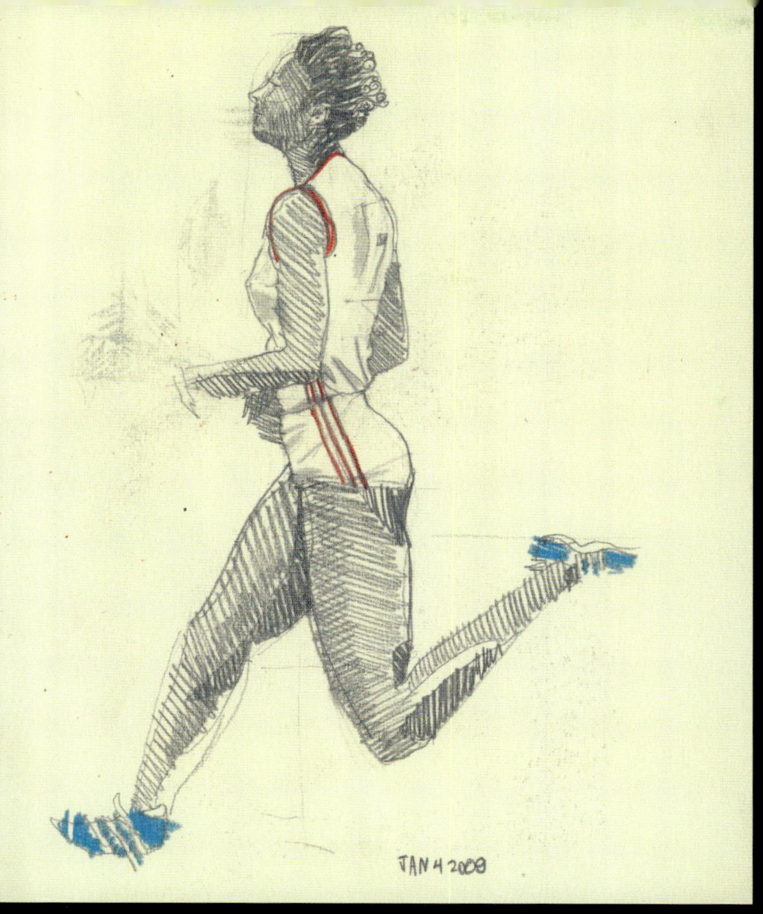

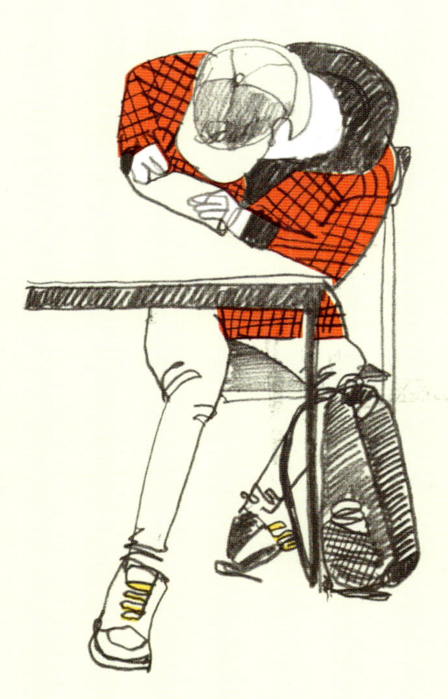

HERO SPOTLIGHT

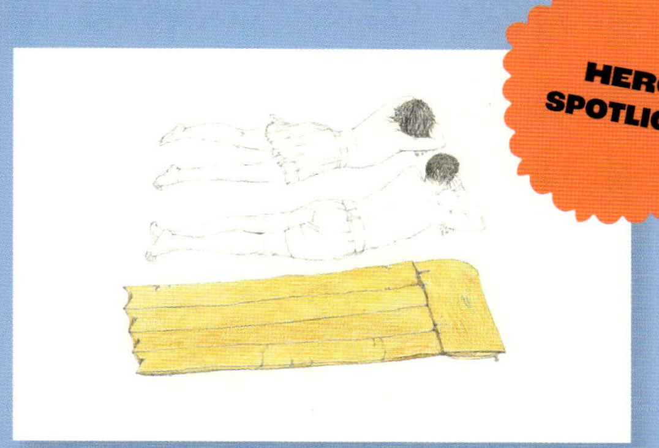

Lauren Nassef was my strongest influence in this period. Drawing in a Moleskine with a mechanical pencil, obsessive hashing, incomplete objects, and adding choice pops of color are all elements that I adopted after discovering Lauren's drawings.

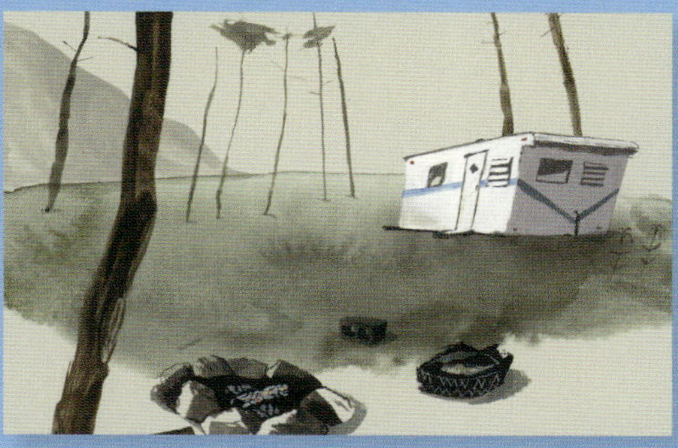

I was captivated by **Kate O'Connor**'s expressive, flowy figures and humorous themes drawn with pen and ink, gouache, and watercolor. You can see her influence in some of my more ink- and watercolor-based drawings from this period.

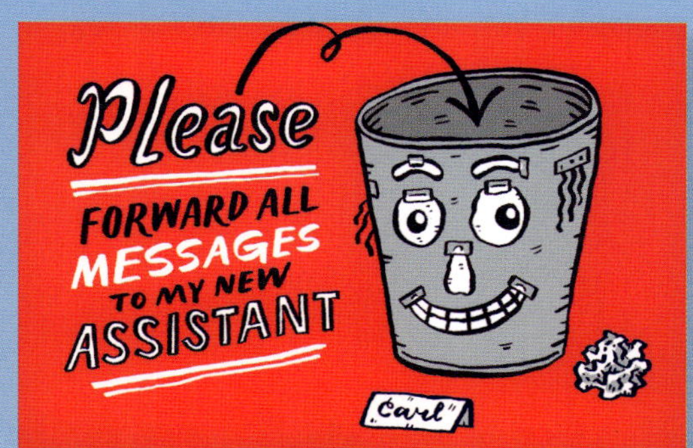

I loved how **Ray Fenwick** combined short little quips and typographically driven images in his drawings and illustrations. You can definitely see me emulating this in my drawings from this period.

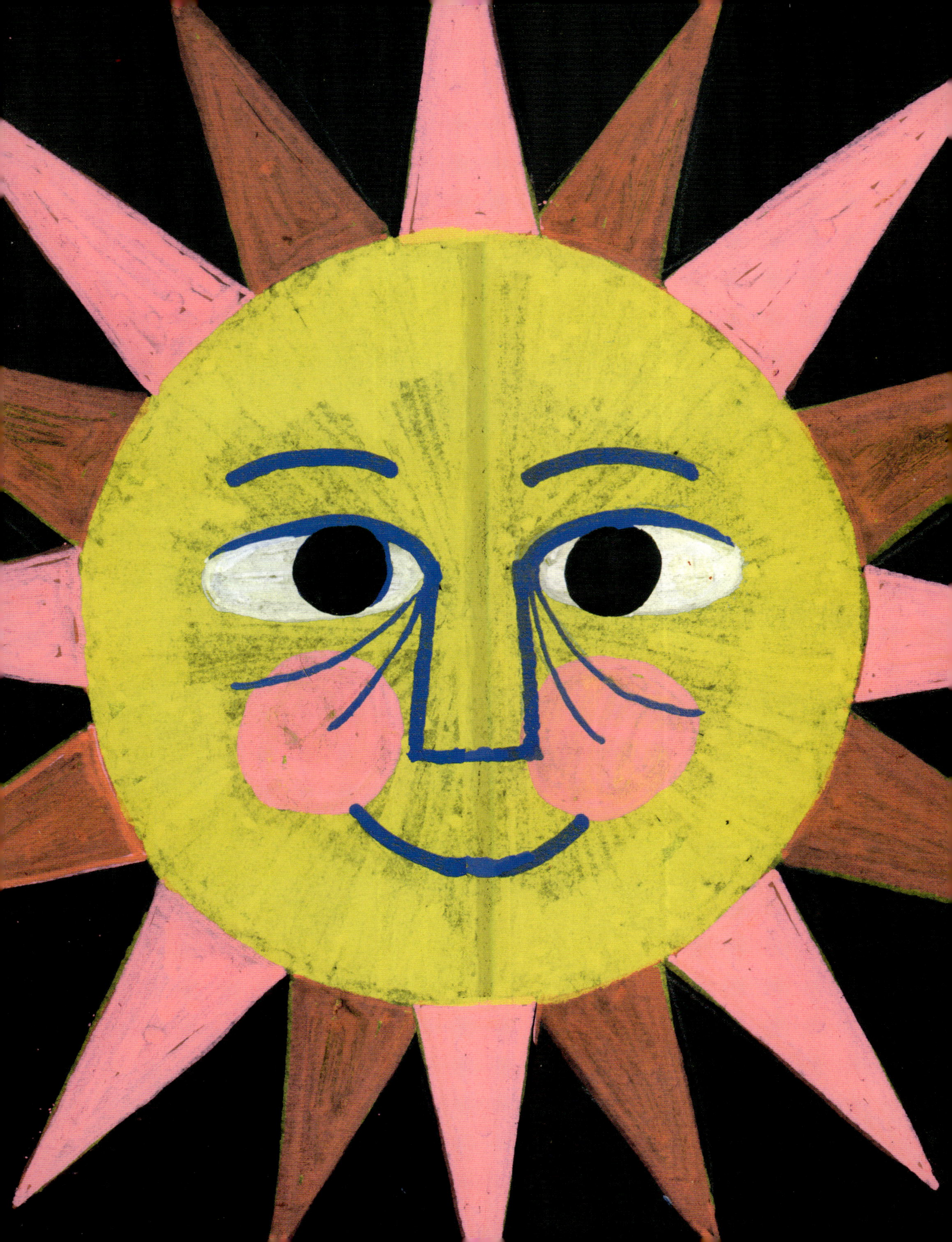

Chapter

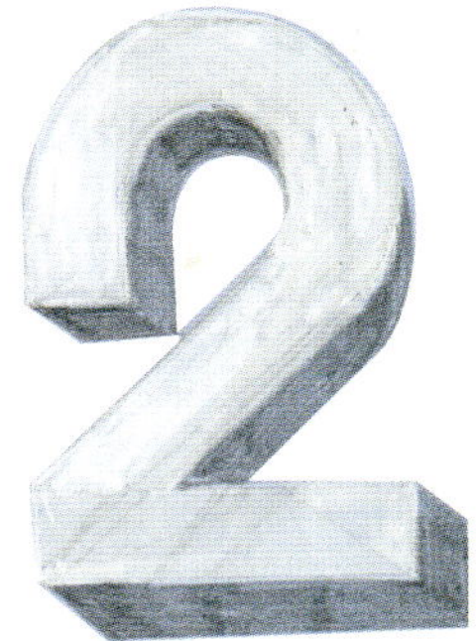

START WITH INSPIRATION

> **"You can't actually find your own voice without being influenced by other artists."**
>
> **Lisa Congdon, *Find Your Artistic Voice***

Every creative journey starts with a spark—that moment when you see something and think, "I want to do that!" This chapter is about finding and understanding that spark for you. We'll explore what inspiration looks like at the beginning of your Daily Drawing Practice and how to use it to guide your early steps. I'll share examples of inspiring practices from others, and you'll begin reflecting on what truly excites you. By the end, you'll have a better sense of what draws you to drawing—and how to use that to stay motivated.

You Are a Baby: Feeding on Inspiration

According to artist and writer Lisa Congdon, we all begin our creative journeys with some kind of initial influence. She calls this first point of discovery a "spark." There is a moment in our lives when we notice something for the first time, and something just ignites our passion for creativity, and this sends us on a lifelong journey of chasing that passion! I've definitely experienced this spark, and for me, it's the moment when something inspired me so much I said, "I want to do that!"

When we are born, we are utterly helpless! Of course, nobody faults us for this. In fact, our only job as babies is to rely on others—to feed and grow bit by bit, over time. Slowly but surely, we grow in our independence, and we learn to express what we need or think, until we are fully independent adults. While there are many parallels between our creative and biological developments, I'll focus here on what it means to be a creative baby. Because most of us are far past the actual baby stage by the time we're thinking about growing creatively, we tend to expect far more of ourselves than perhaps we're ready for. At the very beginning of our creative development, our job is simply to be inspired—that is, to feed on what inspires us most.

If you're at the very beginning, I want to encourage you to give yourself permission to be a creative baby, and to enjoy this stage as much as possible. As a creative coach, I regularly meet with aspiring creatives who are trying to find their voice and find their first steps in the illustration world. As part of my initial questions, I always ask who their top three creative influences are. Not only does this help me understand what drives them—it also helps them know this for themselves. More importantly, knowing who and what inspires you gives you a vision for what's possible.

If you haven't already, I encourage you to identify your creative heroes—people who make work you love—and to let yourself be fully inspired and influenced by them. While later on you will have to find your own unique talents and voice, the only way to begin is by observing others. In *The Creative Habit*, dancer and creative writer Twyla Tharp says, "Before you can think out of the box, you have to start with a box." Finding inspiration and influence in the work of others gives us such a box to start with. This is true not only for a Daily Drawing Practice but also for building any type of creative habit or skill set.

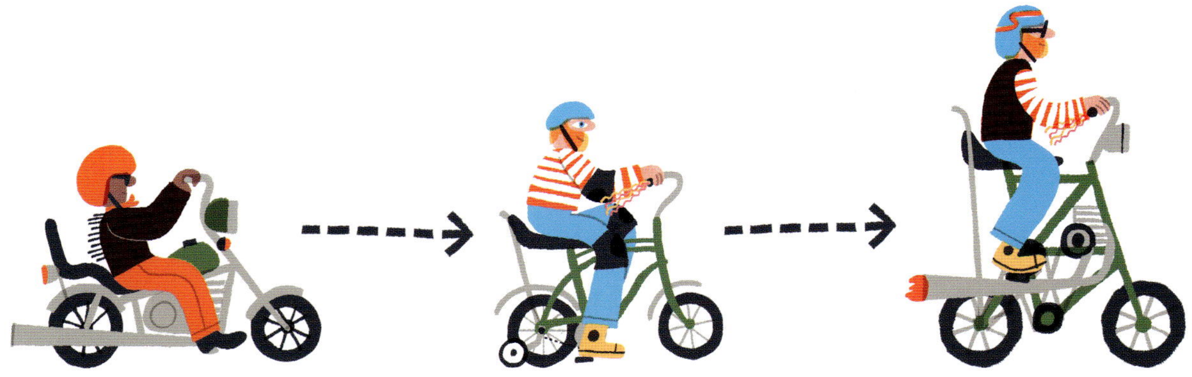

Inspiration

The three stages of finding your voice: inspiration, imitation, and innovation. At first, we discover something that inspires us so much that we say, "I want to do that!"

Imitation

Next, we learn by imitating what we see. This is the necessary imitation stage that Twyla Tharp describes as starting "with a box."

Innovation

It's only after a period of imitating our many influences that we can find a way to bring them all together in our own way. This is the third stage, innovation.

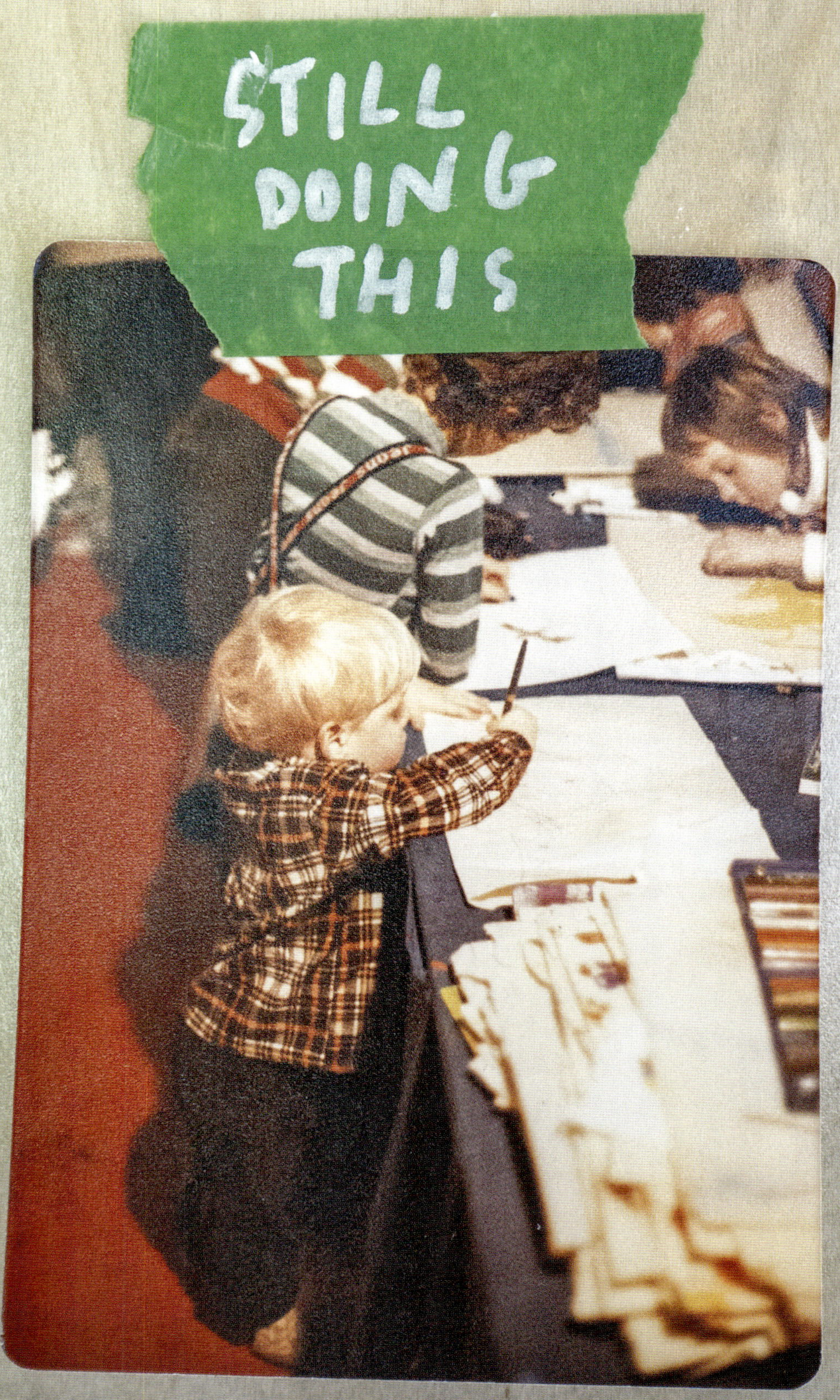

I sometimes imagine what it would be like to travel back in time to tell my younger self that I get to draw for a living. This photo and inscription remind me how cool it is that I'm *still doing this*.

Finding Your Inspiration

In a book like this, sharing examples of what I consider "inspiring" can be tricky. For all I know, you and I might have very different tastes! Instead, I want to help you find what inspires you most, whatever your taste might be! In the next section, "The Inspiration Case Study" (see *page 34*), you'll get a chance to discover just that. However, as your guide, I'll go first and show you some Daily Drawing Practices that have inspired (and still inspire) me over the years! These are examples that have sparked my own Daily Drawing Practice, from my earliest days all the way up to today.

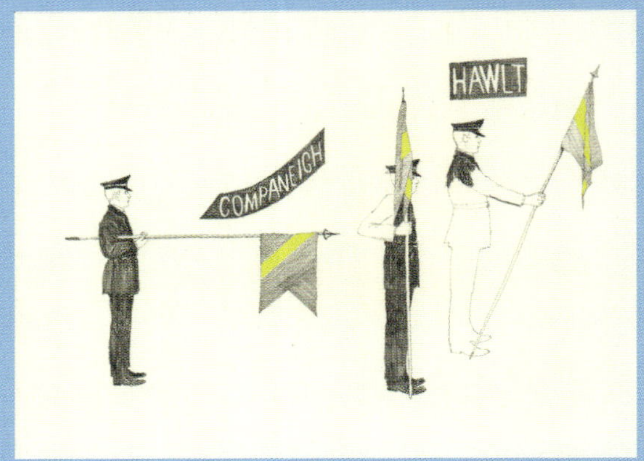

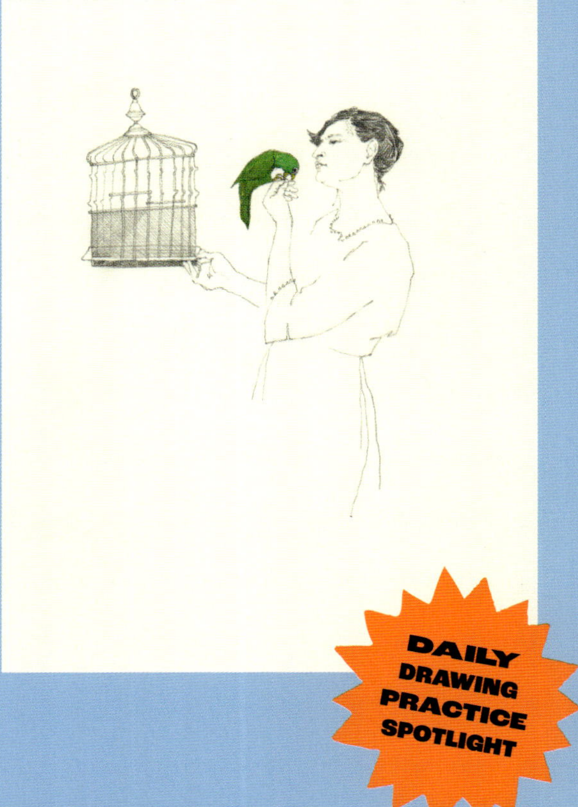

DAILY DRAWING PRACTICE SPOTLIGHT

Lauren Nassef

laurennassef.com

Lauren Nassef is an artist and illustrator living in Chicago. She posted "semi-daily" drawings on her blog from 2007 to 2011. She was a major influence on my own early Daily Drawing Practice. Today, she divides her time between illustration and collections work at the Field Museum of Natural History.

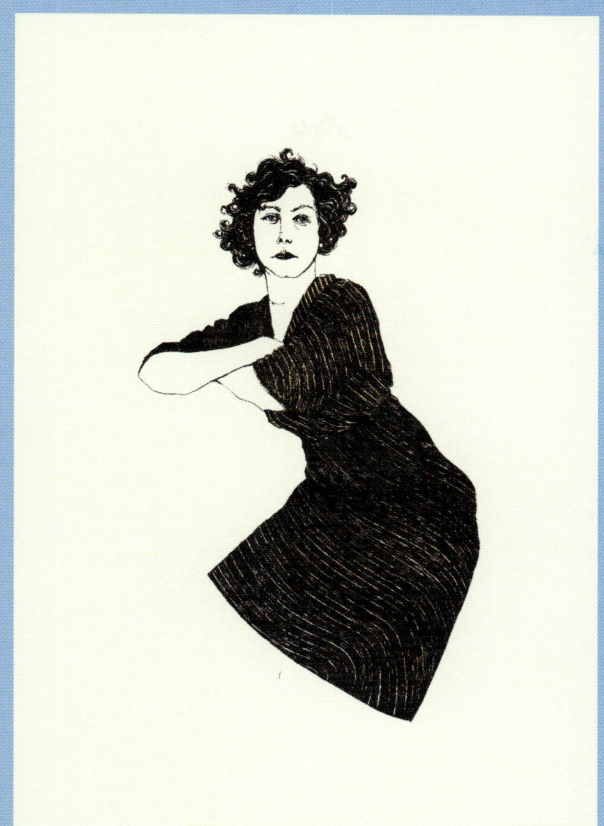

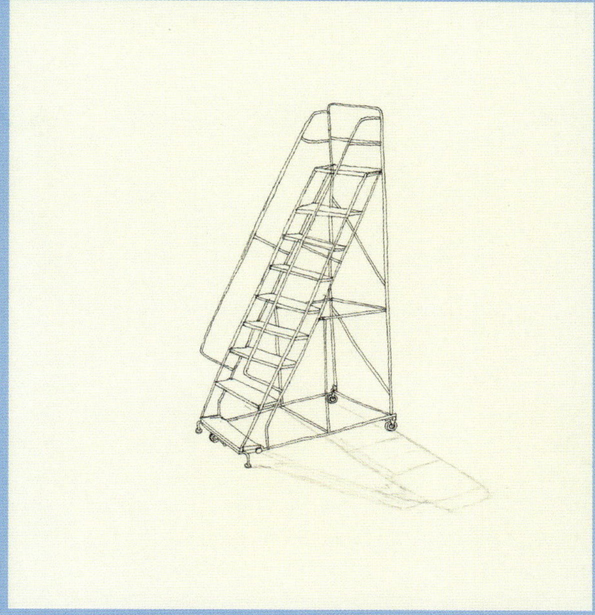

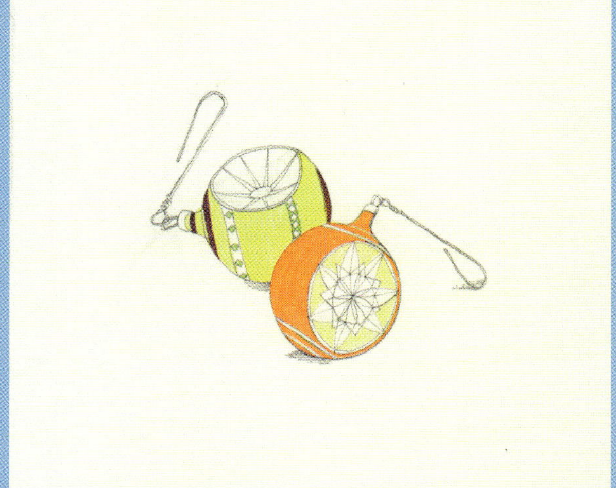

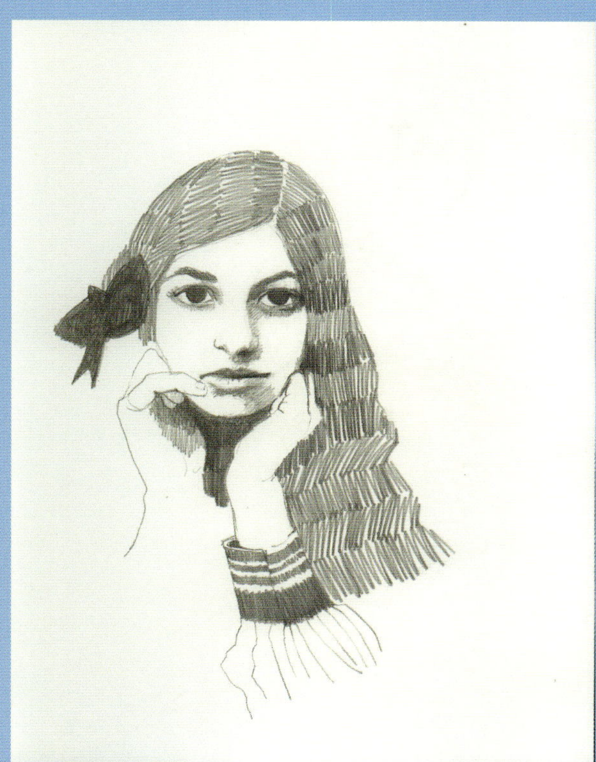

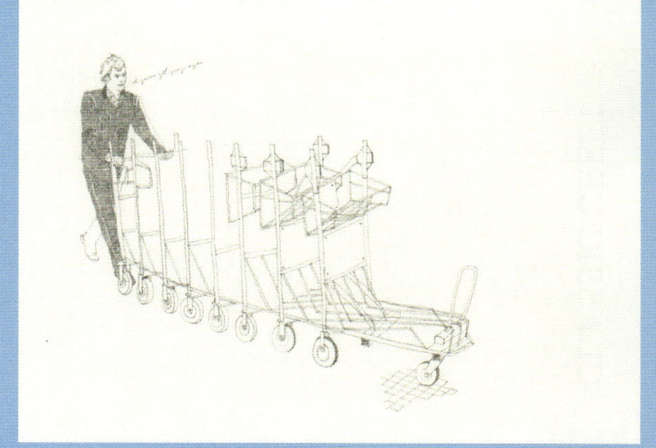

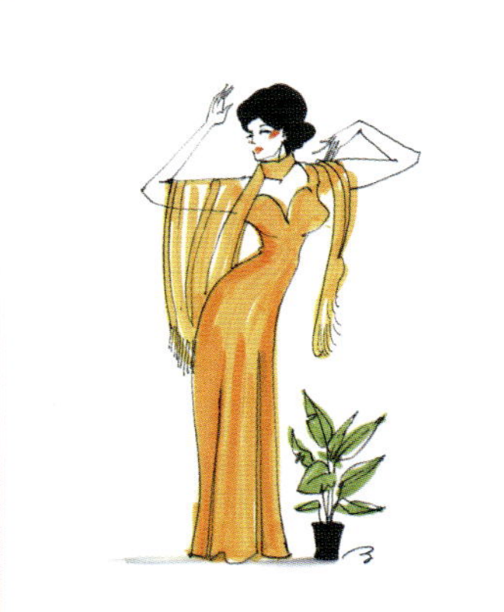
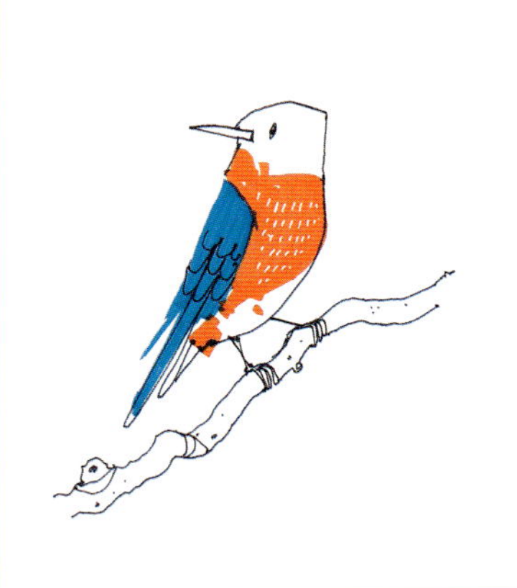
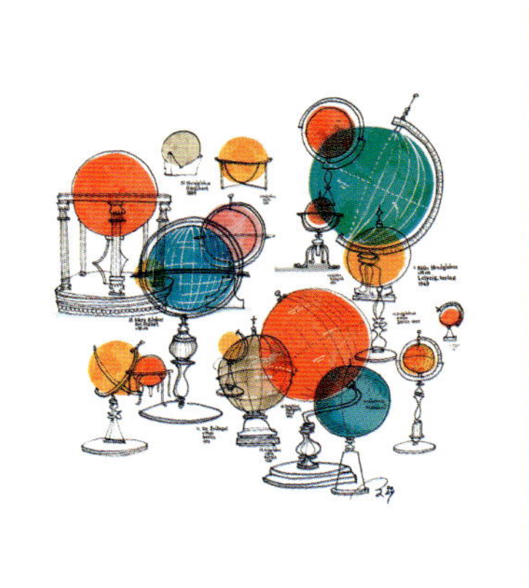
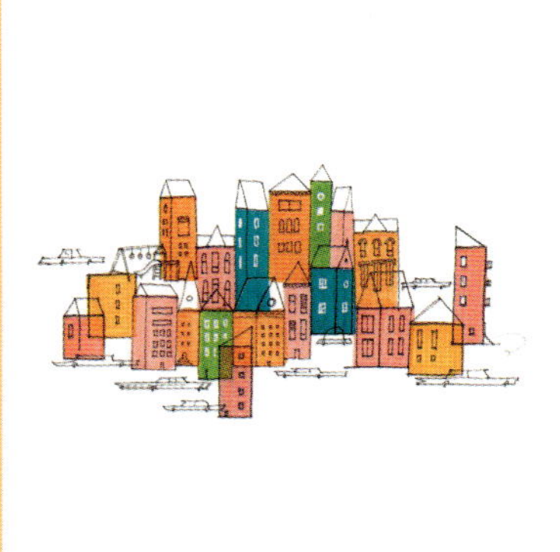
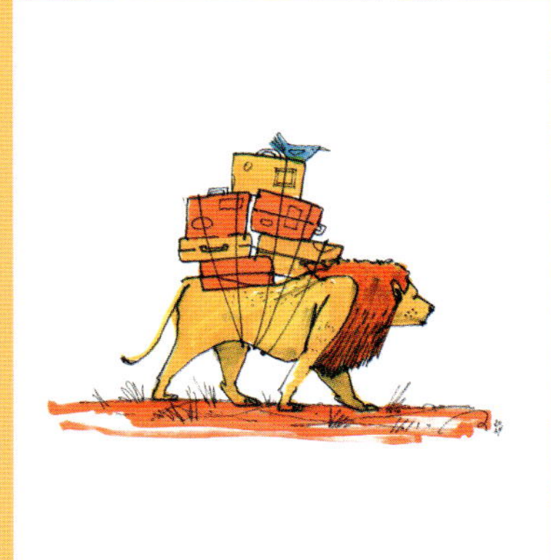
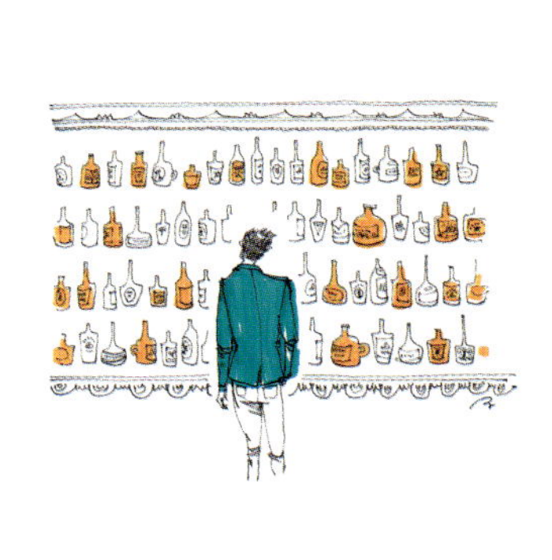

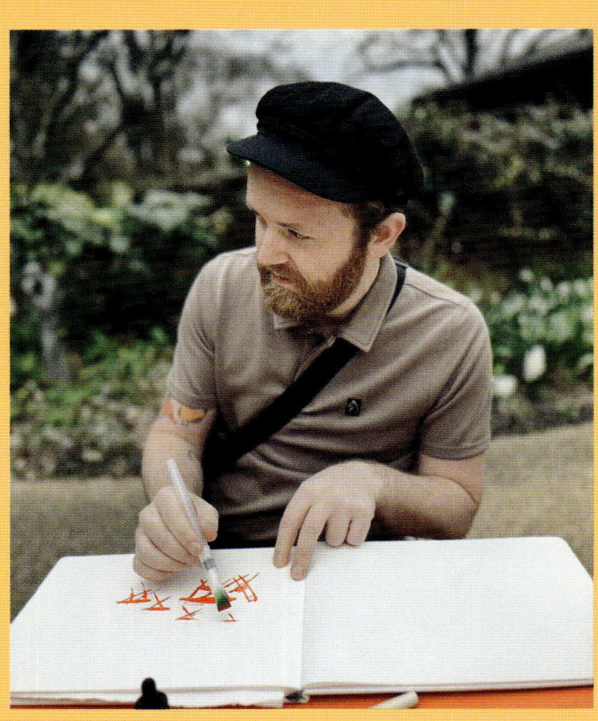

Brandon Campbell

brandoncampbell.tv
Brandon Campbell is an Atlanta-based illustrator. He's built a thriving business around daily retro-inspired drawings, sharing time-lapse videos with well over half a million followers. He sells originals and prints while building a thriving drawing community on Patreon, all using physical media.

How Can You Be Inspired by Influences without Imitating Them?

Do you want to stay a creative baby forever? Of course not! There comes a time when you need to learn to crawl, then walk, and then run. But not so fast! For now, I'm encouraging you to start at the very beginning. Start with inspiration because that's where all creative journeys begin. Without question, beginners start by imitating those who are further along. One day you will find your own way, but not yet.

Think of your inspiration stage as learning to ride a bike. This period of imitating your influences is like having training wheels: They give you support and give you a feeling for riding on two wheels, without the risk of falling over. There's no question that you'll need them at first, but training wheels are designed to be removed. Sooner or later, they must come off.

O- and I-Mode

This progression from imitation to innovation happens throughout our lives in many ways. In my creative process, there are two key stages in coming up with ideas, which I call Observation Mode (O-Mode) and Ideation Mode (I-Mode). In O-Mode, I'm drawing from reference photos or real life. I'm not trying to come up with ideas, but simply "downloading" visual information about my subject. Later, I shift into I-Mode, where I begin working out my own ideas. This stage is always a challenge, but going through O-Mode first makes it much easier.

Likewise, with time and practice, you will naturally find it easier to put your inspiration aside and do things in a more original way. Pablo Picasso reminds us to "learn the rules like a pro so you can break them like an artist." This suggests that taking shortcuts could result in "bad" work, but it also describes the necessary path of every artist from imitation to innovation.

The bottom line: You can and should be copying your influences at first. You've got to imitate to learn. Of course, give credit where credit is due, and don't just rip off your heroes! Remember also that the goal is not to stay in "O-Mode" forever, but to use it as a launching point. In the wise words of the French-Swiss screenwriter Jean-Luc Godard: "It's not where you take things from—it's where you take them to."

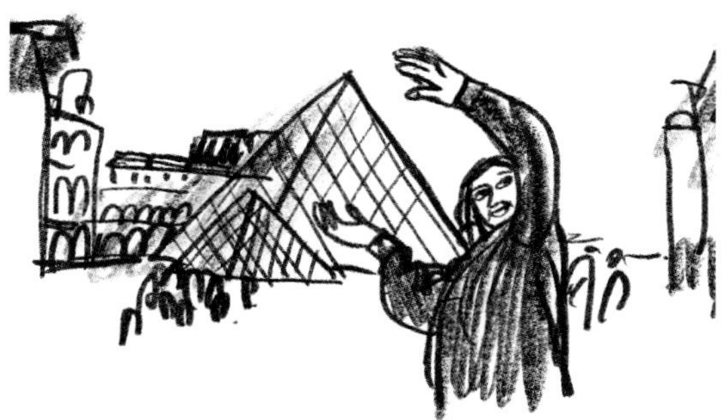

1. O-Mode Drawing

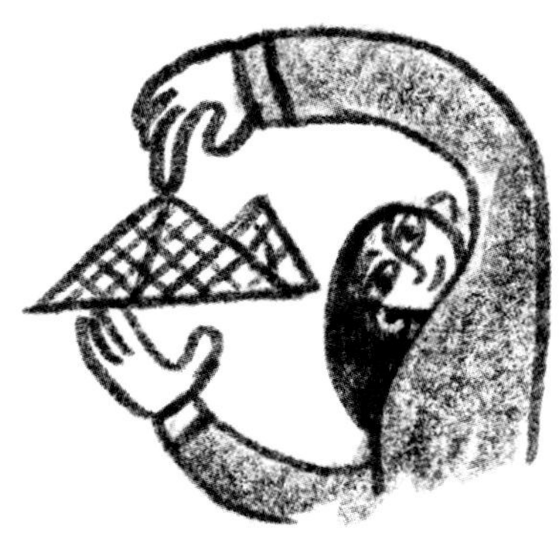

2. I-Mode Drawing

1. In **O-Mode (Observational)** drawing, I allow myself to sketch directly from a reference, from either real life or a reference photo. **2.** Then, in **I-Mode (Ideational)**, I put the reference away and draw completely from my memory and imagination. I accept any quirks and accidents that come up along the way as part of my unique voice.

The Inspiration Case Study

One of my most popular classes is The Style Class: Work Out Your Illustration Style in a Daily Project. In it, I guide students through a month-long Daily Project. A key part of developing your style is identifying the styles you're most drawn to in others' work. Before beginning the full project, I have students complete what I call an Inspiration Case Study—an exercise in mindful inspiration hunting. It's about asking: What inspires me most, and what can I learn from it?

Inspiration is powerful, but without direction, it can feel overwhelming. The Inspiration Case Study gives you a way to channel that energy—to study what you love, learn from it, and begin creating from it.

It's a focused analysis of one artist's work. You can do several, but it helps to start with just one. Ask yourself: What sparked my interest in drawing—and who made it? From there, you can explore how and why that work was made, and how it fits into the artist's larger body of work. This can offer important clues about what you might want to bring into your own practice.

While the exercise is about style in The Style Class, here we're applying it to Daily Drawing Practices. That means we'll be looking more specifically at other people's ongoing creative routines as inspiration for starting our own. The goal is to turn inspiration into action.

How to Do an Inspiration Case Study

Start by choosing one artist's Daily Drawing Practice that really excites you. If you have a few artists in mind, that's great—you can always come back and do more studies!

Setup

You'll need a way to gather and annotate your inspiration—digital is fine for this. While I encourage you to draw using physical tools, digital apps like Procreate or Photoshop work well for this exercise.

Instructions

1. Search for a Daily Project that truly inspires you. Try platforms like Instagram using terms like "daily drawings" or "daily sketchbook" (or hashtag versions).

2. Save five or so of your favorite images—don't overthink it. Just go with what draws you in.

3. Place them in a single document using Procreate, Photoshop, Canva, or even Google Docs.

4. Around or below the images, write:
   a. Artist: Who made this work?
   b. Technique: What materials or methods are they using? Do a little digging if you're not sure—this is an important part of the discovery process!
   c. Context: Where and how are they sharing this work? What seems to be their goal or motivation?
   d. Things I Like: In your own words, list what you enjoy about the work—how it looks, how it makes you feel, and any details that spark your curiosity.

5. Feel free to title your page "Inspiration Case Study: [Artist Name]."

Ironically, too much inspiration can be overwhelming and even paralyzing. The gap between where you are and where you'd like to be can feel too wide to cross. But doing an Inspiration Case Study gives you an actionable step to move forward with—and that alone can break the spell of creative paralysis.

Try This!

INSPIRATION CASE STUDY

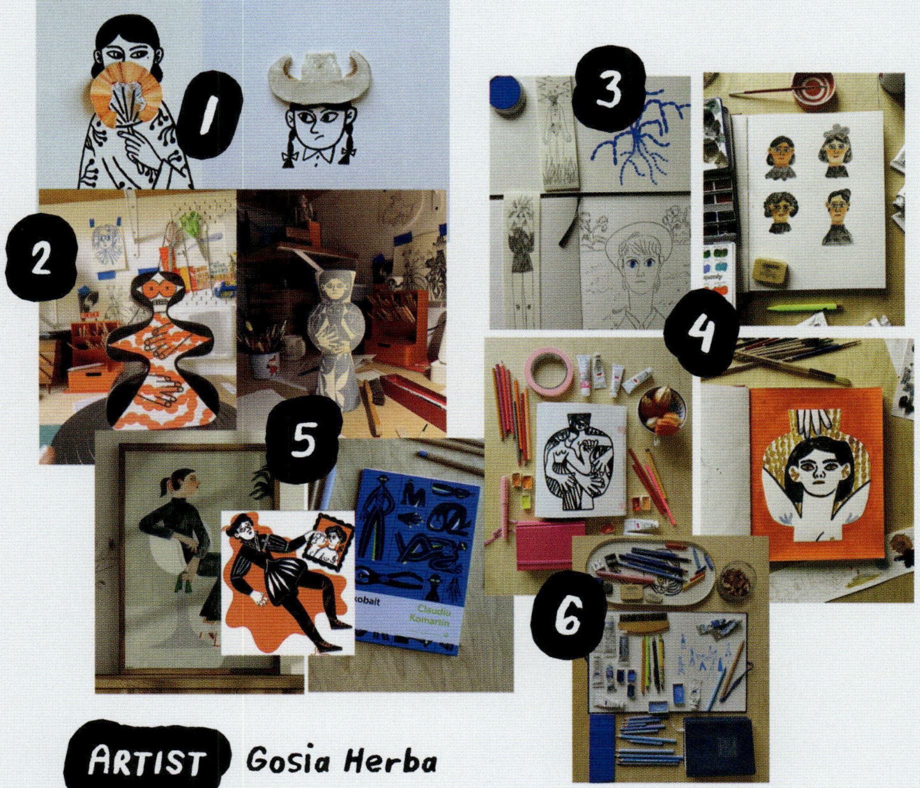

ARTIST Gosia Herba

TECHNIQUES
Gouache/Color media
Pencil and Pen/Ink
Ceramics + Digital

CONTEXT
Instagram

OBSERVATIONS + LIKES

1. Fun experiments with drawing + physical objects
2. Exploring 3D objects (ceramics)
3. Documents drawings with well-lit photos
4. Lots of creative tools/bits reveal the process
5. Also showing finished/client work within the same feed
6. meticulous color coordination

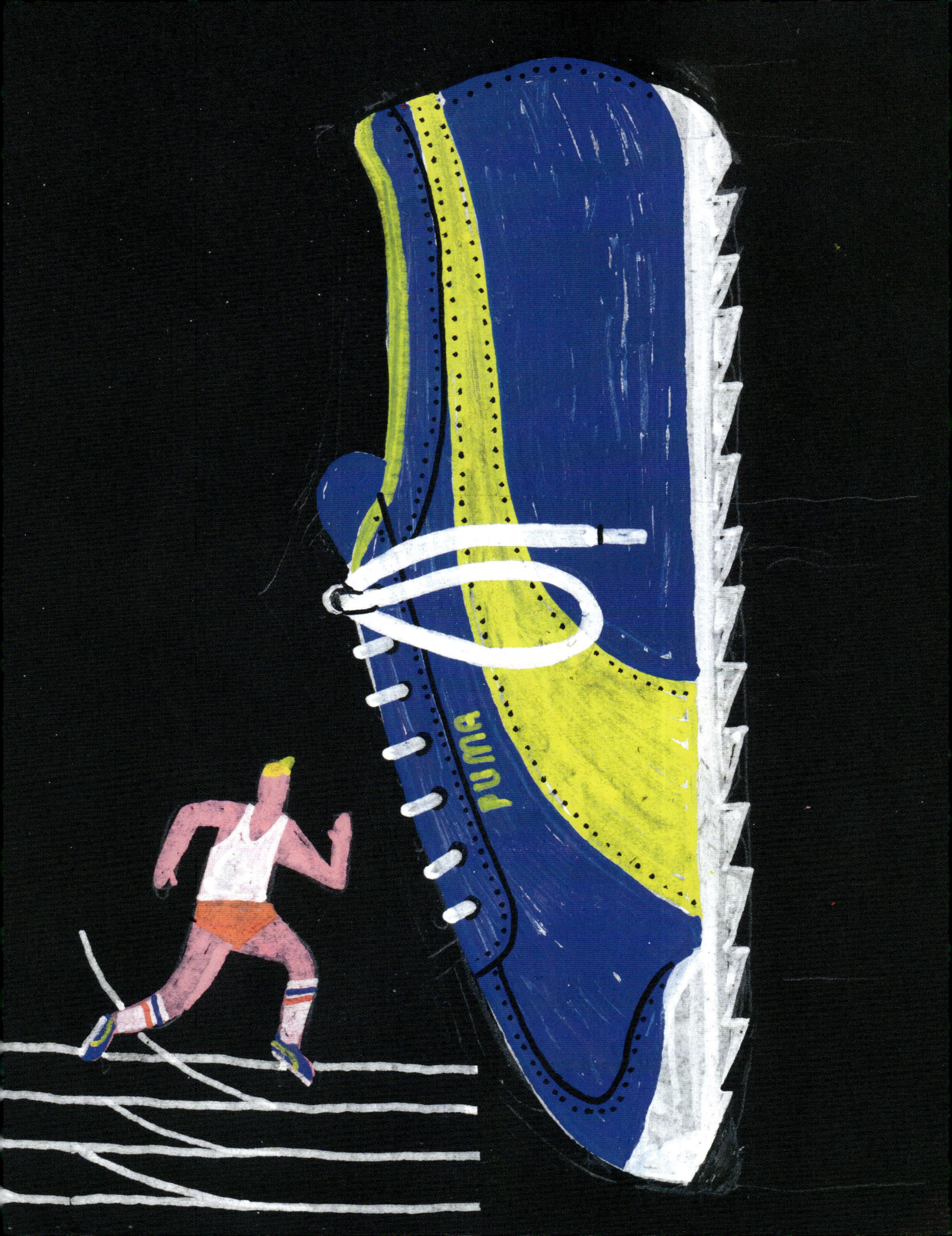
PUMA

Chapter

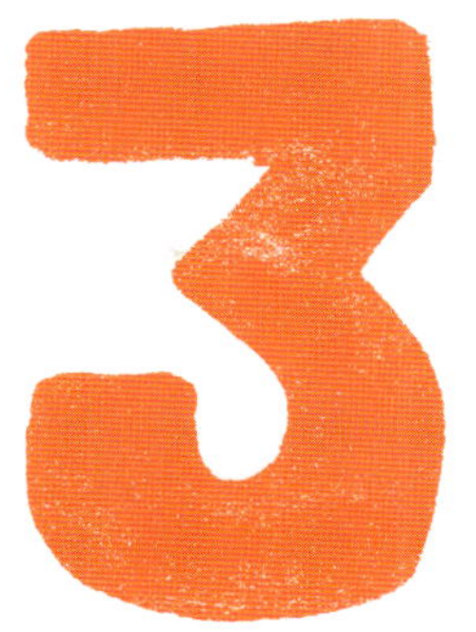

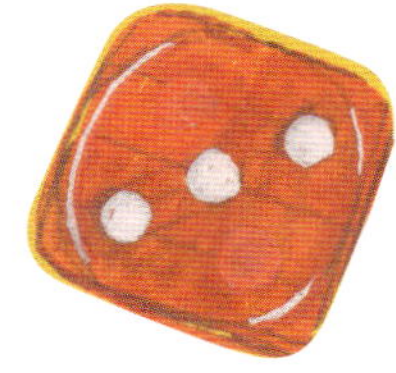

"People often ask me, 'How do you find the time for all this?' And I answer, 'I look for it.'"

Austin Kleon, *Something Small, Every Day*

THE DAILY DRAWING PLAN

While it's possible to start a Daily Drawing Practice without a plan, I wouldn't recommend it. In this chapter, I'll explain why a clear plan is essential if you want your practice to last. You'll learn about the five elements of a Daily Drawing Plan and how to create your own, tailored to your life and goals. With a solid plan in place, you'll be far more likely to keep going when things get tough—and you'll get much more out of the experience.

The Power of the Plan

Have you ever made a New Year's resolution, only to break it a few days later? Perhaps you declared to eat healthier food or go to the gym more. Chances are, as much as you wanted to keep your resolution, you never took the extra step of making a specific plan. Unless we're specific about our goals and the steps we'll take to achieve them, we're almost destined to fail. In the words of Antoine de Saint-Exupéry, "A goal without a plan is just a wish." Likewise, if you wish to have a Daily Drawing Practice, you're going to need a plan.

A Purpose Gets You Started

All big efforts require a plan: A building needs a blueprint, a painting needs a sketch, a successful marathon needs a training plan. It's from this latter example that I have the most experience (outside of drawing), so let me draw from there. In my late thirties, I discovered my love of long-distance running. I had always run for general health and fitness, but the habit came and went depending on the season of life I was in. Things changed when I started working from home and needed to become intentional about getting outside and staying healthy.

I suddenly had a concrete *purpose* for running every day. (As you'll learn later in this chapter, having a purpose is key to building your plan). At first, my runs were fairly short and boring (twenty to thirty minutes, same route). Probably out of boredom, but also out of curiosity, I started using a fitness app to track my runs on my phone. Seeing how far I was running, and how fast, added a new dimension to my running—and made it more interesting. My app was also awarding me little badges for new running achievements, which was oddly motivating! Suddenly I was pushing myself a little harder: I ran 4k yesterday; could I do 5k today? I've run 6k in thirty minutes before, could I do it in twenty-nine? When I ran my first 10k, I was so inspired that I signed up for my first half-marathon (13.1 miles [21.2 km]). Since then, I've gone on to run multiple marathons and even ultramarathons (my farthest distance is 50 miles [80.5 km] so far).

Plans Help You Go the Distance

While it was natural enough getting up to my first 10k, figuring out how to double that was a whole other thing. How on earth do people achieve that kind of fitness? How many weeks would it take? How do I build up my distance each week? Setting my first half-marathon goal led me to discover the *training plan*. It's a simple concept: You set a goal for your distance, and then you find a plan that can get you there, *incrementally*, from where you are now. The plan gives you instructions for each day over the course of a few months (sixteen weeks is a standard training block for a half-marathon). All you have to do is trust the plan and do each day's run—no matter what! If you want to cross the finish line on race day, you need to follow that plan!

Starting and keeping a Daily Drawing Practice is no different. Once you know you want to draw more (and why), the next step is creating a plan to help you get there.

Facing Page: From 5k to 50 miles (80.5 km), I've followed and customized many training plans like this. A plan gives you structure for your daily efforts toward a specific distance and time goal. This one is from my first trail race.

MARATHON TRAIL RUN TRAINING GUIDE

AT LEAST HALF OF YOUR RUNS SHOULD BE DONE ON TRAILS.

	MONDAY	TUESDAY	WEDNESDAY	THURSDAY	FRIDAY	SATURDAY	SUNDAY
WEEK 1	30 min. Hills	4 miles Easy Run	30 min. Tempo Run	Active Rest	3 miles Easy Run	8 miles. Long Run	Rest
WEEK 2	15 min. Speed	4 miles Easy Run	30 min. Tempo Run	Active Rest	3 miles Easy Run	10 miles. Long Run	Rest
WEEK 3	35 min. Hills	4 miles Easy Run	35 min. Tempo Run	Active Rest	3 miles Easy Run	12 miles. Long Run	Rest
WEEK 4	40 min. Hills	5 miles Easy Run	40 min. Tempo Run	Active Rest	4 miles Easy Run	6 miles. Long Run	Rest
WEEK 5	20 min. Speed	5 miles Easy Run	50 min. Tempo Run	Active Rest	3 miles Easy Run	14 miles. Long Run	Rest
WEEK 6	45 min. Hills	5 miles Easy Run	60 min. Tempo Run	Active Rest	5 miles Easy Run	13 miles. Long Run	Rest
WEEK 7	20 min. Speed	6 miles Easy Run	50 min. Tempo Run	Active Rest	4 miles Easy Run	16 miles. Long Run	Rest
WEEK 8	45 min. Hills	5 miles Easy Run	60 min. Tempo Run	Active Rest	3 miles Easy Run	17 miles. Long Run	Rest
WEEK 9	50 min. Hills	6 miles Easy Run	70 min. Tempo Run	Active Rest	4 miles Easy Run	8 miles. Long Run	Rest
WEEK 10	25 min. Speed	5 miles Easy Run	50 min. Tempo Run	Active Rest	3 miles Easy Run	18 miles. Long Run	Rest
WEEK 11	40 min. Hills	7 miles Easy Run	80 min. Tempo Run	Active Rest	3 miles Easy Run	13 miles. Long Run	Rest
WEEK 12	20 min. Speed	5 miles Easy Run	70 min. Tempo Run	Active Rest	3 miles Easy Run	20 miles. Long Run	Rest
WEEK 13	35 min. Hills	7 miles Easy Run	60 min. Tempo Run	Active Rest	4 miles Easy Run	15 miles. Long Run	Rest
WEEK 14	40 min. Hills	8 miles Easy Run	40 min. Tempo Run	Active Rest	4 miles Easy Run	12 miles. Long Run	Rest
WEEK 15	30 min. Hills	10 miles Easy Run	20 min. Tempo Run	Active Rest	3 miles Easy Run	9 miles. Long Run	Rest
WEEK 16	4 miles Easy Run	4 miles Easy Run	3 miles Easy Run	Active Rest	2 miles Easy Run	RACE DAY (26.2 miles)	Sleep.

ALL RUNS (EXCEPT EASY ONES), ALONG WITH HILL WORK, SHOULD BE PRECEDED BY 5 MINUTES OF DYNAMIC WARM-UP AND FOLLOWED BY 5 MINUTES OF COOLDOWN AND 10 MINUTES OF STRETCHING.

The Daily Drawing Plan

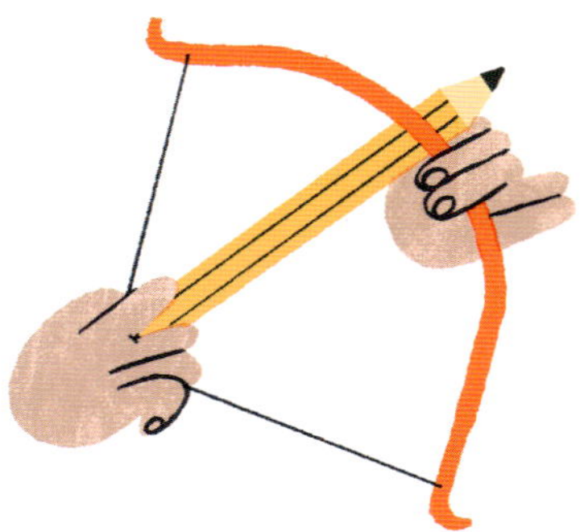

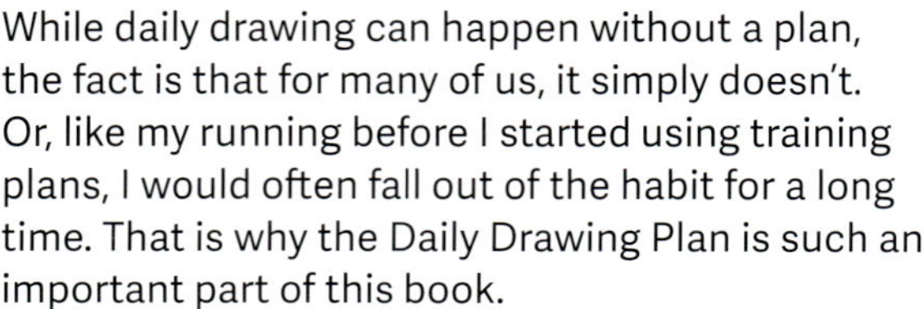

While daily drawing can happen without a plan, the fact is that for many of us, it simply doesn't. Or, like my running before I started using training plans, I would often fall out of the habit for a long time. That is why the Daily Drawing Plan is such an important part of this book.

Fortunately, the Daily Drawing Plan is far simpler than a marathon training plan. You don't have to have a detailed schedule for each day. You don't even need to sweat! There are five simple elements, each one giving you more structure and purpose as you begin your Daily Drawing Practice.

Purpose

If your pain point is lacking motivation, the antidote is finding your purpose. Seriously—why do you want to draw every day? When it comes to doing hard things, without a strong sense of purpose, it can be hard to stay committed (or to even start)! In his book *Start with Why*, Simon Sinek writes, "When we are clear about our 'why,' discipline becomes easier." There will be days that you won't want to draw at all, but simply checking in with your "why" can be enough to motivate you to open your sketchbook and begin.

Media

If it takes too much effort to get set up, you might never get started. I recommend that you declare your go-to media (that is, your favorite drawing tools) ahead of time so you can get right to the drawing without having to think about it in the moment.

I also recommend keeping your tools out and within reach so you don't have to waste time looking for them. If you don't have a dedicated space, you can always keep your tools in a handy travel kit.

When training, when it's time to do my next run, it helps to have my gear ready to go at the front door. On the other hand, if I have to turn the house upside down to find my shoes, sunglasses, water bottle, and such (which happens far too often), not only is this eating at my running time, but it's also opening the door to distractions that could thwart my best intentions.

As for which media to choose, stick with a favorite pairing of sketchbook and drawing media. That's not to say you won't sometimes want to change things up. If your purpose is to try new tools and techniques, then write that in your plan! For more info on media types, see chapter 4.

Sustainable Schedule

In the Daily Drawing Plan, a sustainable schedule helps you set goals that work for you. You can keep your Daily Drawing Practice going by making sure it can fit into your already busy life!

When choosing a race training plan, I need to make sure it fits into the rest of my life. I also need to intentionally build it into my schedule. The more ambitious my goals, the more time I need to dedicate to my training. In busier times I have to scale back my goals. While I'd love to do a 100-mile

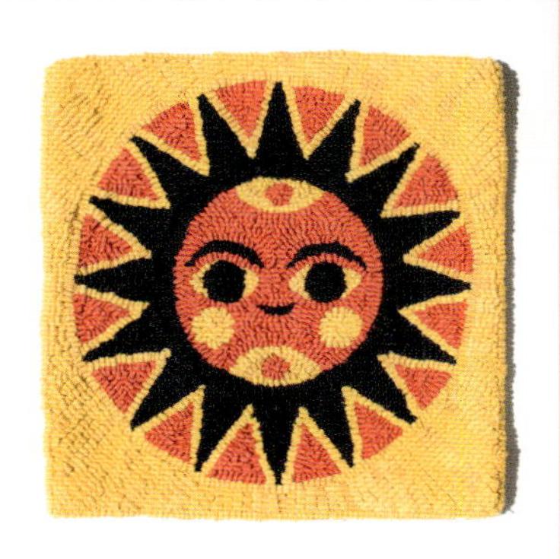

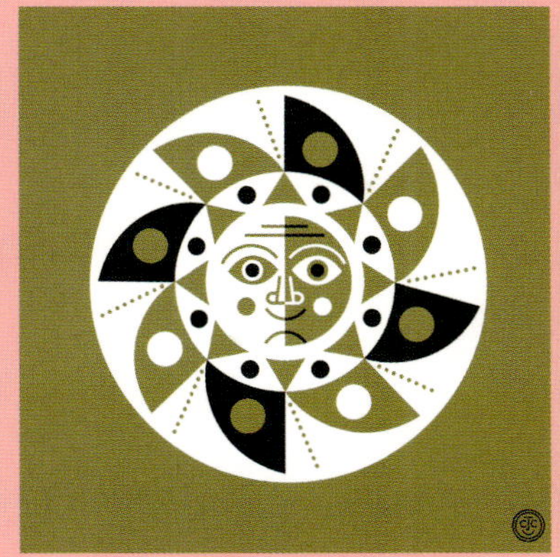

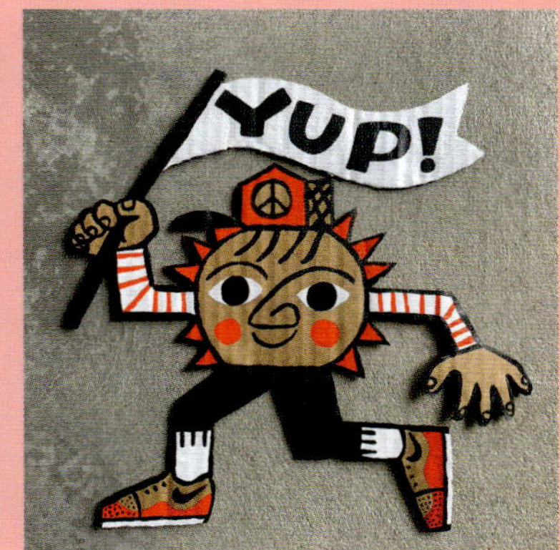

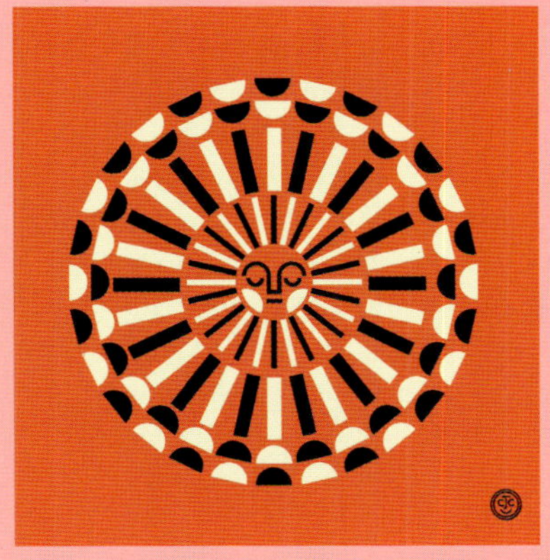

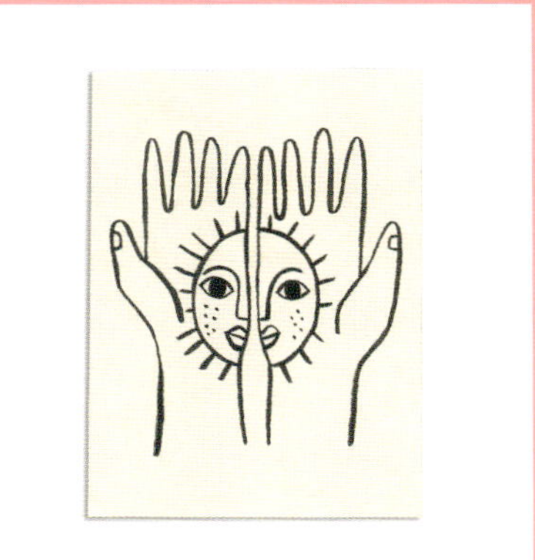

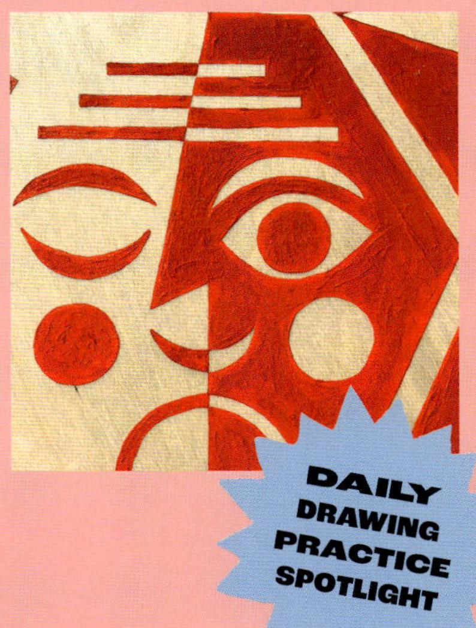

DAILY DRAWING PRACTICE SPOTLIGHT

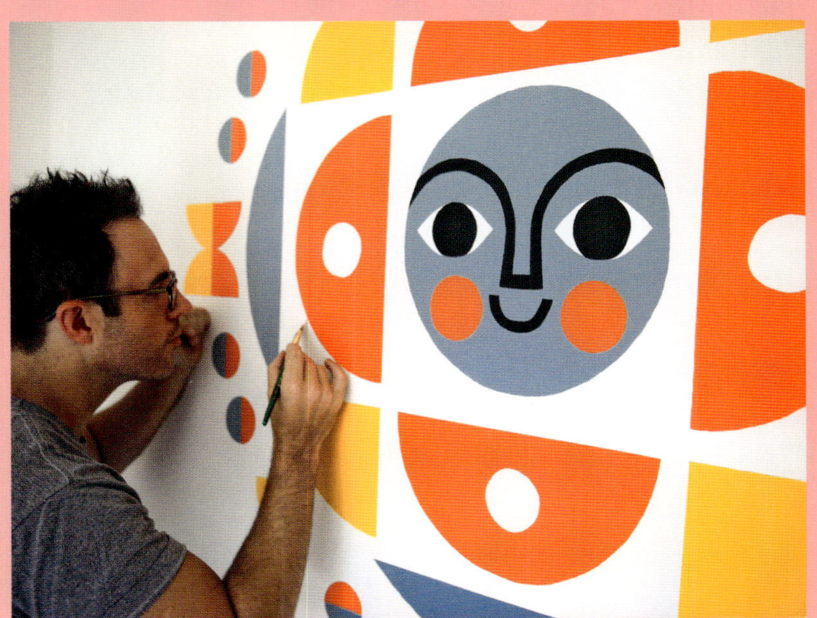

Tad Carpenter

tadcarpenter.com
Tad Carpenter is a designer and illustrator based in Kansas City, Missouri. Tad drew a new sun every week for ten years in a project he called Sunday Suns. While technically more of a weekly project than a daily practice, the principle of consistent, sustainable creativity is no less exemplary. Sunday Suns is an example of how, even with just one image per week, it's possible to build up an inspiringly massive body of work.

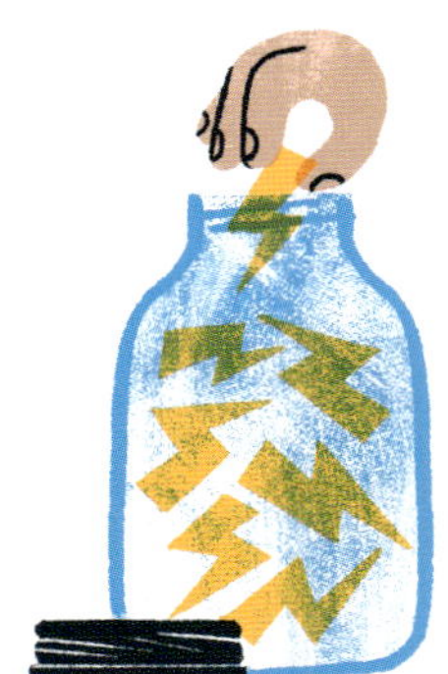

(161 km) ultramarathon before my next birthday, it's just not a practical goal to fit into my life right now. It doesn't have to be all-or-nothing though: I can still pursue my passion for long-distance running with regular marathons!

There are three elements to a sustainable schedule:

Quantity

How much time can you commit to drawing each day? Setting a realistic quantity, in terms of time, can help you stay on track for the long term. But quantity is not just about how long you can draw; it's about giving you a clear finish line. It's also a tool for overcoming your perfectionism. If you don't like how you draw, make it about how *much* you draw. This could be a quantity of time (such as five minutes per drawing) or of space (one page per day). When the five minutes are done or your page is filled, you can say you did the drawing, and this is an accomplishment you can feel good about no matter how you feel about the drawing itself.

Frequency

If you draw too infrequently, it's hard to get into a rhythm. While, of course, daily drawing is the ideal, it's not always possible. Perhaps, like me, five days a week works for you. Tad Carpenter (see *page 41*) added to his ten-year Sunday Suns project just once a week. Many will find three days a week just right.

Duration

Let's be honest. Just because you wrote down a plan doesn't mean it will be easy to keep forever! It's far more reasonable to give yourself a trial period to just see how things go at first. The duration is the span of time in which you intend to keep up with your practice. I recommend setting an initial minimum duration of thirty days. This gives you just enough time to experience the motivational ups and downs of a Daily Practice while also giving your initial ideas and goals a chance to flourish. Do enough of these shorter-term plans, and the lifelong Daily Practice will naturally fall into place. For more details on shorter-term projects, see chapter 7.

Source

Showing up to draw is great, but it can still be hard to know what to draw when you do! For many, this is one of the biggest pain points. The antidote here is to plan what you'll draw ahead of time. Your inspiration could come from a prompt list or a "go-to" source.

A Prompt List

A very common inspiration source for Daily Projects is a prompt list. If you've ever joined a daily drawing challenge like Inktober, you'll be familiar with this. If you have a hard time deciding what to draw each day, you can find daily drawing prompts online, or you can write your own based on a subject you're interested in. For example, maybe you want to improve how you draw hands, so you can spend a month drawing just your hand, or hands of musicians (from photos you find online). If it helps, you can also use AI to generate a prompt list, but remember to do the drawings yourself!

A Go-To Source

Unlike a prewritten list of prompts, a go-to source of inspiration is more variable and less prescriptive. If you want a plan that's a bit more open-ended, as I do, this might be the way to go. For a few years now, I've enjoyed drawing from quirky retail catalogs from the 1970s because they remind me of the stuff that we had in my house when I was a kid. This is my go-to source when I'm out of other ideas, or not doing a shorter-term Daily Project. Each day, I simply open the catalog and draw the first thing that catches my interest.

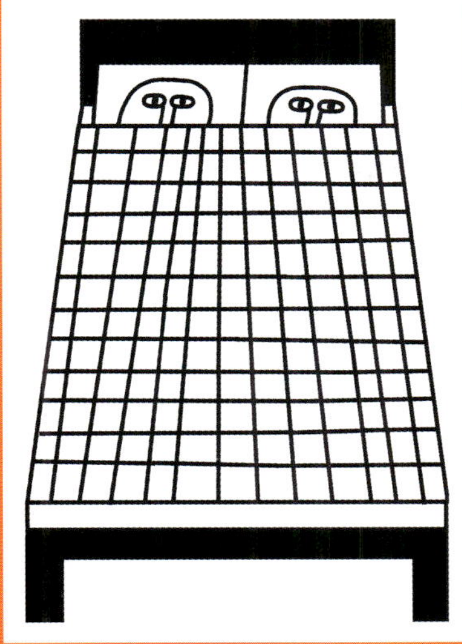

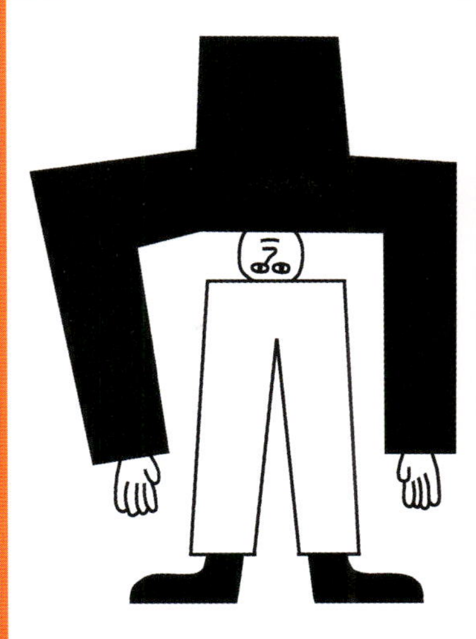

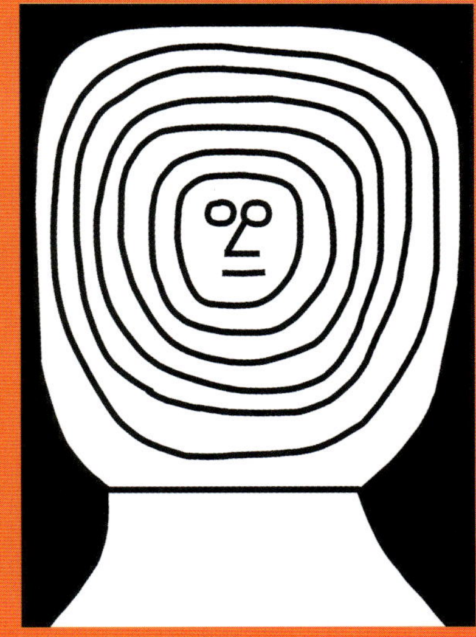

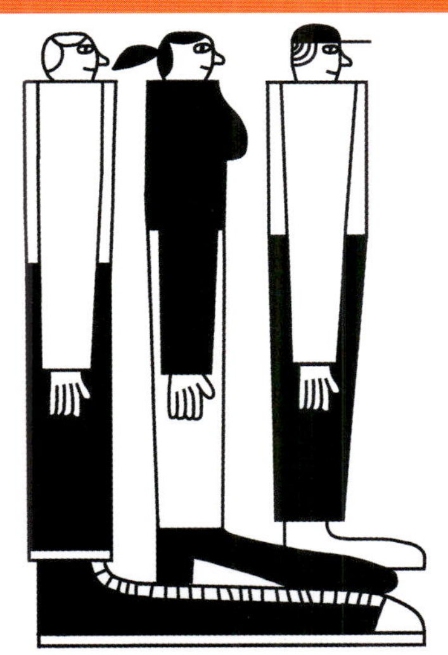

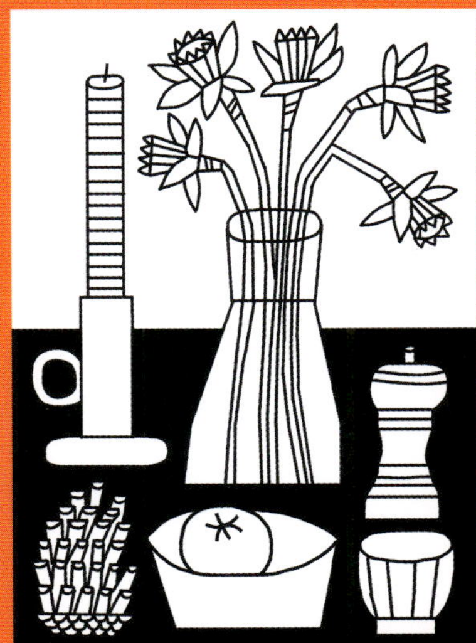

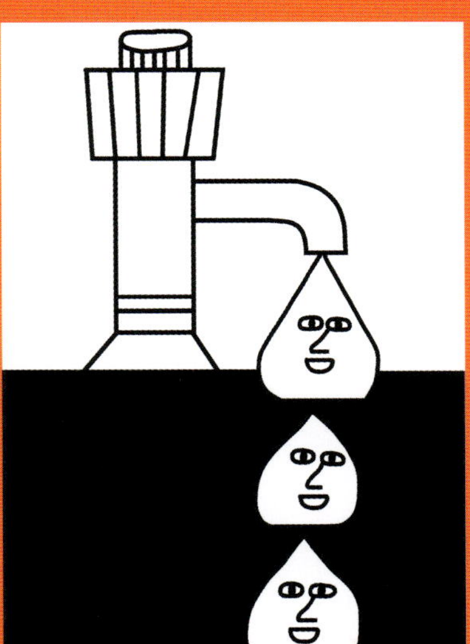

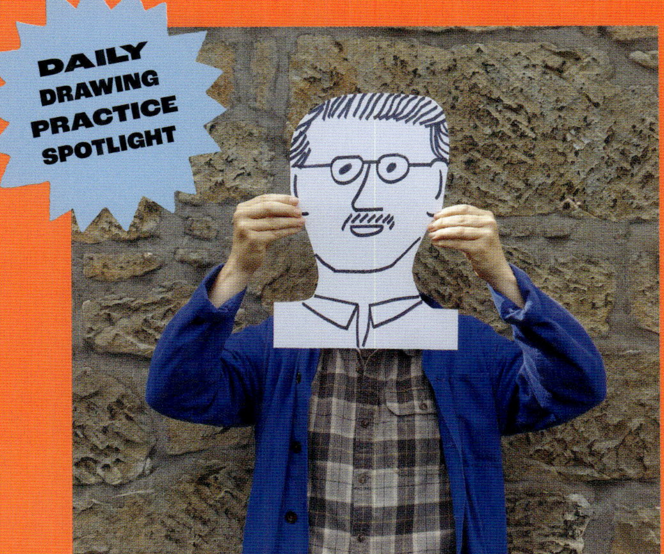

Marcus Oakley

marcusoakley.com
This Dunfermline, Scotland–based artist has consistently carried on with a playful, geometric series of illustrations, mostly figurative, and with simple colors or black and white, but with fun diversions in watercolor and assemblage. Marcus was once a graphic designer for Paul Smith but has since moved on to the world of fine art. His clients include *Anorak Magazine*, *The New Yorker*, and Origin Coffee Roasters.

Sharing

I mention sharing a lot in this book, and that's because I believe it's one of the most powerful ways to stay motivated with and grow through your Daily Drawing Practice. For one, it gives you a bigger reason to show up to draw—people are counting on your next post. For another, it gives you one of the best (and sometimes only) opportunities to get feedback on your work. When making your plan, just write down how and where you intend on sharing. For more insights and tips on sharing, see chapter 8.

Place and Time

Though not essential, I recommend dedicating a specific time and place for your Daily Drawing sessions. If you work out, you do it in the gym. If you practice meditation, you probably know when and where you can do it without distraction. Similarly, knowing ahead of time when and where you'll draw each day can make this part of your day feel more special—and even sacred.

Personally, I like to begin my day with drawing in the hour before my real workday begins. I make some coffee, head out to my backyard studio, sit down at my desk, and do the drawing. This gets my creative juices flowing and fuels me up for the rest of the day.

Does Every Daily Drawing Practice Start with a Plan?

For some lucky people, drawing every day just comes naturally, but that's not a reliable approach for everyone. Nor do all daily creative types feel the need to state a plan or work by a specific schedule. For example, Brandon Campbell (*see page 32*) says he just kind of found his groove and kept going. A Daily Drawing Plan—and this entire book—is for those who would like to start drawing more but can't seem to find their groove. These are just tools to help you build up some initial momentum. From there, you may find it was just the push that you needed to keep going.

After working with a Daily Drawing Plan for a while, like riding a bike, you may find you can ease in and out of seasons of daily drawing more naturally. This is certainly true for me. Now that drawing is a long-established habit, I'm able to hit pause when things get busy, and then get right back into it as soon as things clear up.

Facing Page: Use this example to structure your own Daily Drawing Plan. Be sure to write it in your own sketchbook if you borrowed this book from the library!

MY DAILY DRAWING PLAN

Make a Plan!

PURPOSE

Why do you want to start a daily drawing practice?

MEDIA

What will your go-to tools and sketchbook be?

SCHEDULE

☐ TIME-BASED ☐ SPACE-BASED

Quantity	Frequency	Duration
How much will you draw per session?	How many days per week will you show up to draw?	For how long will you commit to this particular plan?

SOURCE

☐ PROMPT LIST ☐ GO-TO SOURCE

Write your prompt list or go-to source below.

SHARING

How will you digitally capture or document your drawings?
Where will you share them?

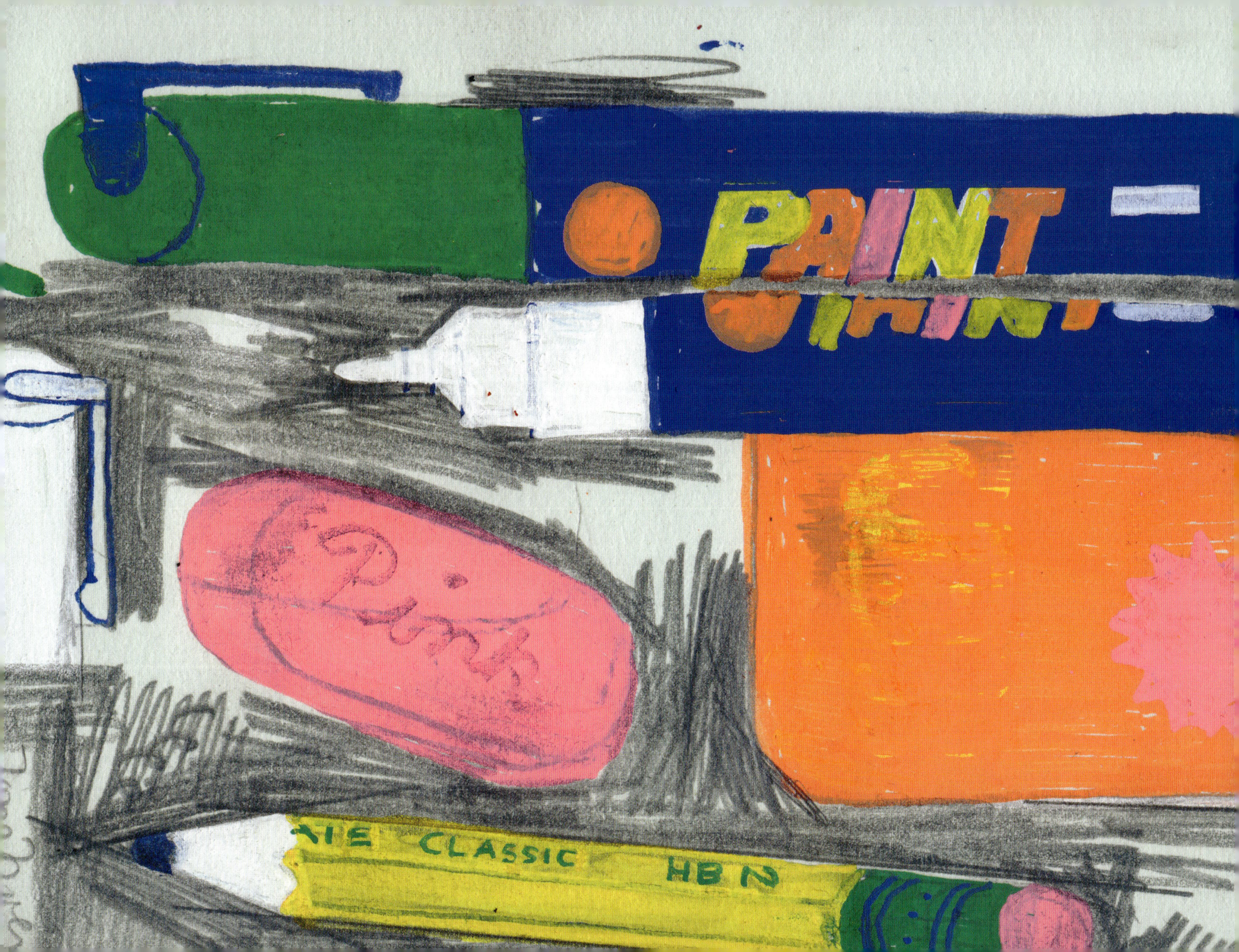
PAINT
Pink
CLASSIC
HB 2

Chapter

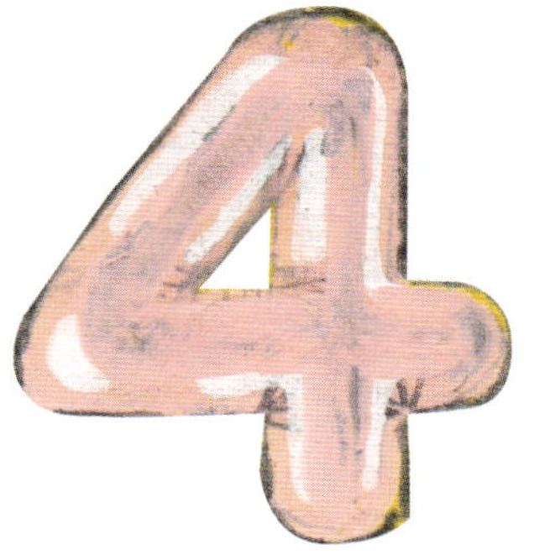

> "Want to draw more? Put your pencils, pens, notebooks and drawing tools on top of your desk, within easy reach."
>
> **James Clear, *Atomic Habits***

TOOLS AND TECHNIQUES

Having the right tools makes it easier to draw consistently—and enjoy the process. In this chapter, we'll focus on identifying your ideal set of daily drawing tools. I'll share why it helps to keep things simple, consistent, and always within reach. You'll learn how to choose tools that not only fit your goals and lifestyle but also bring you joy. By the end of the chapter, you'll have a stronger understanding of the right tools for you—to reduce creative friction and keep you focused on the actual drawing.

Set It and Forget It

We're far more likely to keep up with our practice when the steps involved become automatic. As James Clear puts it in *Atomic Habits*, "It is human nature to follow the law of least effort, which states that when deciding between two similar options, people will naturally gravitate toward the option that requires the least amount of work." Every added decision or demand on your willpower becomes a potential point of failure. Since your drawing tools are essential to your Daily Drawing Practice, I recommend automating—or better yet, eliminating—the decision about what tools to use as much as possible.

As a long-distance runner, I go through more shoes—and more types of shoes—in one year than most people do in a decade. When I first got serious about running, I had no idea different shoes were designed for different kinds of runs. But the deeper I got into it, the more I learned how things like drop height, tread depth, cushioning, and weight can affect performance. Some shoes help you run faster; others support you over longer distances. Some are made for trails, others for pavement.

With so many brands and styles out there, I quickly felt overwhelmed. I even used to dread shopping for shoes—the clerk's questions felt more like a cross-examination than friendly customer service. But over time—and thanks to many hours of YouTube shoe reviews—I learned to navigate the world of running footwear. Today, not only do I know how to match shoes to different runs, but I actually look forward to talking gear with fellow running nerds. Best of all, when it's time to head out the door, I don't have to think twice about what shoes to wear.

Fortunately, drawing supplies are much cheaper than running shoes, and there's far less pressure to find the "perfect" ones. There are no rules about what you should or shouldn't use in your Daily Drawing Practice. What matters most is keeping your tools simple, consistent, and easy to grab. Just as important, you should *enjoy* using them. Like running shoes, having go-to tools makes it easier to dive into your Daily Practice and keeps things simple when it's time to restock.

Because a Daily Drawing Practice thrives on consistency and focus, using a single type of medium can also help your work feel more cohesive over time.

Choosing Your Tools

With thousands of options for paper, pens, paints, markers, and pencils, how could you possibly narrow it down? The truth is, finding what works best for you takes time and experimentation.

To start, keep it simple. Use what you already know and enjoy. Once you're ready to explore, it helps to know what to look for. In this section, I'll share six media types—combinations of tools and materials—that I've enjoyed using in my own Daily Drawing Practice. This is not a definitive guide but just a bit of inspiration to help you on your way to finding the right tools for you.

DAILY DRAWING Starter Pack

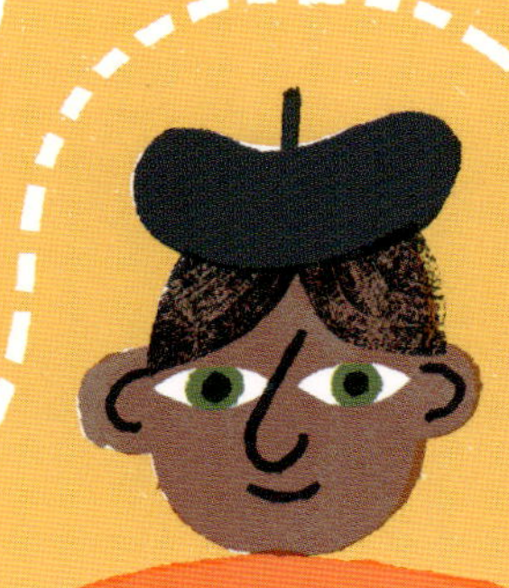

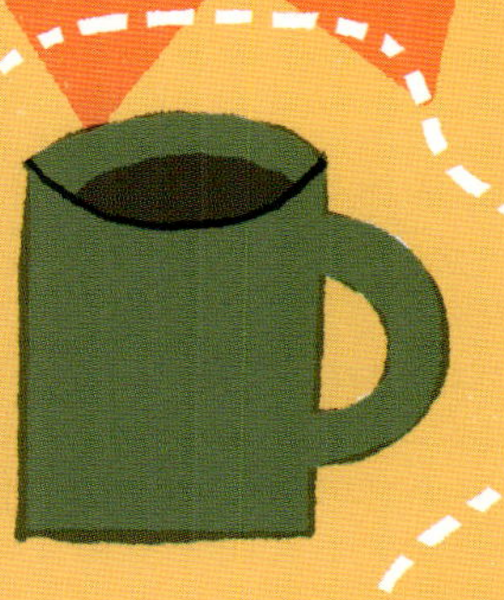

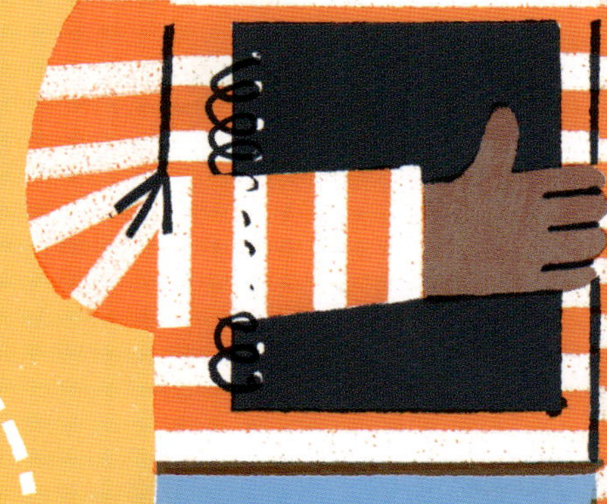

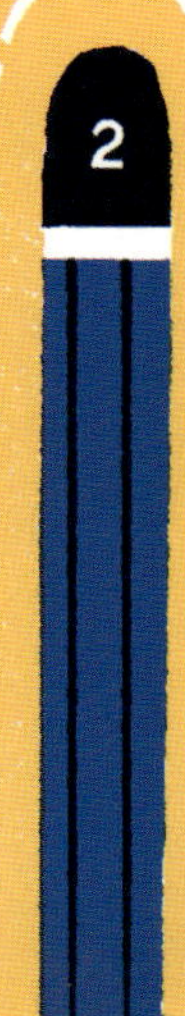

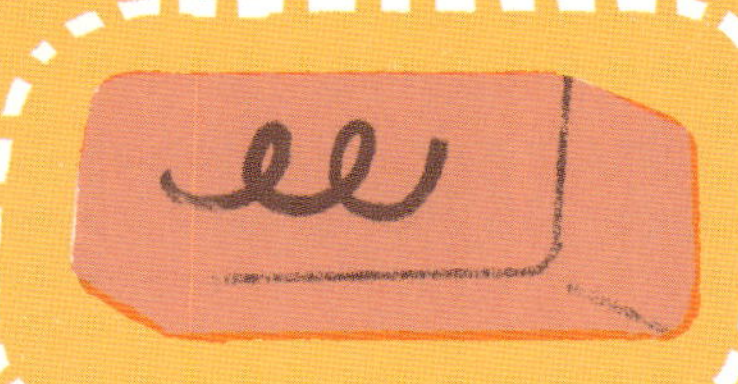

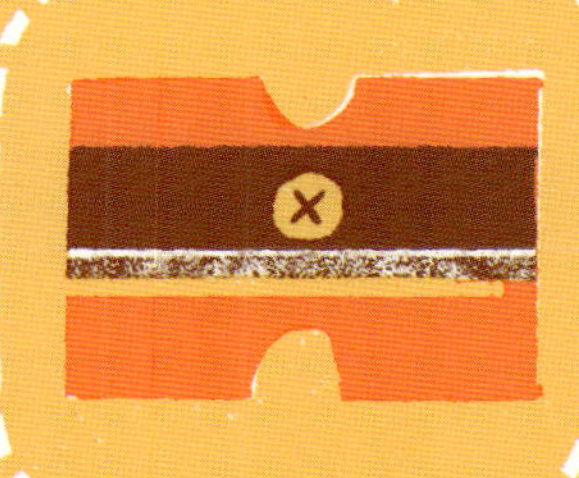

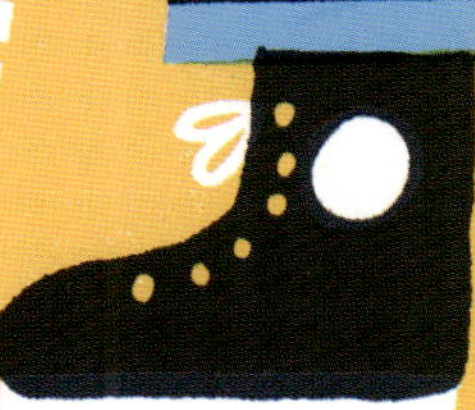

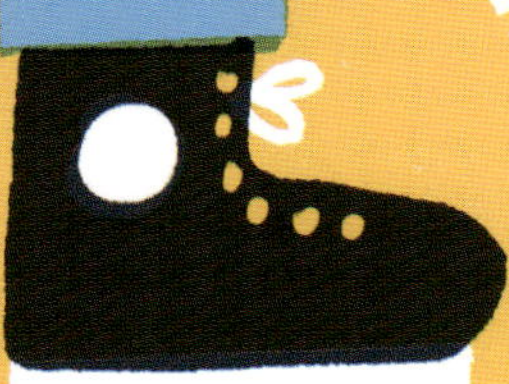

Choosing Your Go-To Sketchbook

As the place where all your drawings go, your sketchbook plays a pretty important role in your practice! While you'll want to choose one that works well with your chosen media, there are some general things to keep in mind. Honestly, a lot of this comes down to personal preference, but here are some basic things I look for (and avoid) when picking a sketchbook:

Things I Look For in a Sketchbook

- It lies flat while I'm drawing.
- It's easy to photograph or scan.
- It has quality paper that suits my media.
- It's small enough to carry around.
- I love it as an object, but I'm not afraid to mark it up.
- Consistent form factor: looks good on a shelf and packs neatly.
- Reliably available when it's time to purchase a new one.

Things I Avoid

- Bulky "artisanal" sketchbooks (e.g., fancy binding styles, handmade paper).
- Large formats that feel awkward in public or overwhelming to fill.
- Spines on the short edge, making it unwieldy when opened.
- Coil bindings: They get in the way of my drawing hand, are difficult to scan, and snag easily.
- Perfect-bound books that don't lie flat without pressure.
- Generally, any sketchbook that's an outlier in size or shape from my usual set.

Over the years, I've tried all kinds of sketchbooks—hardbound, coil-bound, artisanal, dollar-store—but I keep coming back to just two: Moleskine and Uglybooks.

Moleskine

Though pricey, I love how Moleskine notebooks lie flat on every page. The creamy off-white paper is thin yet strong, allowing for many pages per book. I also love the back pocket for tucking in little keepsakes, and how they form a clean, matching set over time. Mine play triple duty as sketchbook, planner, and journal.

Uglybooks

Uglybooks are a recent discovery, but I'm hooked for life. Their bold, colorful pages are perfect for Posca paint pens, which really pop on the surface. I prefer the saddle-stitched type: They lie flat, scan easily, and have plain covers that beg to be customized—which over time are very satisfying to look at as a set.

To Tell You the Tooth

Paper comes in smoother or rougher textures. The rougher it is, the more *tooth* it has. Toothier paper absorbs media better—especially pencil, pen, and wet media—but wears down tools faster. It can also create a more expressive texture. Smoother paper, by contrast, is less abrasive but more prone to smudging, especially with dry media like pencil.

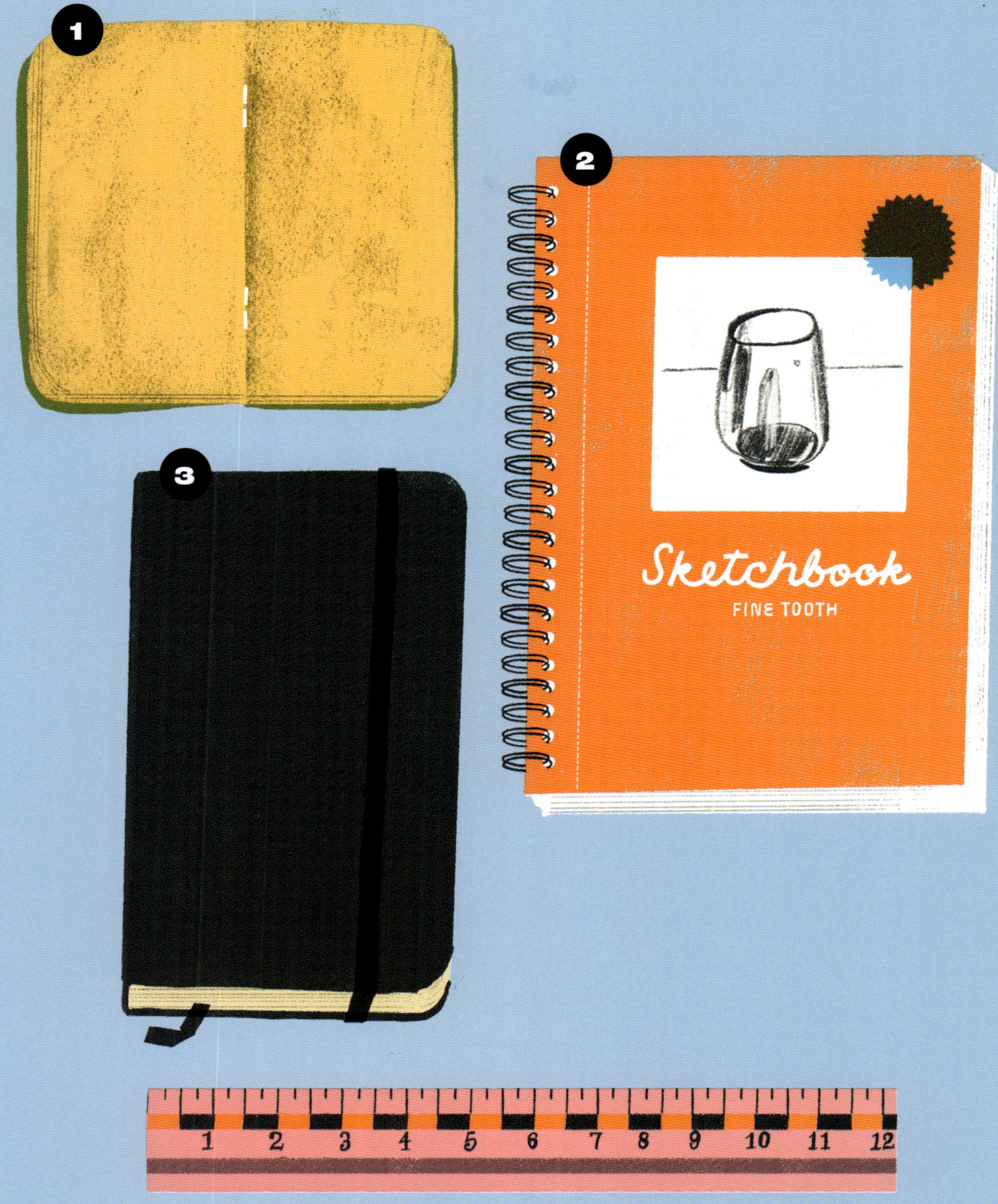

1. Uglybooks No. 1 Saddle Stitch. Comes in a 3-pack. (4 × 5.75 inches [10 × 14.5 cm]). Opens along the short edge, making it really long (or really wide) when opened.

2. Coil-bound sketchbooks like these often have good-quality paper for most drawing media, and they keep a small footprint while drawing. But there's a "catch"—the wire or plastic coils often come unbound, meaning loose sheets and awkward snags.

3. Moleskine Classic Notebook, Large, Plain, Black, Hardcover (5 × 8.25 inches [13 × 21 cm]). Comes in grid and dot grid varieties too (I switch between these just to keep things interesting).

The Six Media Types

While there are thousands of artistic tools and techniques out there, I've boiled down the most common into six basic categories or types. If choosing your tools is a sticking point, I recommend choosing one of these to start.

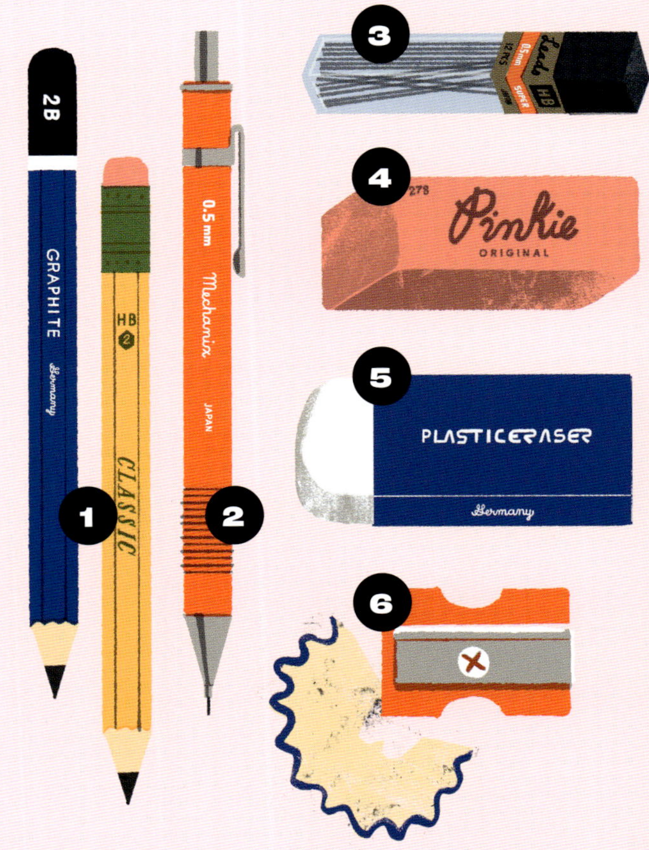

Basic Pencil and Paper
Pencil and paper are the staple tools of drawing. Some use pencil primarily for rough sketches, others as their main media. Pencils come in two basic forms: wooden shafts with lead cores **1** and mechanical pencils **2** that take refillable leads **3**. "Leads" are actually made of graphite, which varies in hardness and is measured on a scale from H (hardest) to B (softest). The higher the number in either direction, the more extreme the quality—6H is very hard, and 6B very soft. Right in the middle is HB (also known as No. 2), which works just fine for most people! For daily drawing, I prefer a 0.5 mm mechanical pencil, but if a dull IKEA pencil is closer, I might just use that instead. While I love the iconic Pink Pearl eraser **4** for its looks, I recommend a white plastic one, like the Staedtler Mars Plastic **5**. Don't forget about a decent-quality pencil sharpener **6**. For sketchbooks, almost any with white or whitish paper works. Moleskine notebooks **7** have thin, smooth, but surprisingly strong paper. They come in pocket, large, and extra-large sizes. If in doubt, go with large (5 × 8.25 inches [13 × 21 cm]).

Pen and Ink

Pen and ink is technically a specific artistic technique, but here I'm using it more broadly to include any ink-based drawing media. This includes micron or fineliner pens **8**, ballpoint pens, nib pens **9** with India ink, calligraphy pens, and even permanent markers **10**. (There is too much variety in this category to cover it all!) When I started drawing years ago, I loved the precise, black line quality of micron pens. In my illustration work, I sometimes use a nib pen or paintbrushes **11** with India ink, especially when I want more spontaneous, unpredictable marks. India ink **12** is water-based and requires having a jar of water **13** on hand for rinsing or making washes. Finally, you'll want to match your sketchbook to your pen type. Many pens will bleed through thinner pages (even Moleskine), so here I would recommend a general-purpose or mixed-media sketchbook **14** with at least 70 lb (114 gsm) paper.

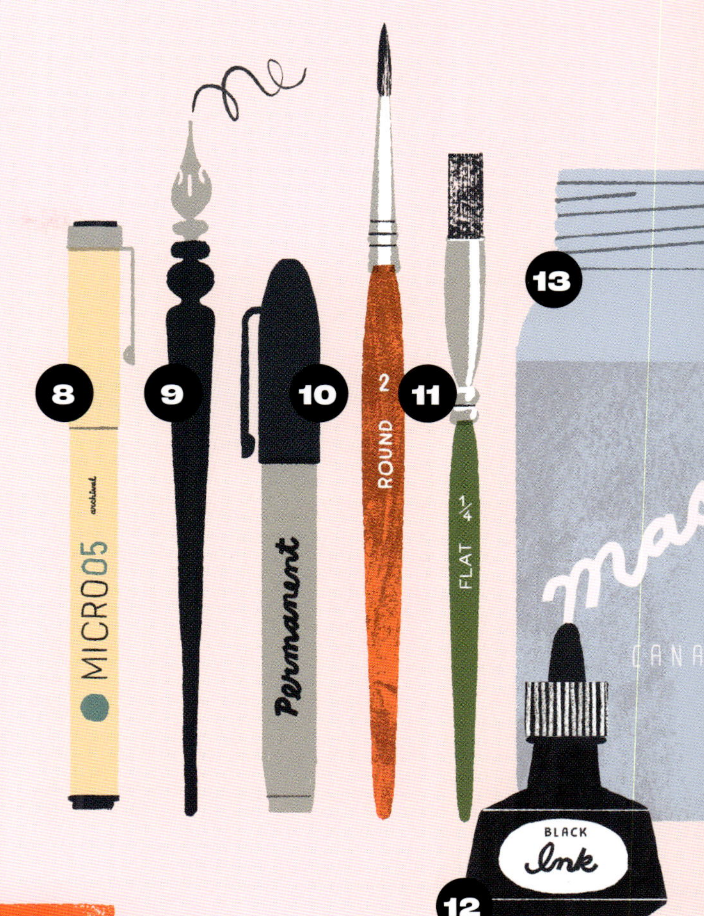

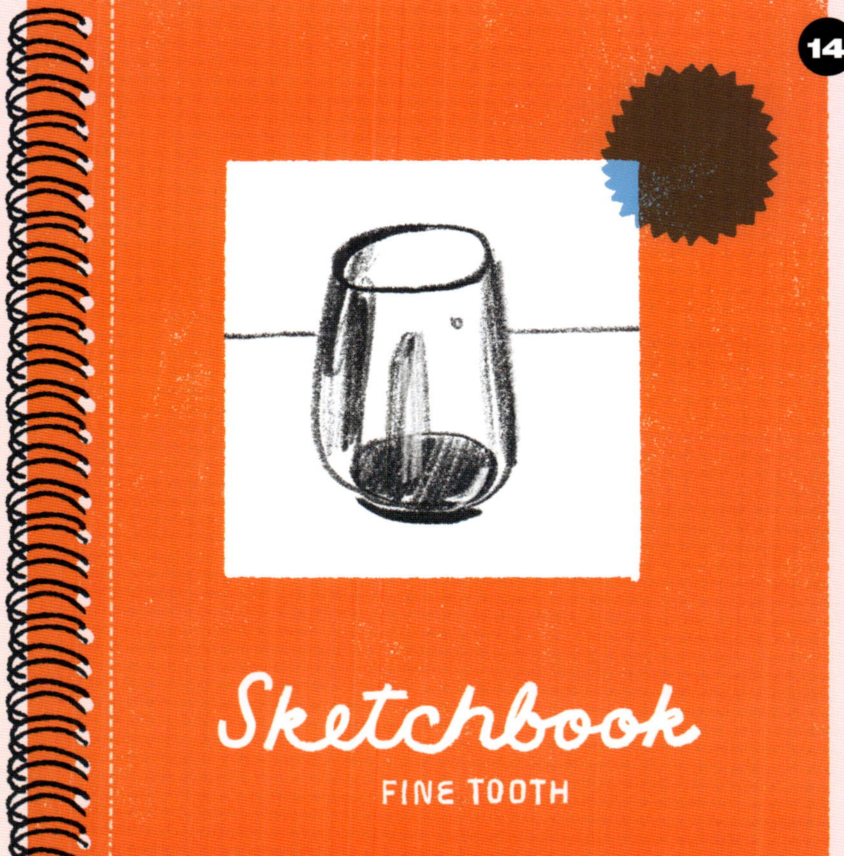

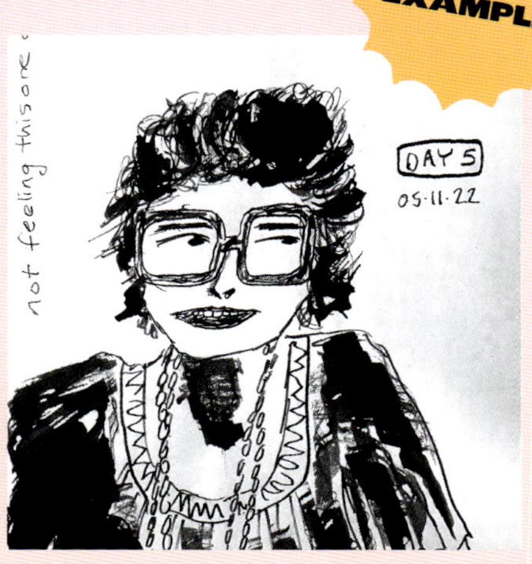

Pen and ink drawing by Nicola Thwaite

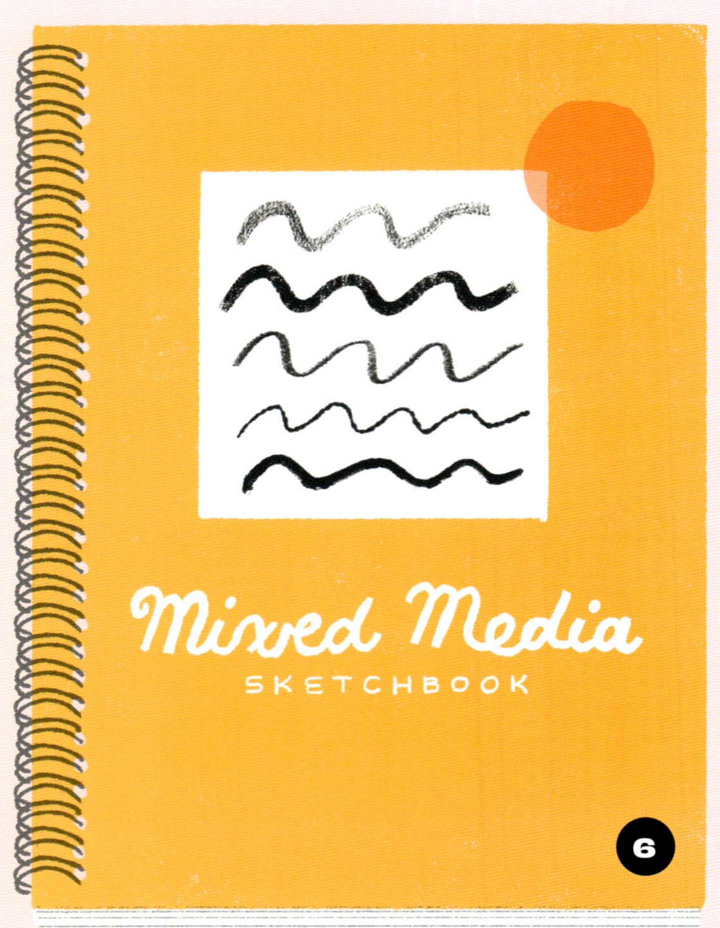
6
Mixed Media
SKETCHBOOK

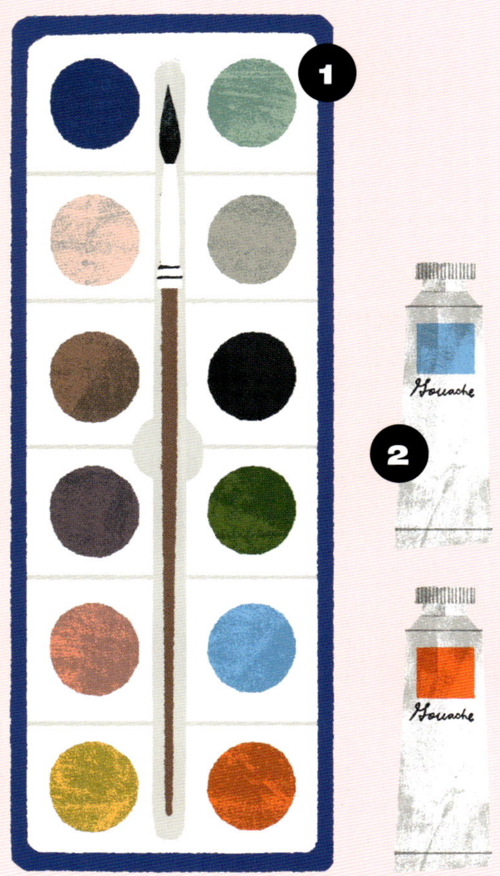
1
2
Gouache
Gouache

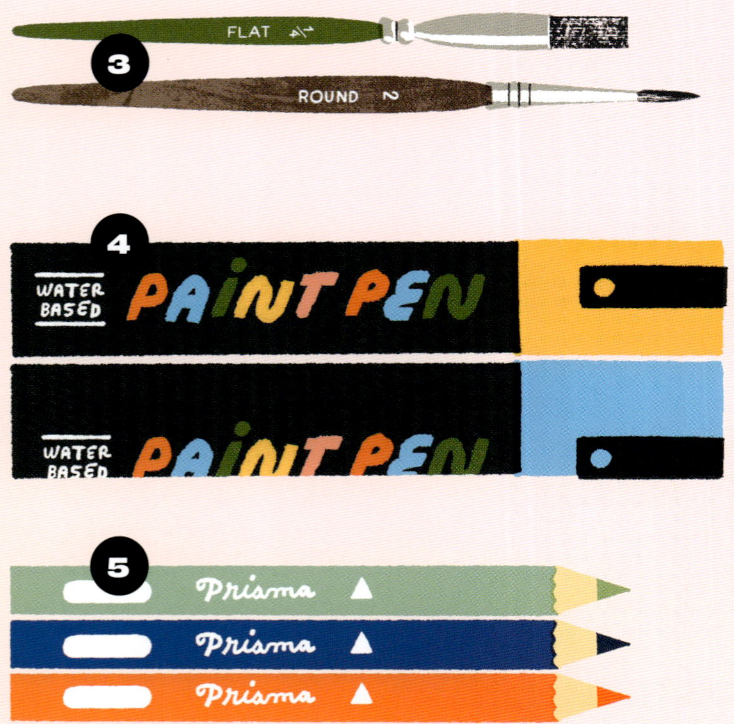
3
FLAT
ROUND 2
4
WATER BASED
PAINT PEN
WATER BASED
PAINT PEN
5
Prisma
Prisma
Prisma

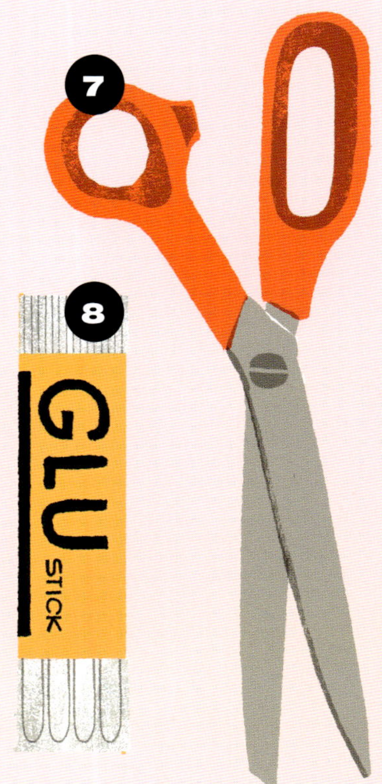
7
8
GLU
STICK

Painting and Color Media

In the context of daily drawing, painting is less about mastering technique and more about adding color. While I'm not a painter, I've worked with watercolor and gouache—I especially enjoy the latter. Watercolor **1** is transparent, allowing layers to show through, while gouache **2** is opaque, covering previous layers completely. For sketchbooks, small round and flat brushes **3** are ideal. My favorite color media are Posca paint pens **4**, which use an opaque, acrylic-based pigment similar to gouache. Paint pen ink dries quickly and can be layered in minutes. There are all kinds of markers available, including oil-, water-, and alcohol-based. Tips can be fine and firm, more brushlike, or chisel-shaped. Colored pencils **5** and oil pastels also fall into this category. Transparent media work best on heavier, whiter, toothier paper. Opaque media are more versatile and pair well with construction paper, Bristol board, or my beloved Uglybooks. Avoid thin papers that wrinkle when wet. When in doubt, go with a mixed-media sketchbook **6**.

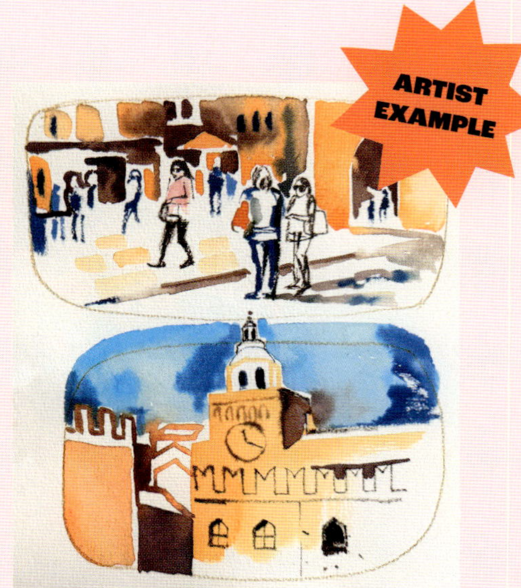

Watercolor sketch by Ohn Mar Win

Mixed Media and Collage

As you might have guessed, mixed media can involve any combination of different media types. If you're drawing, painting, and gluing bits of paper into your daily drawings, you're working with mixed media. Collage, the art of gluing scraps of paper and found materials onto the page, is a type of mixed media. For a classic sketch journal or travel sketchbook look, mixed media is a great choice. It's also a way to get yourself out of your head if more "pure" drawing scares you. By nature, the possibilities of mixed media are endless, but the basics are simple: good-quality scissors **7**, an acid-free glue stick **8**, and scraps from magazines or paper bits **9**. Try using tape **10** for an even scrappier look. Be sure to find a sketchbook that works well with mixed media—often it will say so right on the cover.

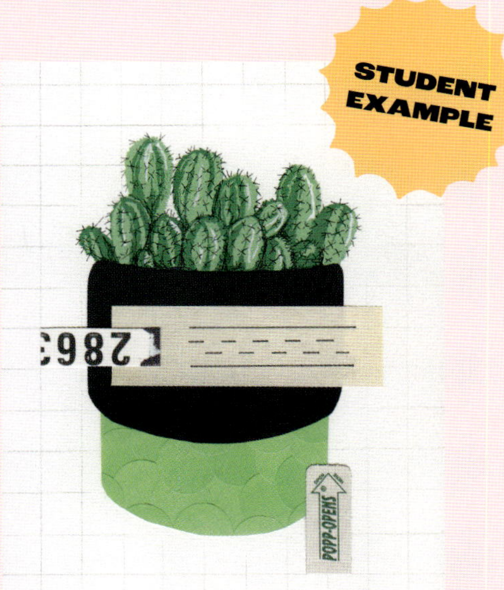

Mixed media example by Mariah Knight

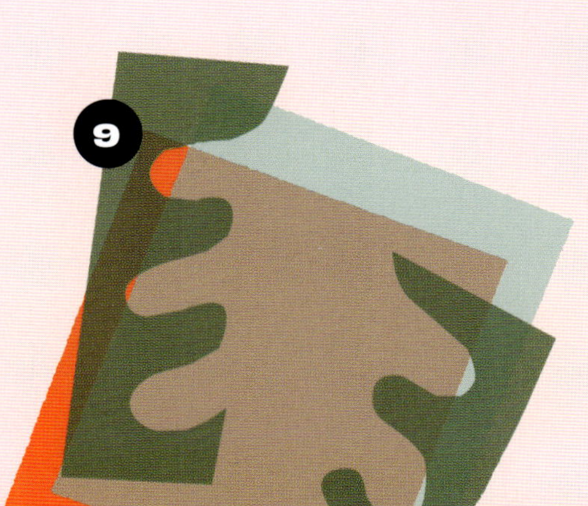

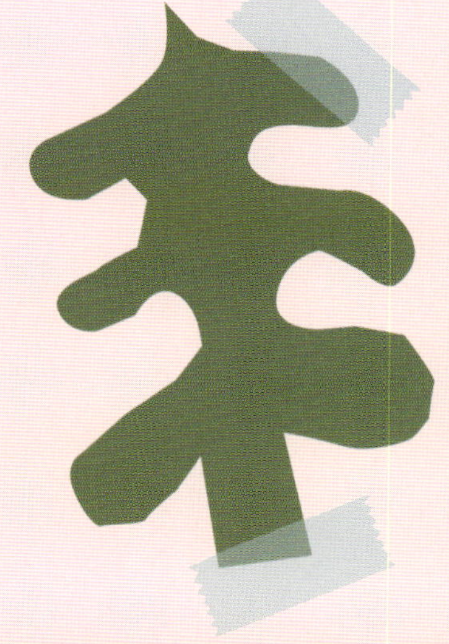

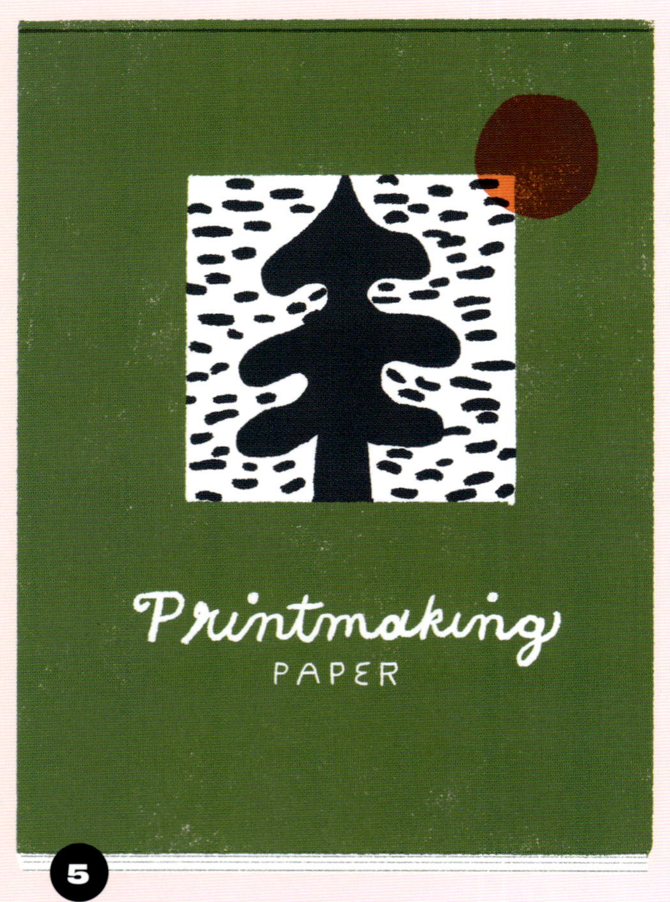

Printmaking

Although printmaking isn't typically included in lists of drawing or sketchbook techniques, it can be a wonderful addition to your Daily Practice. At its core, printmaking is any process that transfers an image from one surface to another—usually using ink and paper. A great entry point is block printing, where an image is carved into a surface known as a carving block **1**. Ink is then applied—often with a roller or brayer **2**—and clings to the raised areas of the design. When pressed onto paper, only those raised areas transfer ink, creating the image. Block printing supplies are relatively affordable and widely available at most art stores. Basic tools include carving knives **3**, rubber or linoleum blocks, block printing ink **4**, brayers, and inking surfaces (a small sheet of glass or smooth plastic works). You don't have to use traditional tools here—ready-made stamps, stamp pads, and virtually any object could work! If you can stamp it, you can use it. For best results, use a sketchbook with a smooth to medium surface, or just get a block of purpose-made printmaking paper **5**.

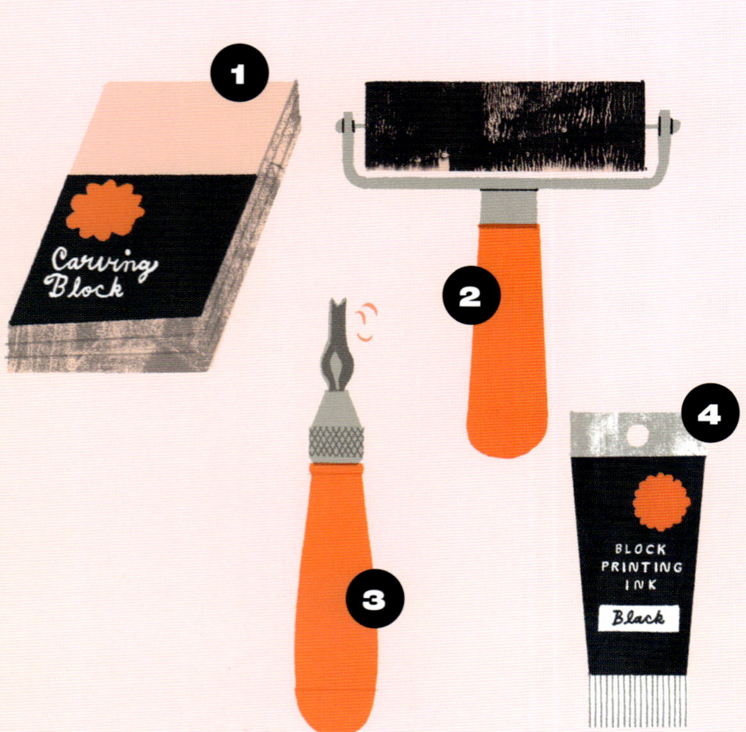

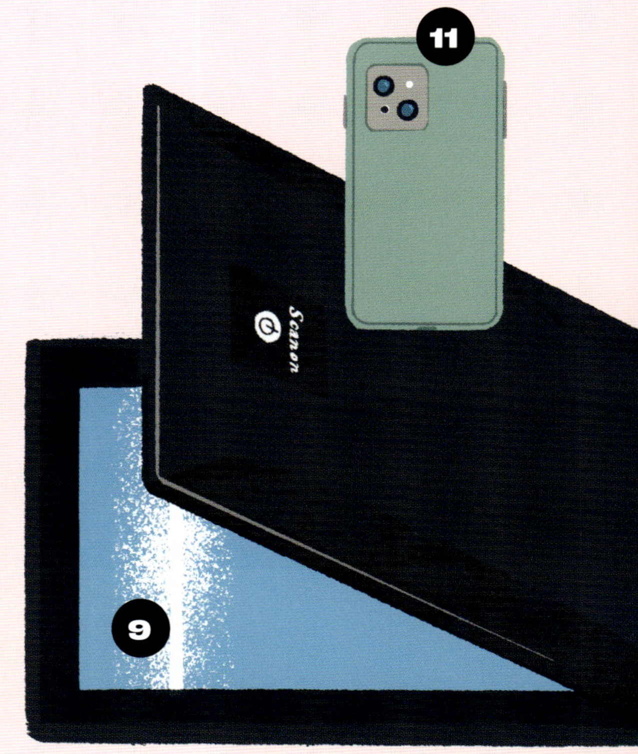

Digital

While this book emphasizes analog drawing media, digital tools are worth mentioning—especially since I often use them in my Daily Drawing Practice and even more so in my shorter-term Daily Projects (*see chapter 7*). It's also important to acknowledge that some people prefer to draw digitally, and several of the projects featured in this book use digital workflows. Digital drawing requires a digital art app like Procreate on an iPad (tablet) **6** and a stylus **7**. Use a palm rejection glove **8** to avoid accidental taps and gestures. I use a flatbed scanner **9** to digitize my drawings, and then make small color adjustments, edits, and cleanups in Photoshop on my Mac **10**. No scanner? No problem—your smartphone camera **11** will likely do just fine.

That said, my Daily Drawing Practice always begins with pencil on paper. My drawings take up space: They fill sketchbooks, and those sketchbooks fill my shelves—and that's a deeply satisfying and tangible archive to look back on over time. Digital sketchbooking is perfectly valid, but it's worth considering how you'll access it in the long term: Will the file formats or devices needed to view them still be around in twenty-five years?

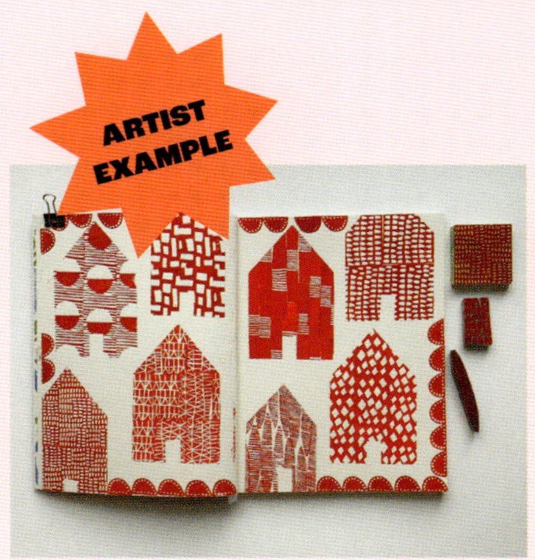

Block printing example by Jeanne McGee

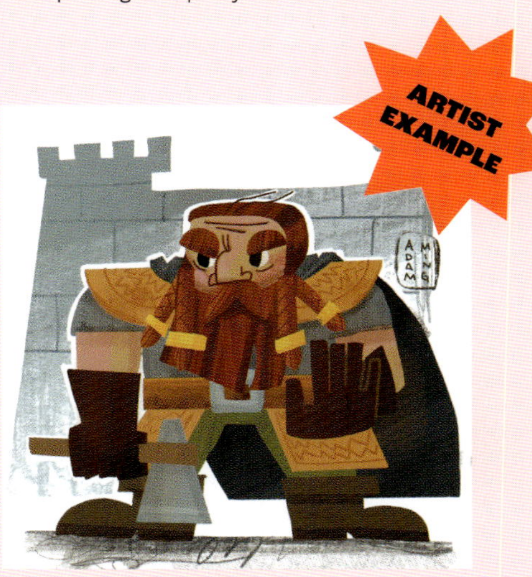

Digital drawing by Adam Ming

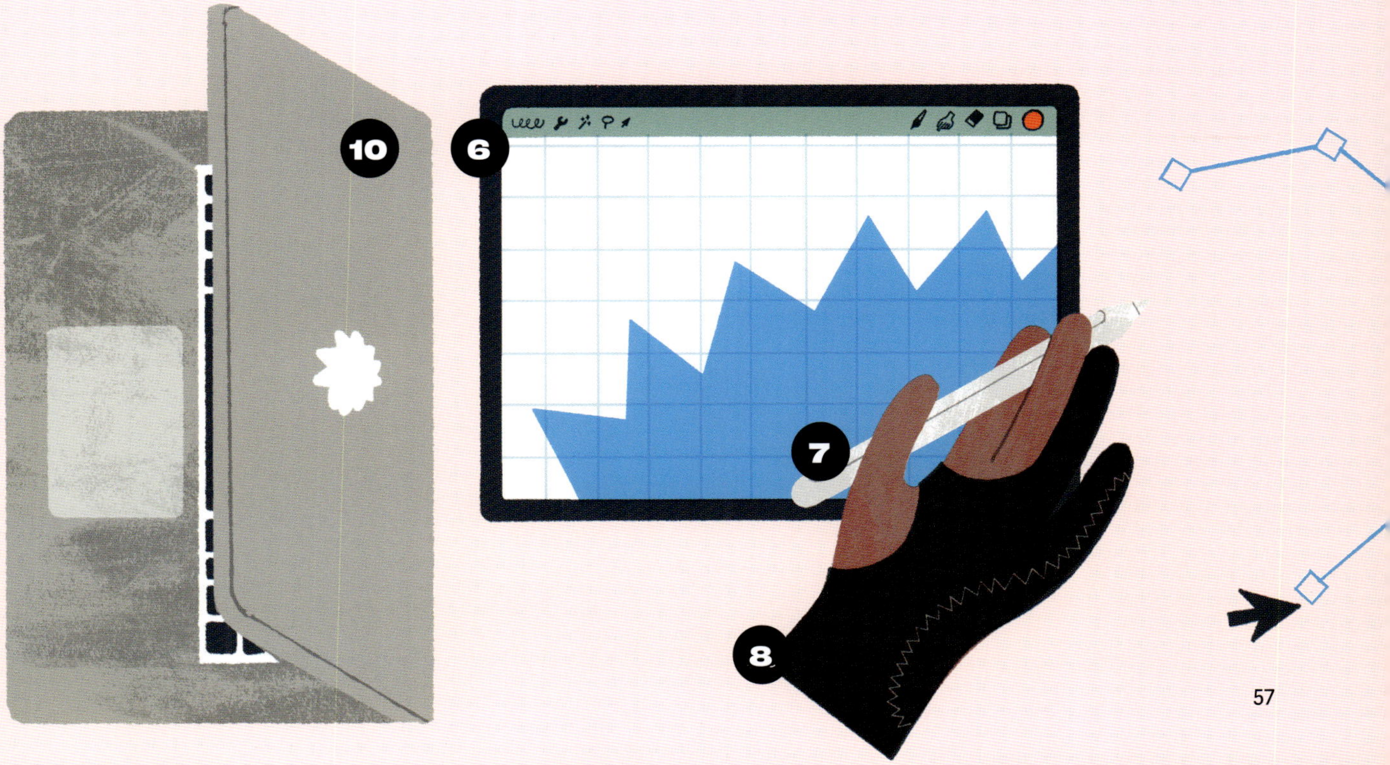

Interlude II

The Reboot

A few years into my illustration career, things were going well—I was getting steady work and even making a name for myself. But as my workload grew, so did my roadblocks. Certain subjects felt impossible to execute within the style and techniques I'd developed over the years. To push past these limits, I turned back to drawing regularly.

I picked up where I left off—observational drawing with my go-to tools: a 0.5 mm pencil and a Moleskine notebook. But I also experimented with tools like markers, brushes, gouache, pen, and ink. As a huge fan of Czech illustrator Miroslav Šašek, I drooled over his mix of organic textures and crisp edges and wanted to develop a similar balance in my own work. It was around this time that I encountered a poem my friend Lance Odegard wrote, called "At the Pool We've All Got Bodies." While I'm not much of a poetry buff, this piece—part observational humor and part life metaphor—stuck with me. It inspired a recurring series in my sketchbooks that I informally called my "Swimming Studies." I had hoped to create a picture book based on the poem, which never materialized, but the intuition to work my idea out in a Daily Drawing Practice was correct. It was during this period that I started to take sharing my art on social media more seriously, and being more intentional about how I did this.

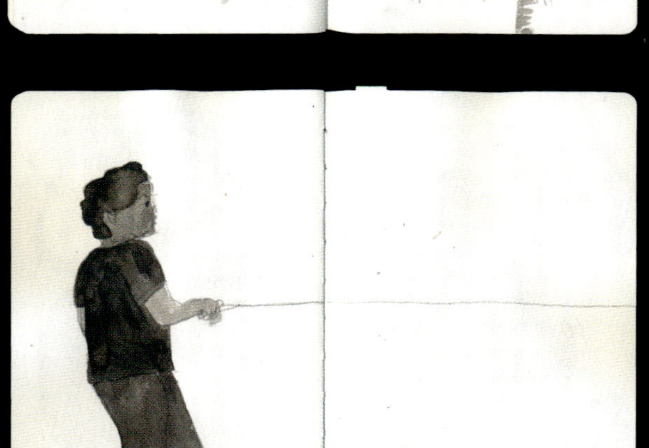

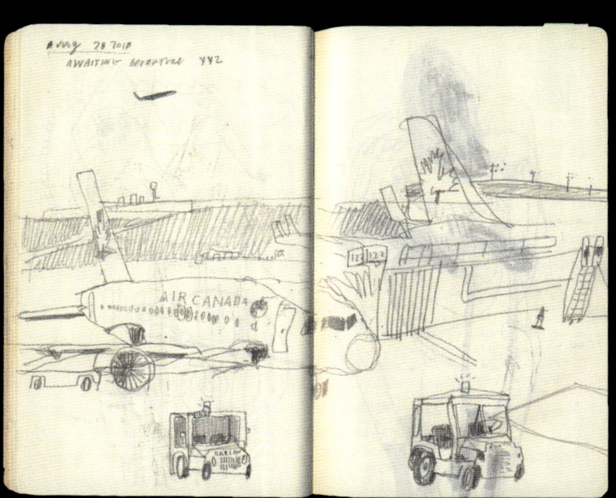

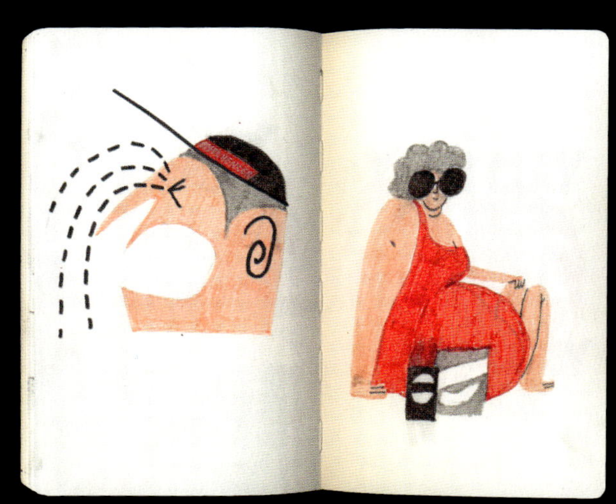

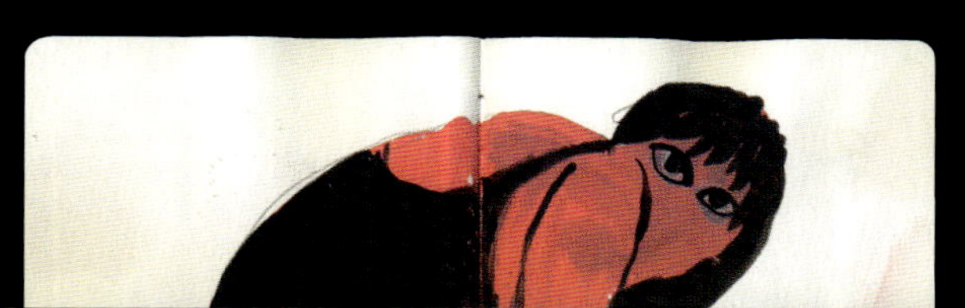

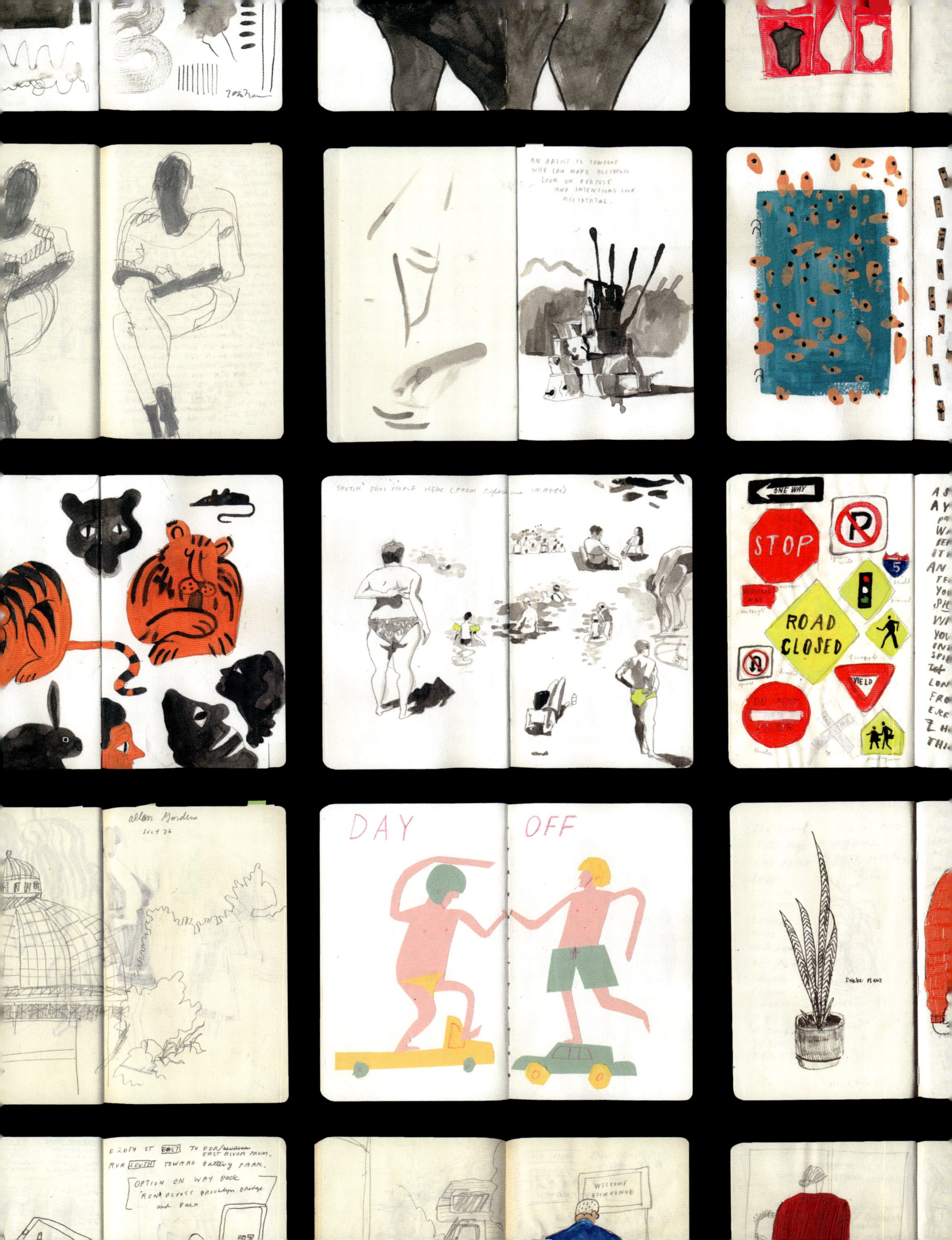
AN ARTIST IS SOMEONE WHO CAN MAKE ACCIDENTS LOOK ON PURPOSE AND INTENTIONS LOOK ACCIDENTAL.
ONE WAY
STOP
ROAD CLOSED
YIELD
Allan Gardens
DAY
OFF
Snake plant
E 20TH ST EAST TO FDR/ EAST RIVER PROM.
RUN SOUTH TOWARD Battery PARK.
OPTION ON WAY BACK
RUN ACROSS BROOKLYN BRIDGE and BACK
WELCOME
BIENVENUE

While I became more deliberate about sharing my drawings again, I hadn't yet settled on a more consistent approach to my practice. This was a time of trying different media, which I think is important, but it also meant that both my body of work and my commitment to showing up were inconsistent.

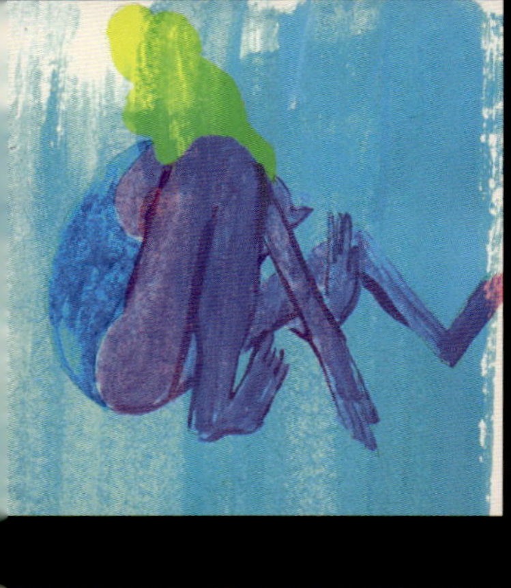

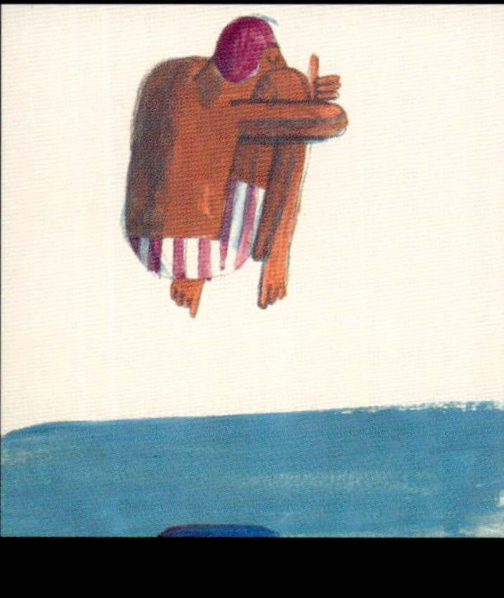

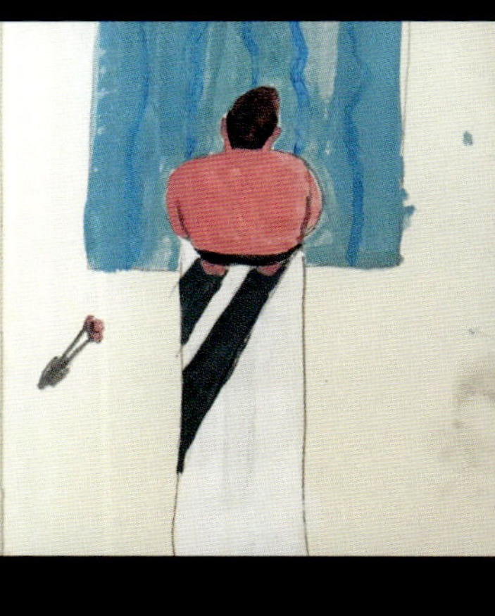

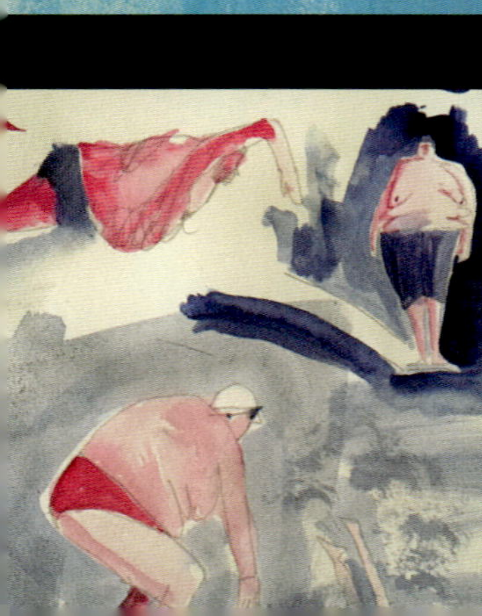

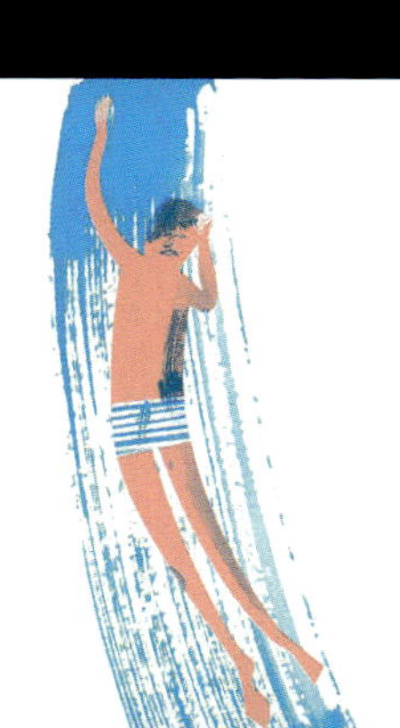

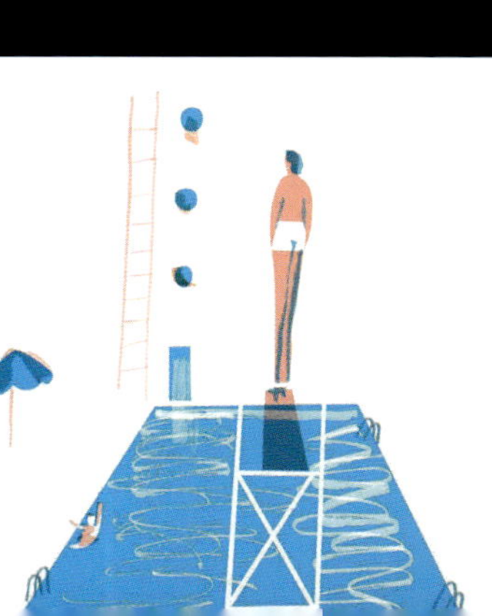

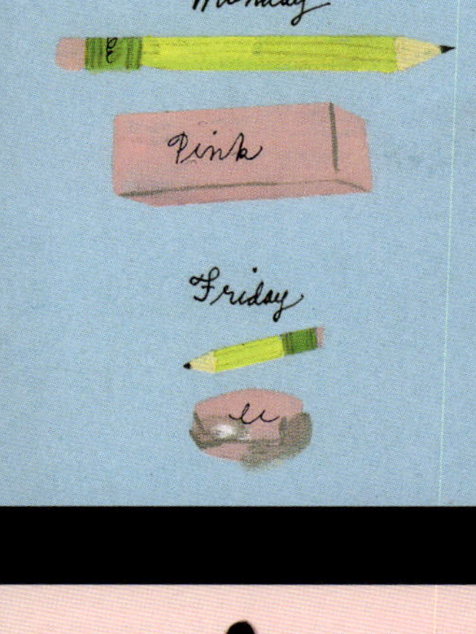
Monday
Pink
Friday

INK

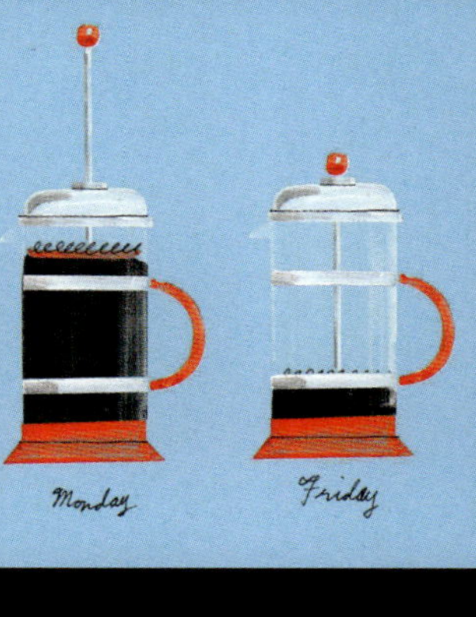
Monday
Friday

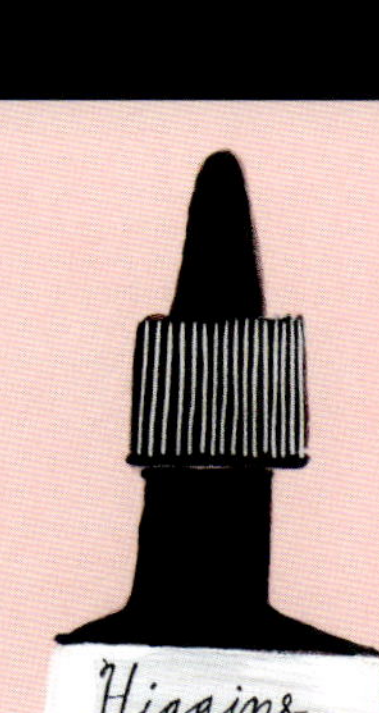
Higgins

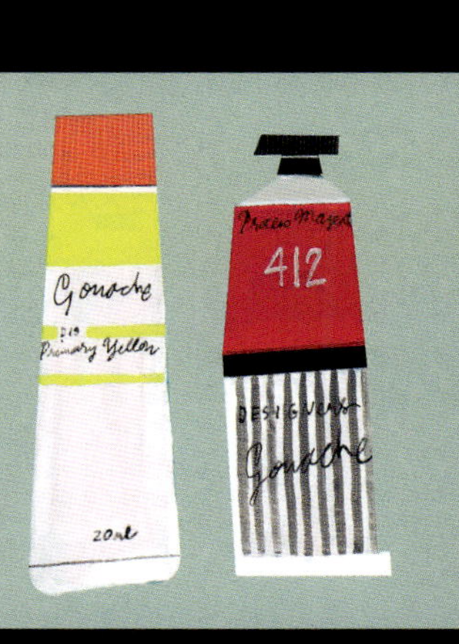
Gouache
Primary Yellow
20ml
412
Gouache

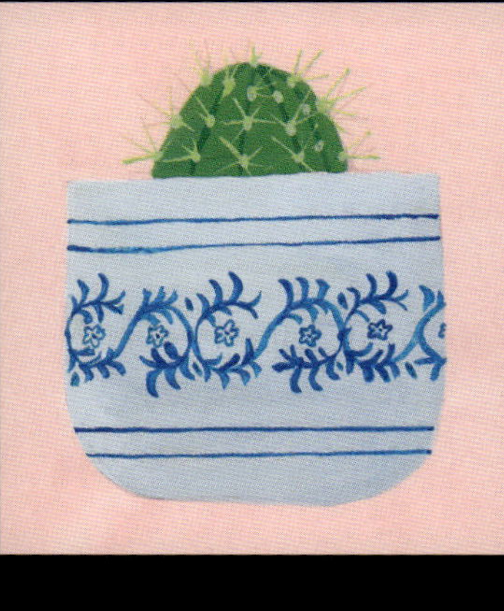

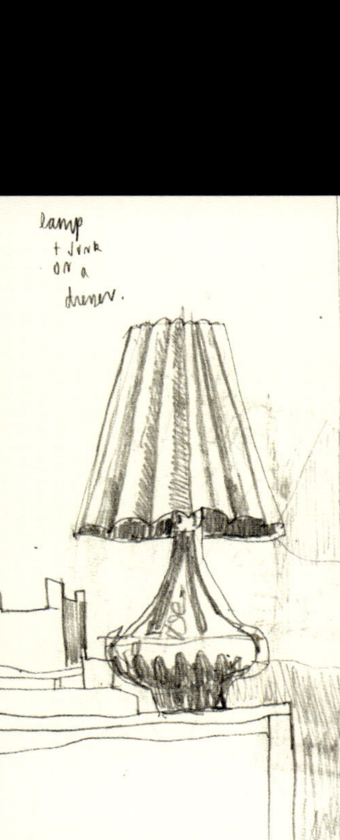
lamp
+ junk
on a
dresser.

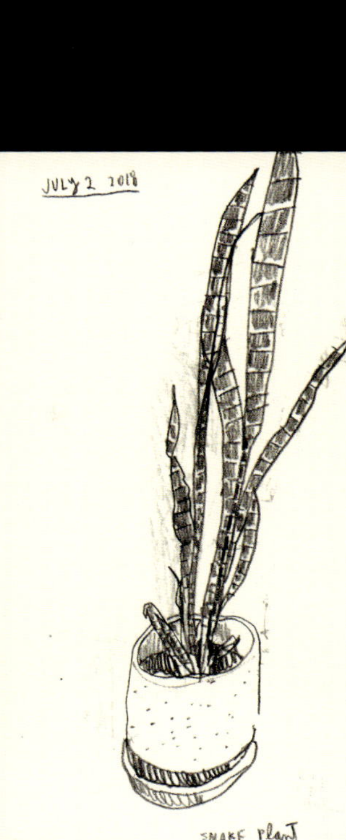
JULY 2 2018
SNAKE PLANT

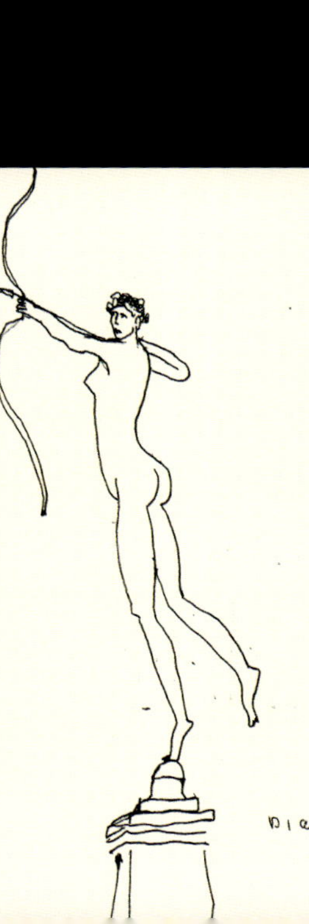
Diana

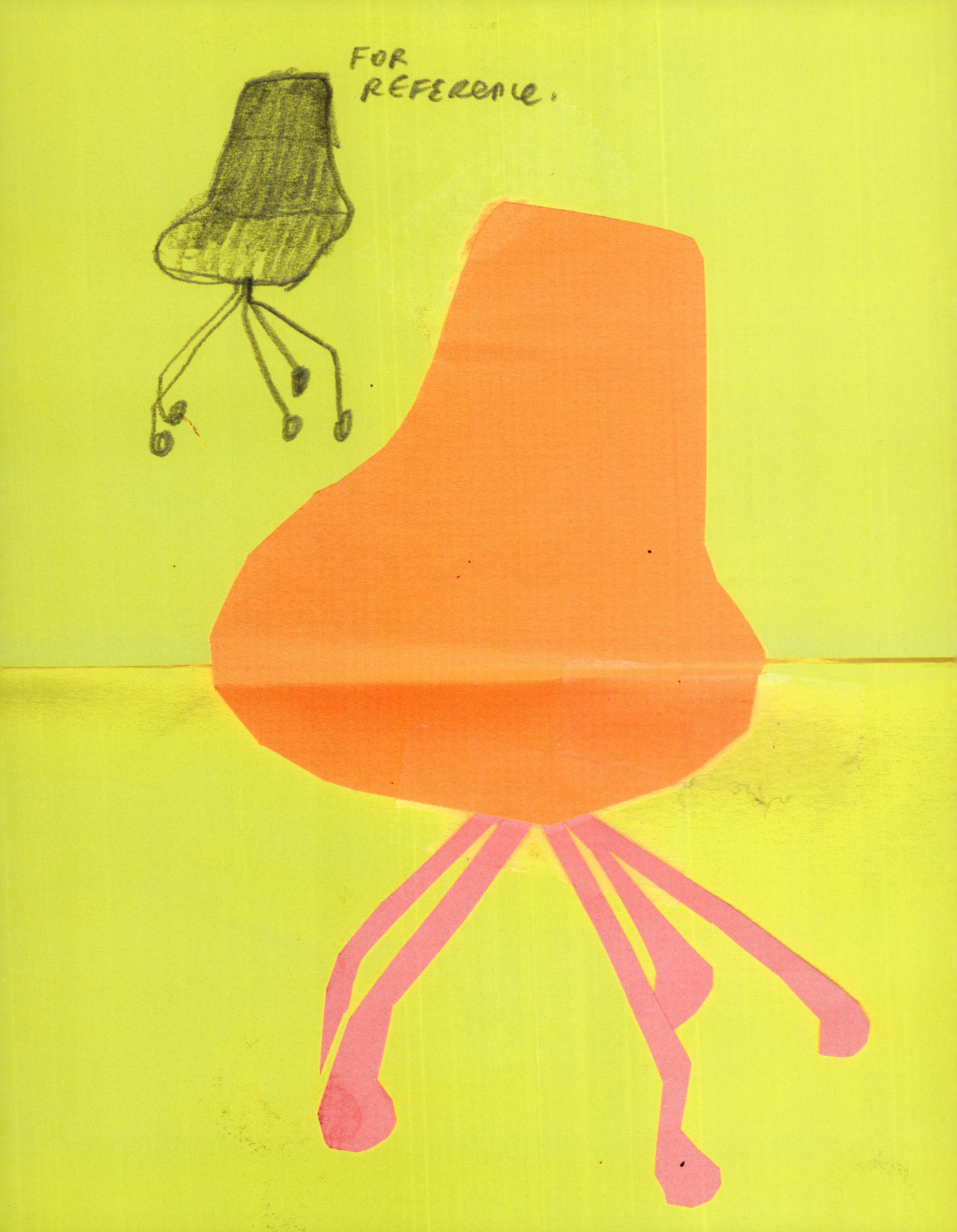
FOR
REFERENCE.

> "As soon as we realize that it's not our job to be perfect, everything gets easier and more honest and more true."
>
> Adam J. Kurtz, *You Are Here (For Now)*

Chapter 5

STARTER KITS FOR BEGINNERS

If you're starting from scratch, even making a plan can feel overwhelming. This chapter offers five simple starter kits to help you begin drawing right away—no overthinking required. Think of them like ready-made training plans: short, focused, and designed to get you past the hardest part—getting started. Along the way, I'll share inspiring examples from past students who used similar setups to gain confidence and momentum in their daily drawings. By the end of this chapter, you'll have at least one clear path you can get started with today.

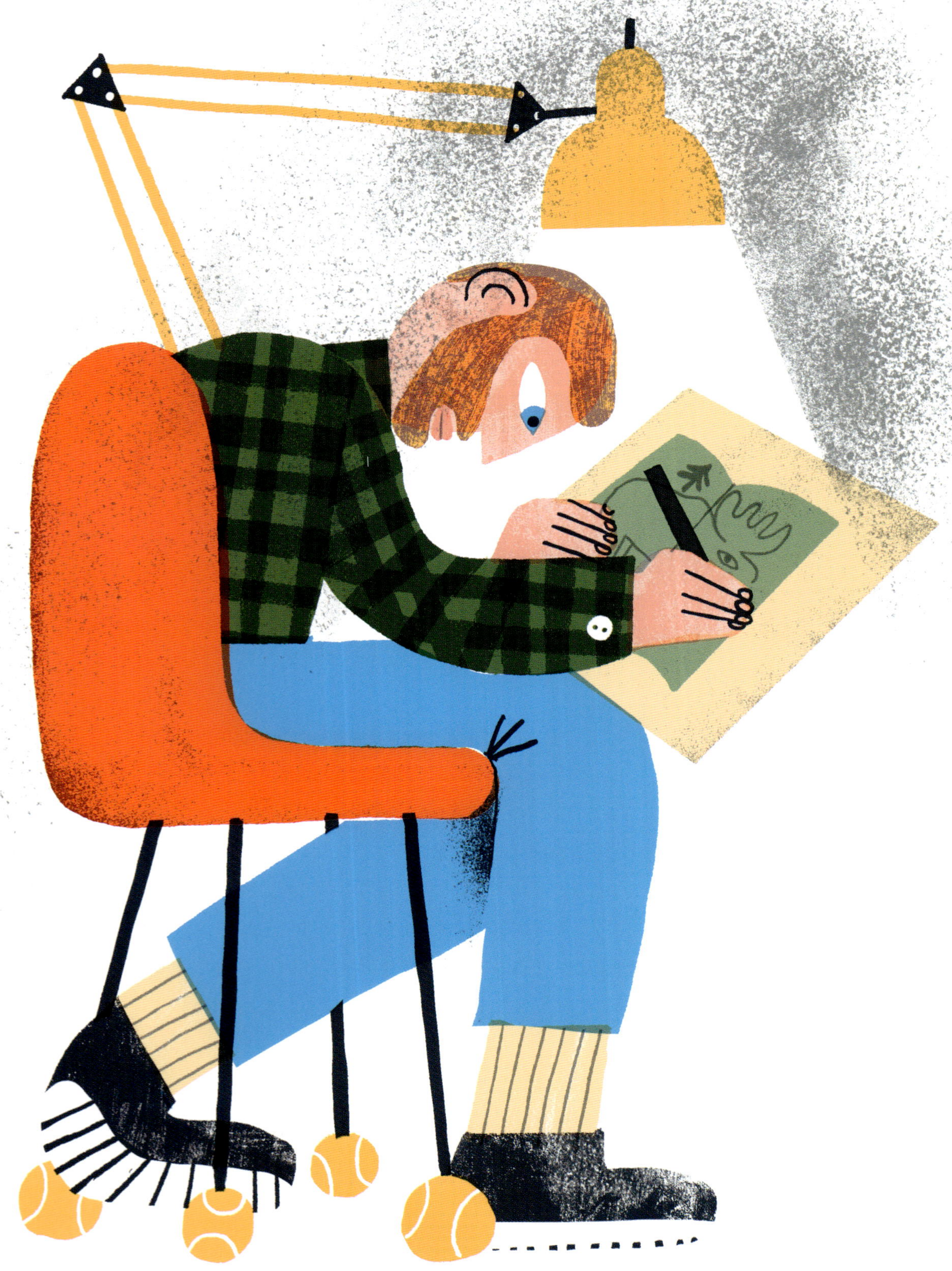

Five Off-the-Shelf, Short-Term Plans to Get You Started

What was the first meal you ever made on your own? Chances are, it wasn't paella from scratch—it was more likely boxed mac and cheese. (In Canada, we call it Kraft Dinner.) It might not be your proudest culinary moment, but it was a great place to start. The box came with almost everything you needed, and all it took was a pot of water, a spoon, and a little milk and butter. No special knowledge, no fancy equipment—just a few simple steps, and voilà: dinner.

Kraft Dinner is a starter kit. And starter kits exist for just about everything: embroidery, LEGO, home repair, back-to-school supplies—you get the picture. They're designed to help you ease into something new without needing to know everything up front.

That's what this chapter is about. Think of the following starter kits as off-the-shelf Daily Drawing Plans: They're easy to begin, require only basic materials, and give you a taste of what drawing every day can feel like—without the pressure. Just add water.

Overcoming Your First Obstacle

Even simple choices can feel weirdly hard at first. I'm sure there was a time when Kraft Dinner dominated the instant mac and cheese market. But now? The options are endless. Do you want organic? Gluten-free? Vegan? High-protein? Low-carb? Name brand or store brand? Classic cheddar or gourmet white cheese with truffle oil?

I don't know about you, but I can spend ten full minutes just staring at the shelf before picking a box. So if you're having a similar experience—standing at the metaphorical shelf, not sure which Daily Drawing Plan to try—I get it. And I've got you.

Keep these things in mind:

1. **There's no "right way" to start.** Just choose a starter kit today, and if it's not working, try something else!

2. **You don't have to stick to just one.** If you want to do them all, you can! Just do one at a time, and then move on to the next.

3. **You don't have to be good.** At first, you probably won't be. Embrace it and know that this is the first step toward getting better!

4. **Sharing is optional.** While sharing is part of the full Daily Drawing Plan, it's not required at this stage. Some people find it motivating; others find it paralyzing. Do what's right for you!

5. **Start with inspiration.** Just like the photo on the mac and cheese box gets your mouth watering before you even leave the store, it helps to see what's possible for these starter kits. That's why I've included a few inspiring student examples from my Drawing Is Important class to help you choose a plan and dive in.

Starter Kit No. 1

Good Old Pencil and Paper

There's no better way to get started than with the basics, and it doesn't get more basic than good old pencil and paper.

PURPOSE
To get in the habit of daily drawing.

MEDIA
Pencil, eraser, and plain sketchbook

SOURCE
Draw one object that you can see from where you are sitting.

SCHEDULE
5 minutes / day
5 days / week
for 2 weeks

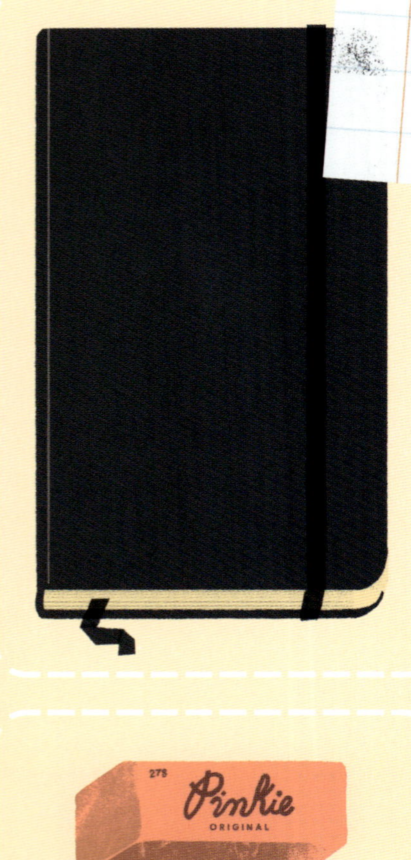

SHARING TIP
Using your phone camera, take a photo of your drawing in good light. If your pages don't stay flat, you can clip them down, hold them with one hand, or opt to hold your book up and purposefully include some of the background.

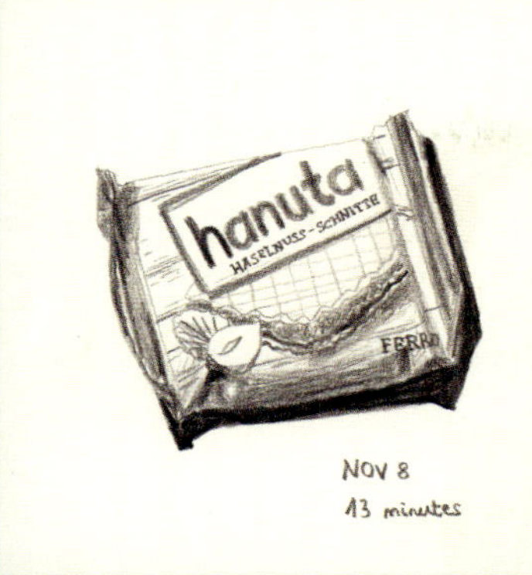

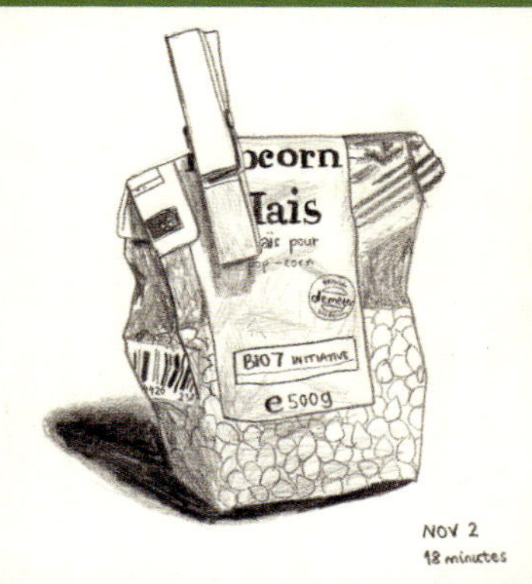

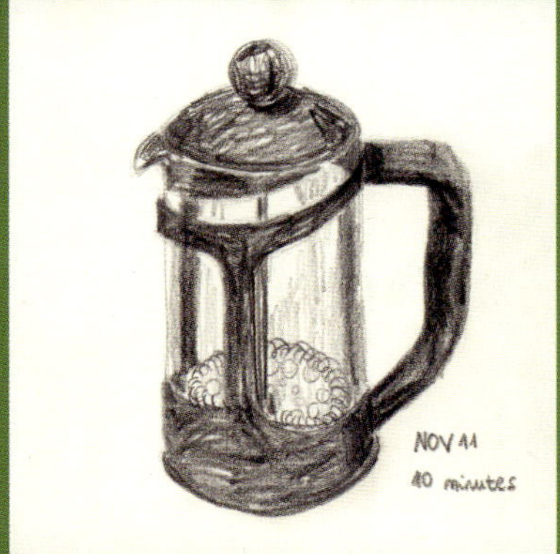

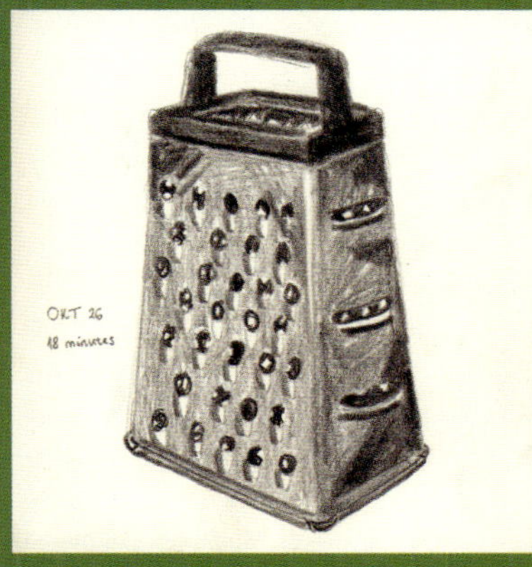

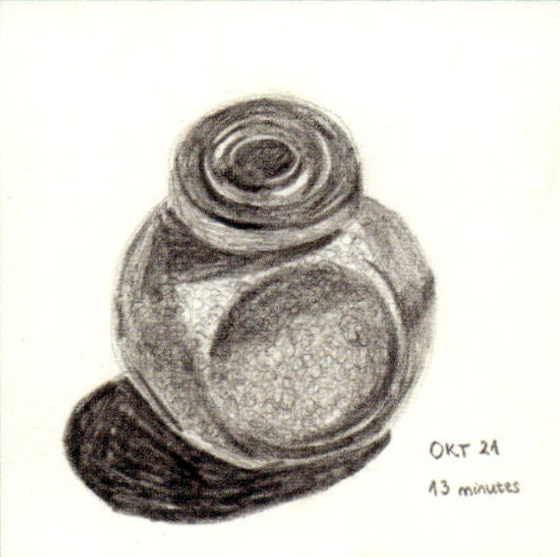

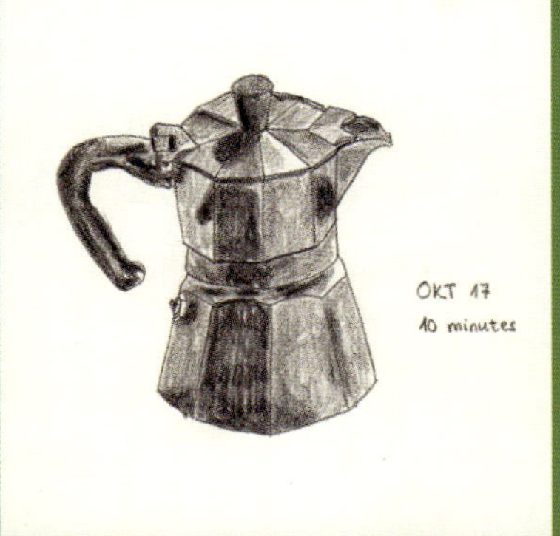

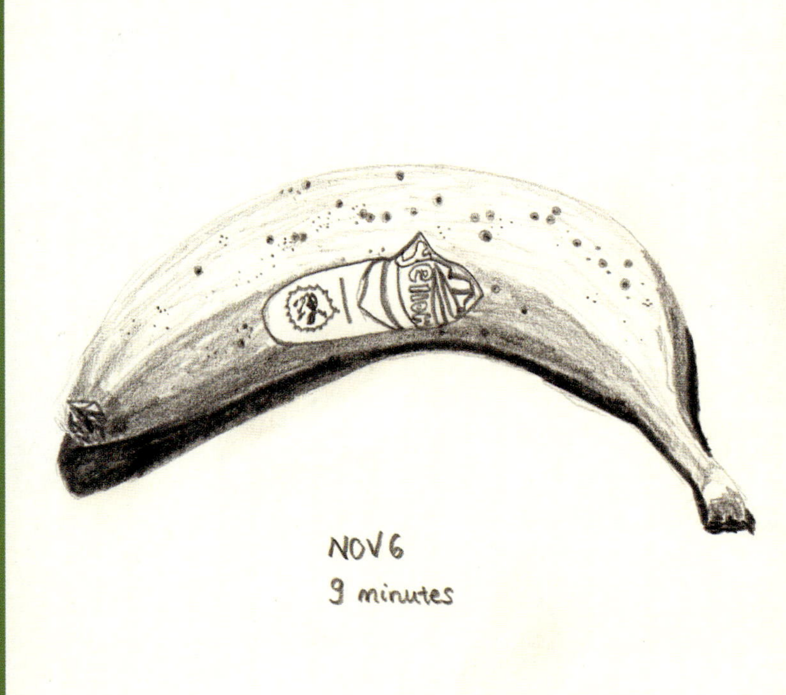

STUDENT SPOTLIGHT

Flóra Gábor

@flora_gabor
Flóra Gábor wanted to use her thirty-day project to help explore her style. Using a Moleskine square notebook and a graphite pencil as her go-to media, she drew one small object from her kitchen per day. She used a scanner to digitize her drawings, and then cropped each drawing for a tidy, focused look. Flora shared her drawings both on the class projects page and on Instagram.

Starter Kit No. 2

Paint Pens and Uglybooks

If you're interested in working with color media but don't know where to start, this is one of the easiest and most satisfying ways to begin. Create instantly eye-popping effects with opaque ink on colored paper.

PURPOSE

To experiment working with color media.

MEDIA

Paint Pens and Uglybooks sketchbook, pencil (for preliminary sketches), and eraser (to remove pencil after)

SOURCE

Write a series of prompts based on a theme before you start, or have a go-to source, such as an old catalog.

SCHEDULE

15 minutes / day
5 days / week
for 30 days

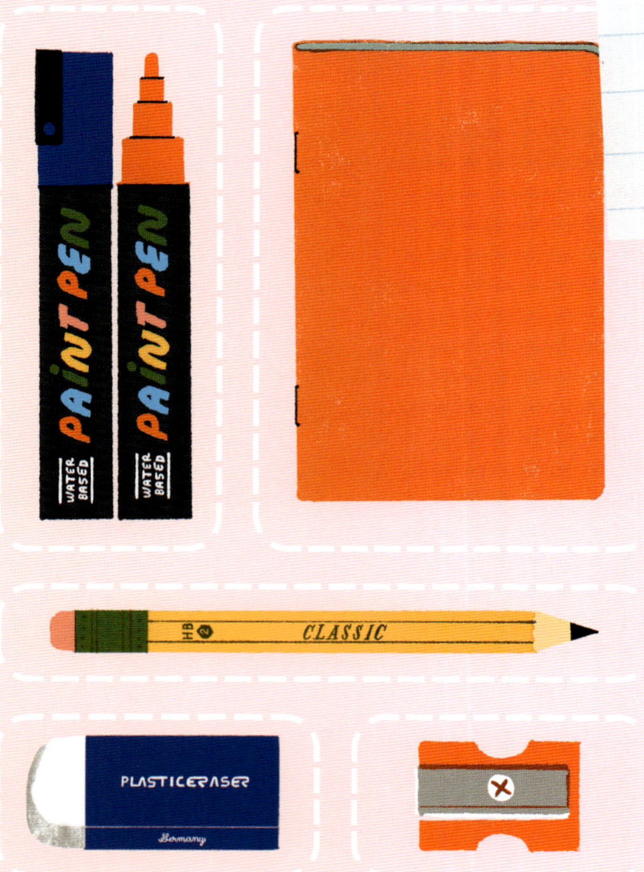

SHARING TIP

Wait for the paint to dry, then scan in RGB at 300 dots per inch (dpi) on a clean flatbed scanner. You can put a larger sheet of white or colored paper overtop as the background, which will look nicer than whatever is on the underside of the scanner lid. Send to your phone to crop, and adjust the contrast and saturation a bit to suit.

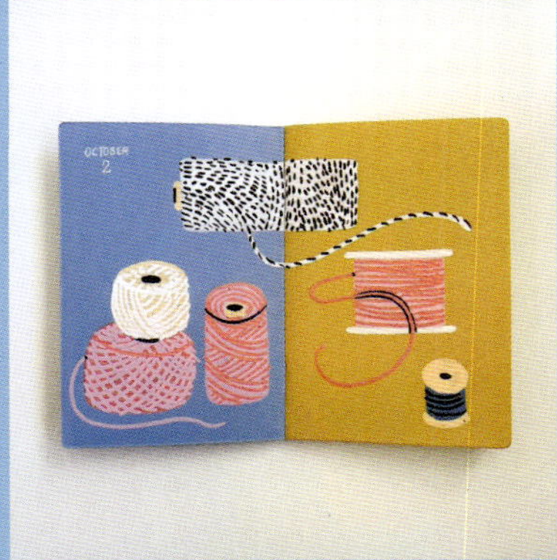

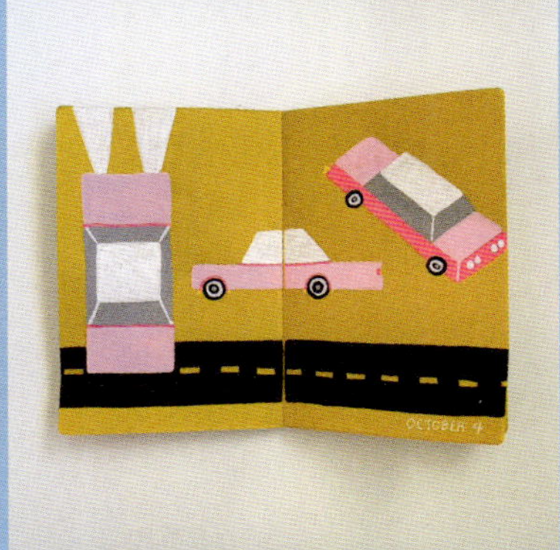

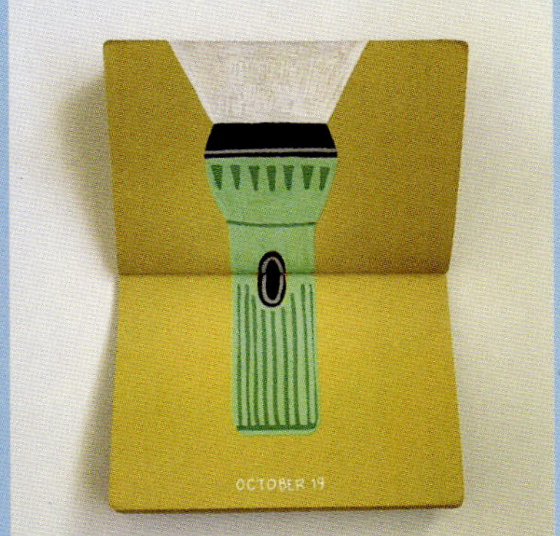

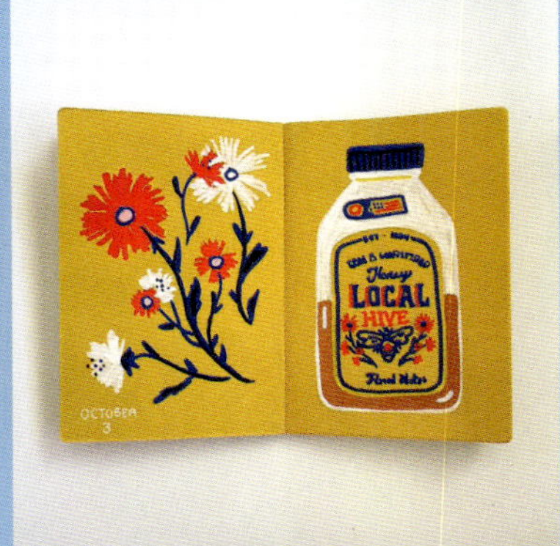

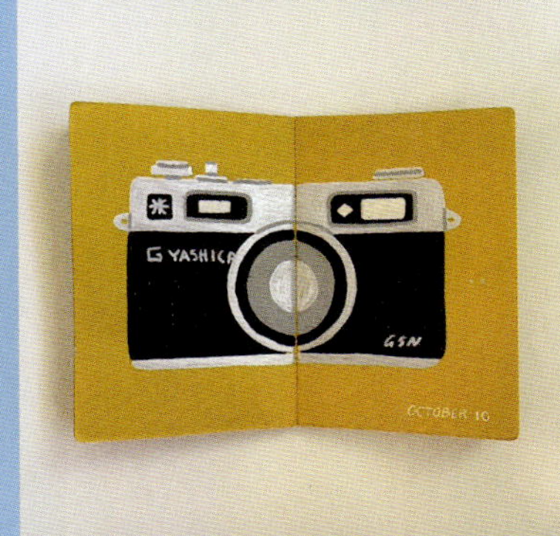

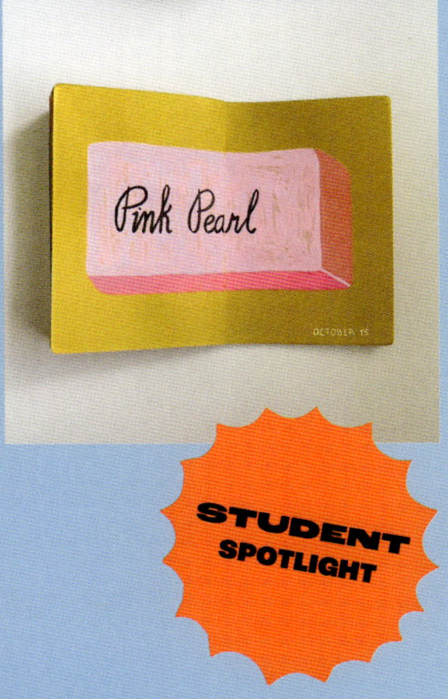

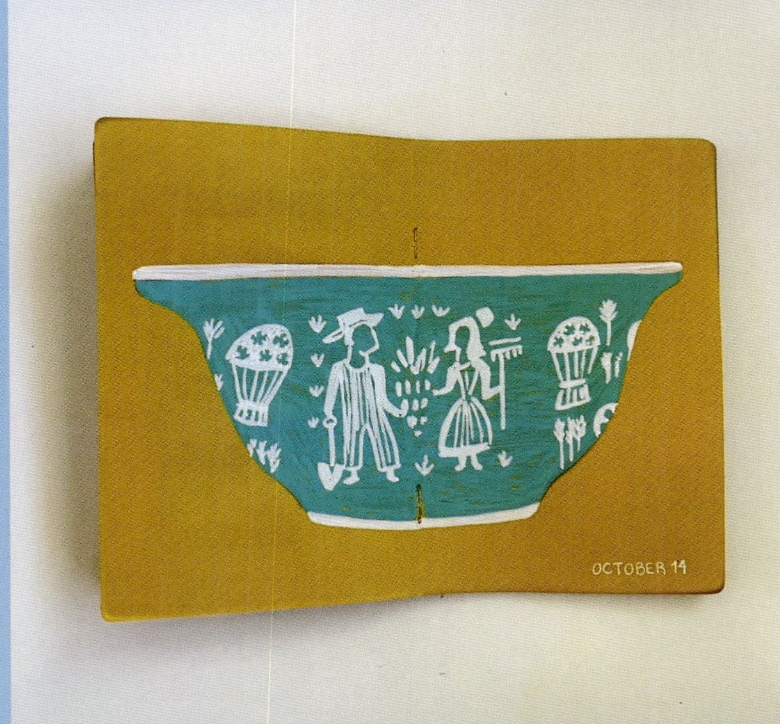

Ez Pudewa

ezpudewa.com

This California-based illustrator used her thirty-day drawing project to "shake off creative burnout" and experiment with new materials. With a goal of drawing for at least ten minutes each day, she used Posca paint pens and Uglybooks to draw ordinary objects from around her home. To share her drawings, she photographed each one on a clean surface, with bright, even light.

Starter Kit No. 3

Big Fat Sharpie

If you get stuck on the fine details, how about using a tool that makes this impossible? Free yourself from overthinking, and focus on the bigger picture with this in-your-face, impossible-to-erase starter kit!

PURPOSE

To practice drawing more simply and loosely.

MEDIA

Black Sharpie with a broad rounded tip, sketchbook with heavier paper.

SOURCE

Draw something (like your hand) every day, in a contour drawing style.

SCHEDULE

5 minutes or 1 page / day
5 days / week
for 2 weeks

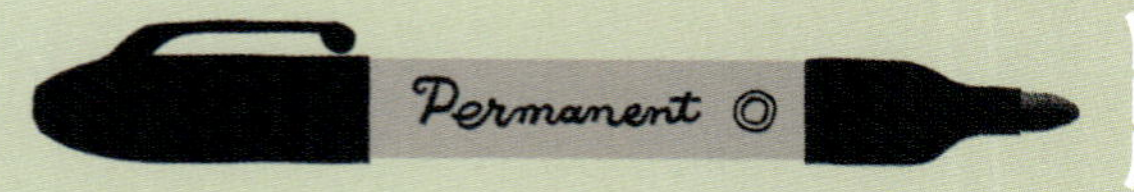

SHARING TIPS

Draw on right-hand pages only, placing a sheet of paper underneath to protect the next right-hand page from bleed-through.

Scan or photograph in black and white only to reduce "color casting." Crop to your sharing platform's preferred aspect ratio (e.g., square, 4:5, 16:9).

For a cleaner look, aim for more contrast, making the black as black as it can be and the white as white as it can be—ultimately removing any surrounding paper texture.

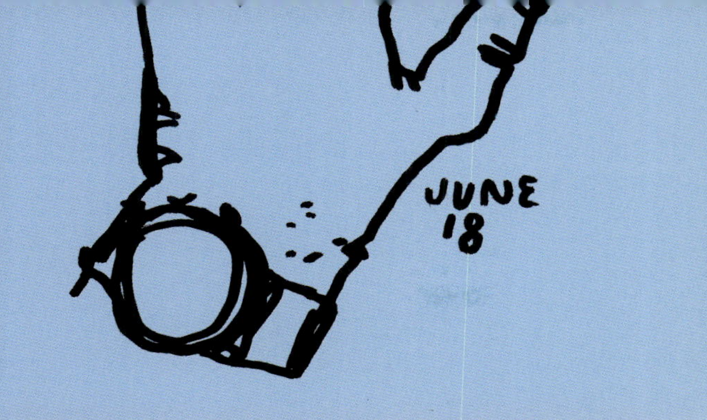
JUNE
18
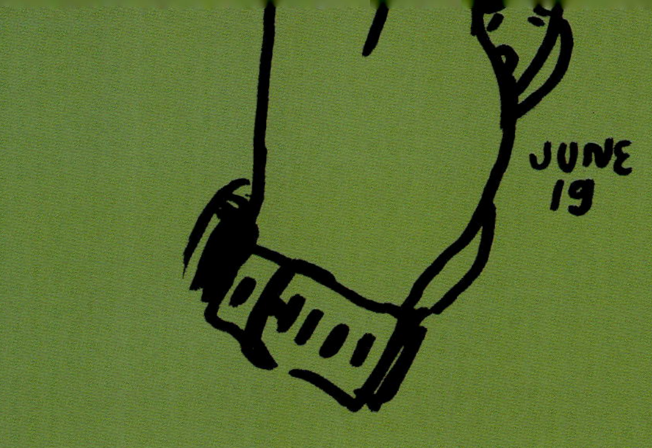
JUNE
19
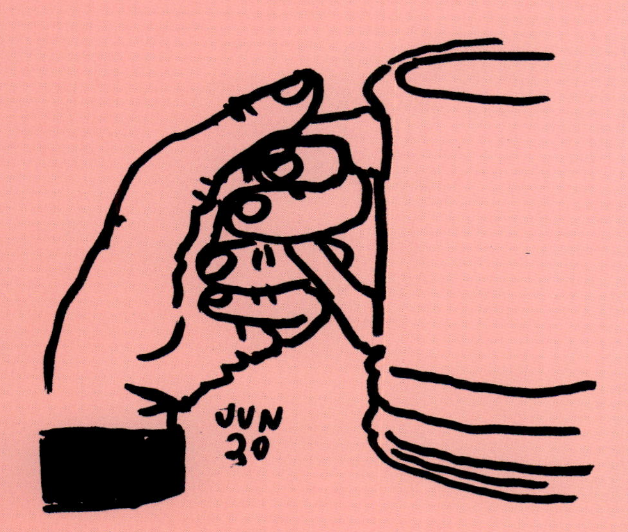
JUN
20
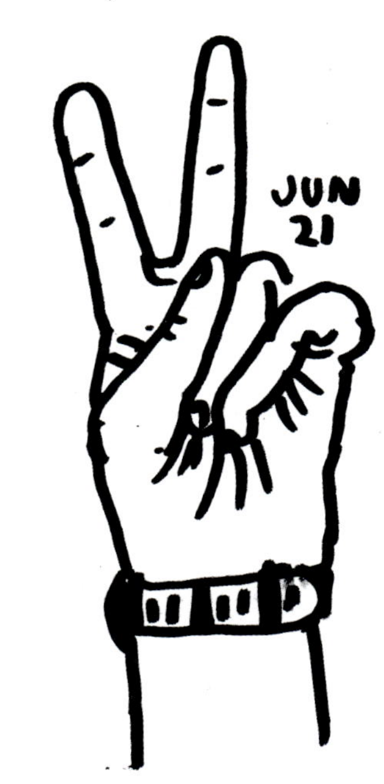
JUN
21
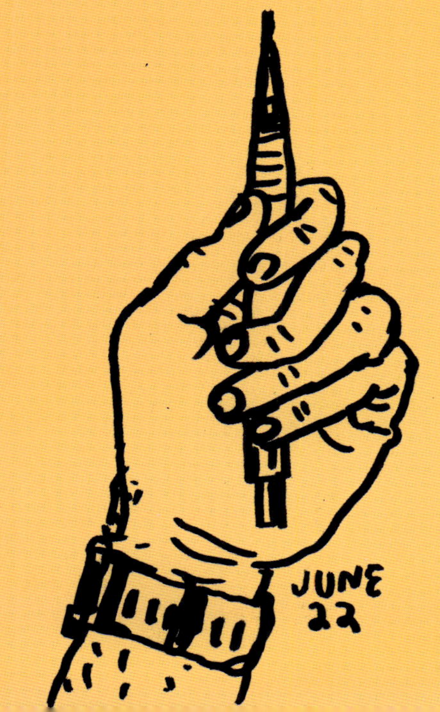
JUNE
22
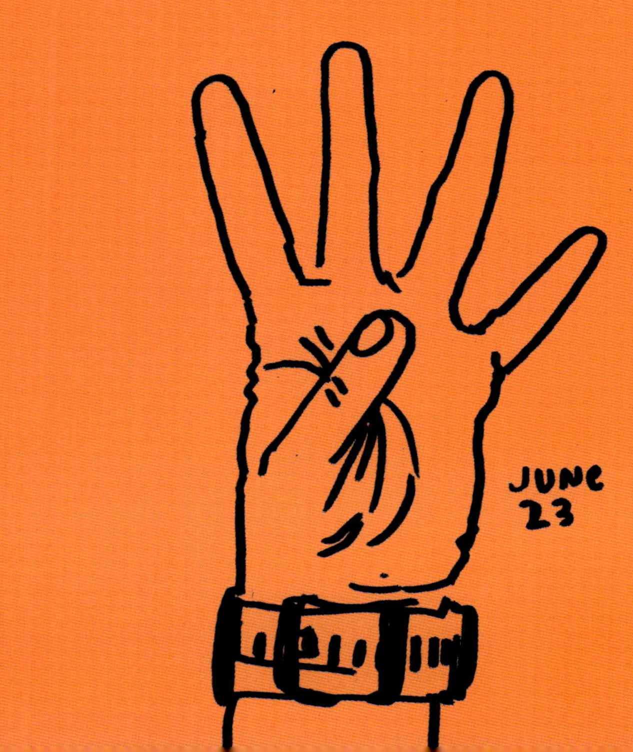
JUNE
23

Starter Kit No. 4

Drawing with Scissors

Are you a relentless perfectionist? Completely sidestep your inner critic by using the worst possible drawing tool: scissors! This one is great for escaping the pressure to be a "good" drawer altogether.

PURPOSE
To loosen up.

MEDIA
Any pencil or pen.
Any sketchbook.

SOURCE
Stream of thought.
See what random ideas pop into your head as you flow.

SCHEDULE
10 minutes / day
5 days / week
for one week

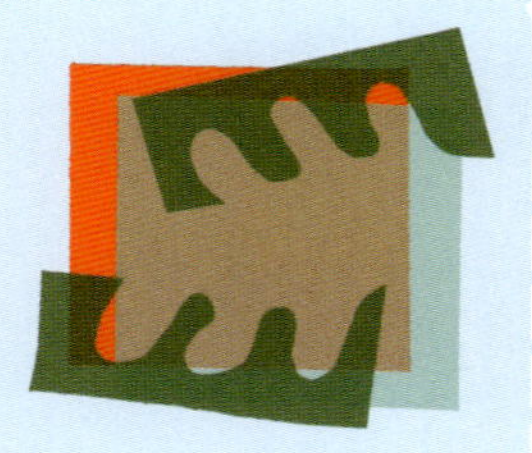

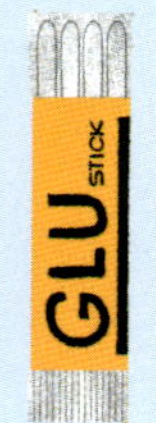

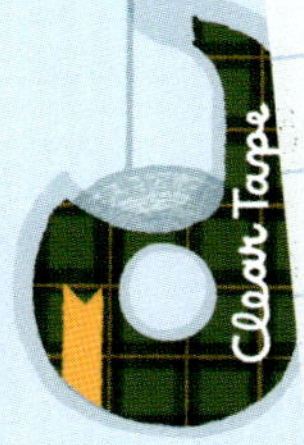

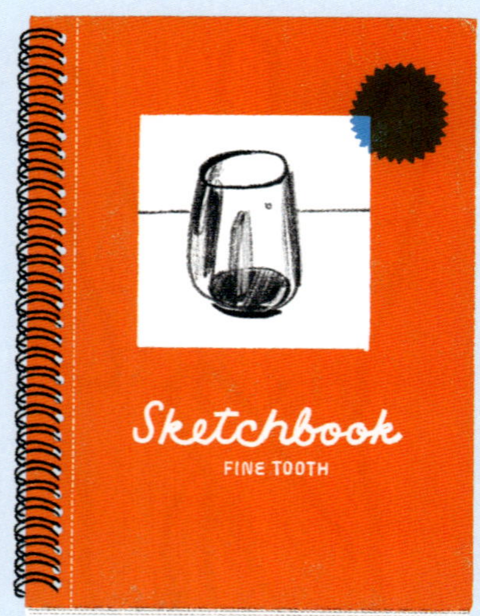

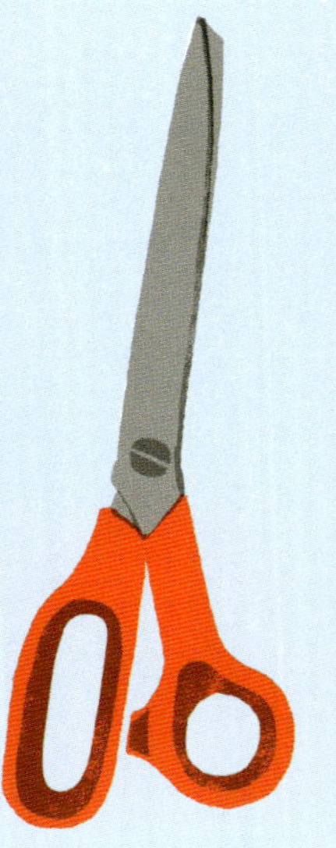

SHARING TIPS
For a clean look without shadows, use a scanner to digitize your work.

For a more creative, scrapbooky feeling, take a picture of your open sketchbook directly on your work surface, leaving in some of the tools and scraps from the process. (Make sure your space is well-lit.)

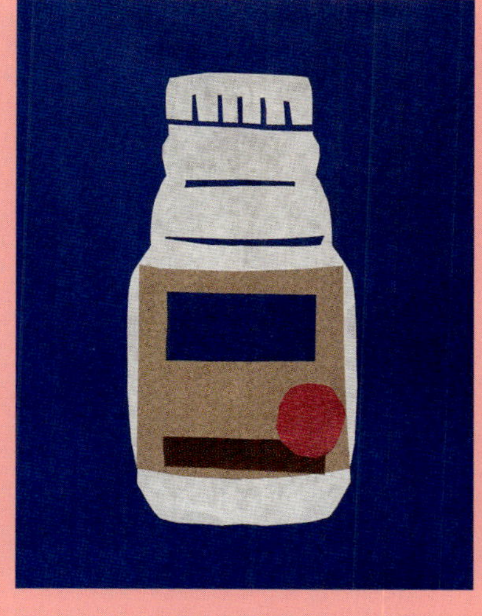

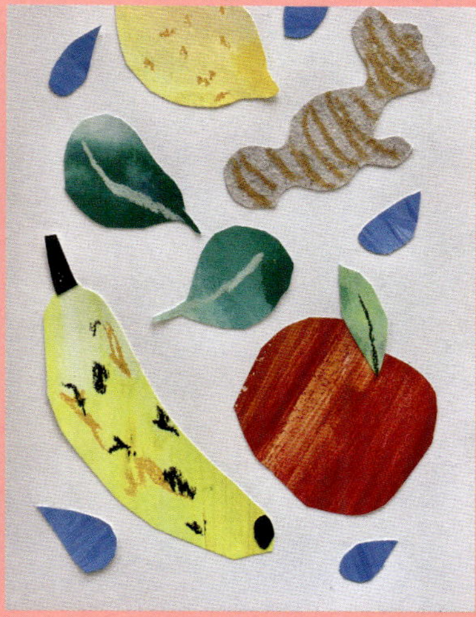

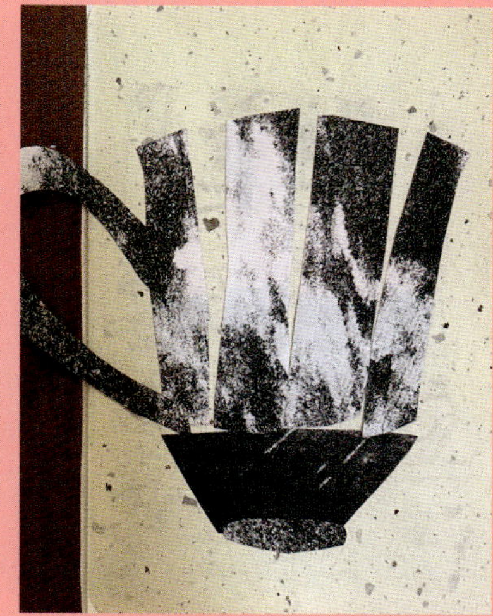

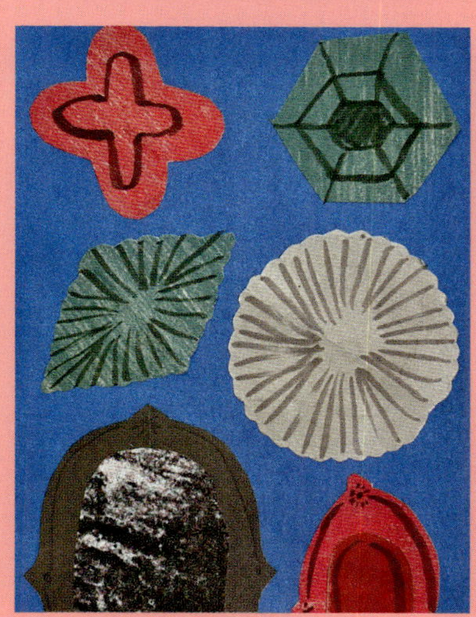

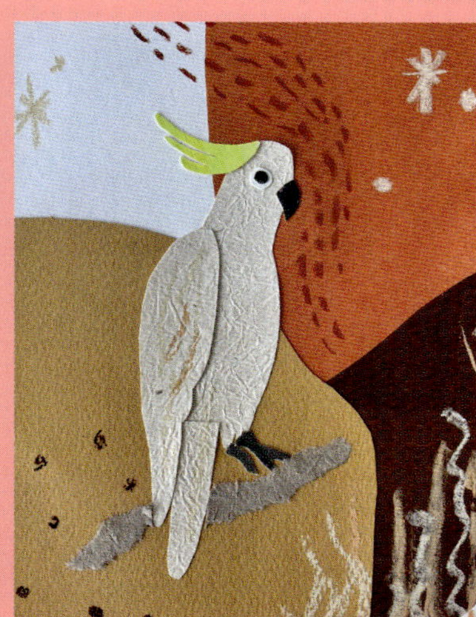

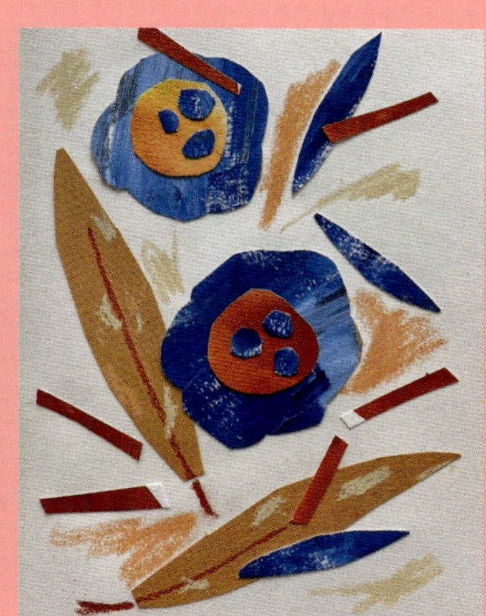

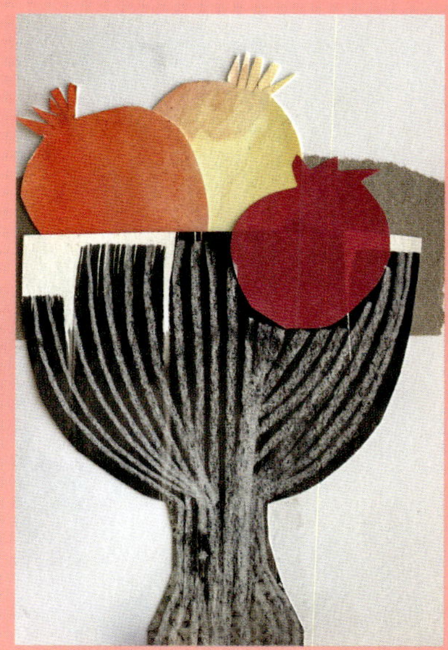

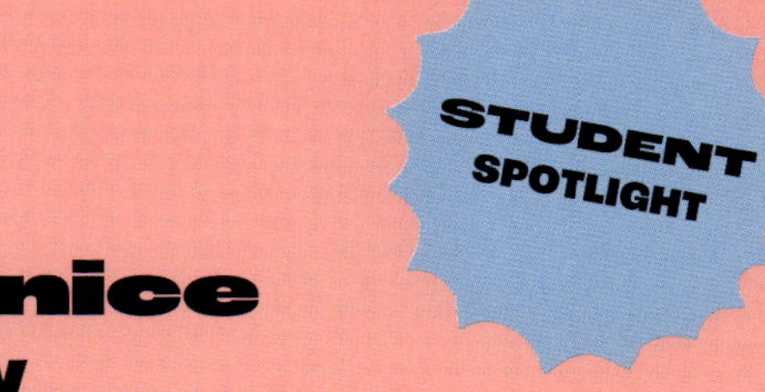

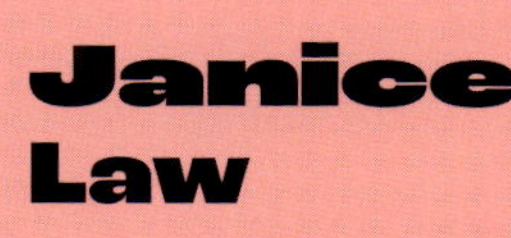

Janice Law

janicelaw.design

For her Daily Project, Janice Law "drew" from everyday life objects using scissors and scraps of paper. She even created some of the textures herself, which reminds me of American children's book illustrator Eric Carle. Janice said she enjoyed the freedom and fun of this technique so much that she kept going after the thirtieth day.

Starter Kit No. 5

Word Salads

Word salads are a Dada-inspired, stream-of-thought exercise for when words seem to come more easily than pictures. It's also a fun way to tap into your subconscious. If you're feeling creatively stuck, this creative roughage might just be the thing to get you flowing again.

Here's how: Write out, in smallish letters, whatever words come to your mind—no matter how silly they might be. Then, without hesitation, begin to draw a shape or doodle around them, responding to the meaning or feeling of the words. Then find a nearby place to do this all over again. Keep doing this until you fill the page. Another option is to play a podcast or song and just write out whichever words or phrases seem to stand out to you.

Your Choice: Let your drawings be loose and unartful, or use this to explore and get better at hand lettering.

PURPOSE
To creatively loosen up.

MEDIA
Any drawing tool and a sketchbook.

SOURCE
Stream of thought.

SCHEDULE
10 minutes / day
Once / week for 1 month

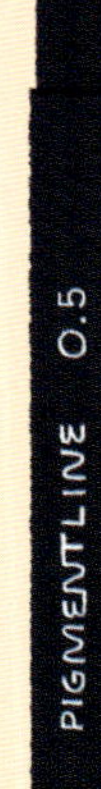

SHARING TIP
Share your word salad as a whole, or isolate it into separate little badges.

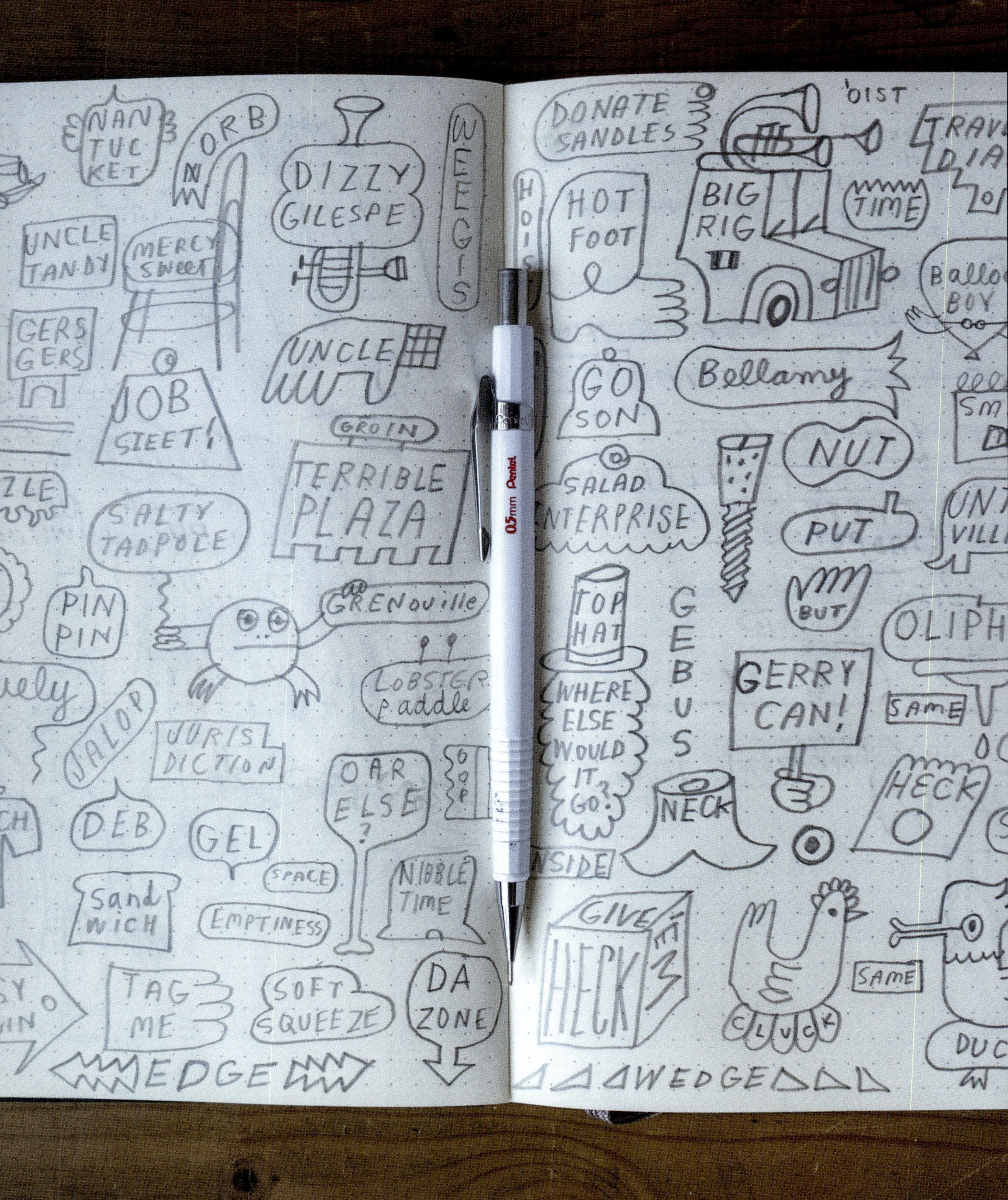

NAN TUC KET
ORB
DIZZY GILESPE
WEEGIS
UNCLE TANDY
MERCY SWEET
GERS GERS
UNCLE
JOB SIEET!
GROIN
TERRIBLE PLAZA
SALTY TADPOLE
PIN PIN
GRENouille
LoBSTER paddle
JALOP
JURIS DICTION
OAR ELSE?
DEB
GEL
SPACE
NIBBLE TIME
Sand wich
EMPTINESS
TAG ME
SOFT SQUEEZE
DA ZONE
EDGE
DONATE SANDLES
OIST
HOT FOOT
BIG RIG
TIME
Bellamy
GO SON
NUT
SALAD ENTERPRISE
PUT
BUT
TOP HAT
GEBUS
WHERE ELSE WOULD IT GO?
GERRY CAN!
SAME
NECK
HECK
GIVE HECK
SAME
CLUCK
WEDGE
0.5mm Pentel

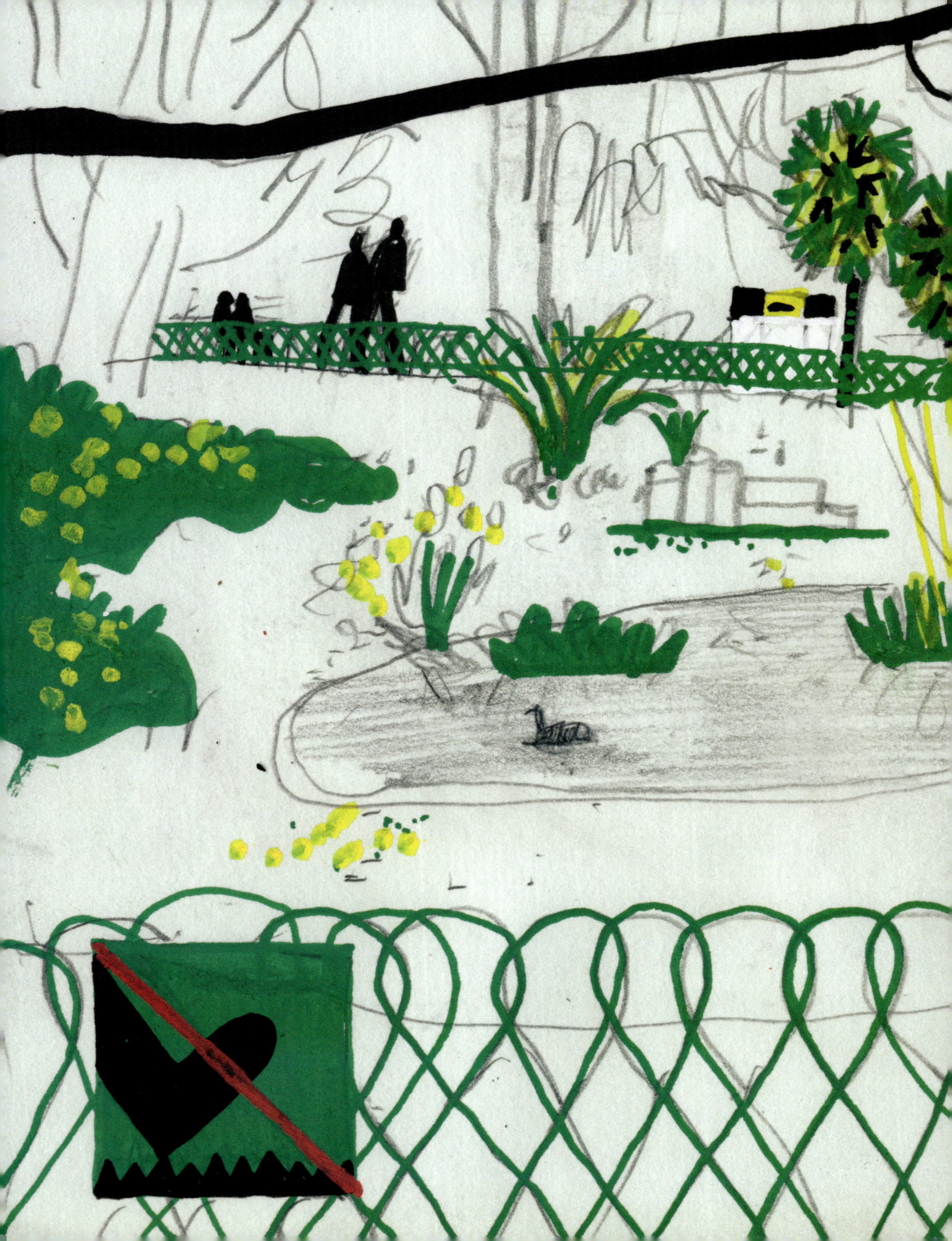

Chapter

> "I can admit, even as a professional artist, there are days I feel stuck... until I open my sketchbook."
>
> **John Hendrix, *Drawing Is Magic***

WHEN DRAWING IS YOUR DAY JOB

You might assume professional illustrators just naturally keep in the habit of drawing for themselves—but that's not always the case. In this chapter, we'll look at how working artists maintain a personal drawing practice, even when creativity is already their day job. I'll share examples of different approaches—some that separate daily drawing from client work, and others that blend the two. By the end, you'll be better equipped to decide how your Daily Drawing Practice can support, rather than compete with, your creative career.

Why Make Time for Personal Drawing When You Already Draw for a Living?

"I don't have time" is one of the most common reasons professional creatives give for not drawing for themselves. "I get to draw all day long—and get paid for it. Why would I want to draw even more?" might be another. For the latter types, whether a personal Daily Drawing Practice is worth adding to your life is up to you. But if time feels like the main barrier, I believe it's actually less about time and more about belief—belief that drawing is worth your time. If you're still not convinced, here are some reasons to make more space for drawing in your life, even if you already draw or create for a living.

To Stay Inspired

Having a personal Daily Drawing Practice will ensure that you always stay in touch with your creative impulses, regardless of how things are going in your main line of work. I find it's easy to stay in autopilot with client work, while drawing makes me more intentional about staying creatively challenged and inspired.

To Develop Your Style

Once we become known for a style, it's hard to break out of it, especially in our client work. Over time, we can start to feel boxed in. Having a personal Daily Drawing Practice gives you a sacred space to experiment and discover new frontiers. Through my Daily Drawing Practice, I'm constantly finding new ways to push my style, just a little bit at a time, so nothing ever feels like a huge departure.

To Let Off Some Steam

One surprising function is to help you preserve your usual style for client work. If "Don't fix it if it ain't broke" is your mantra, but you'd like to keep evolving as an artist, a Daily Drawing Practice can be a safe place to try new things, relieving the pressure you might feel to freak out and abandon the style you've worked so hard to become known for.

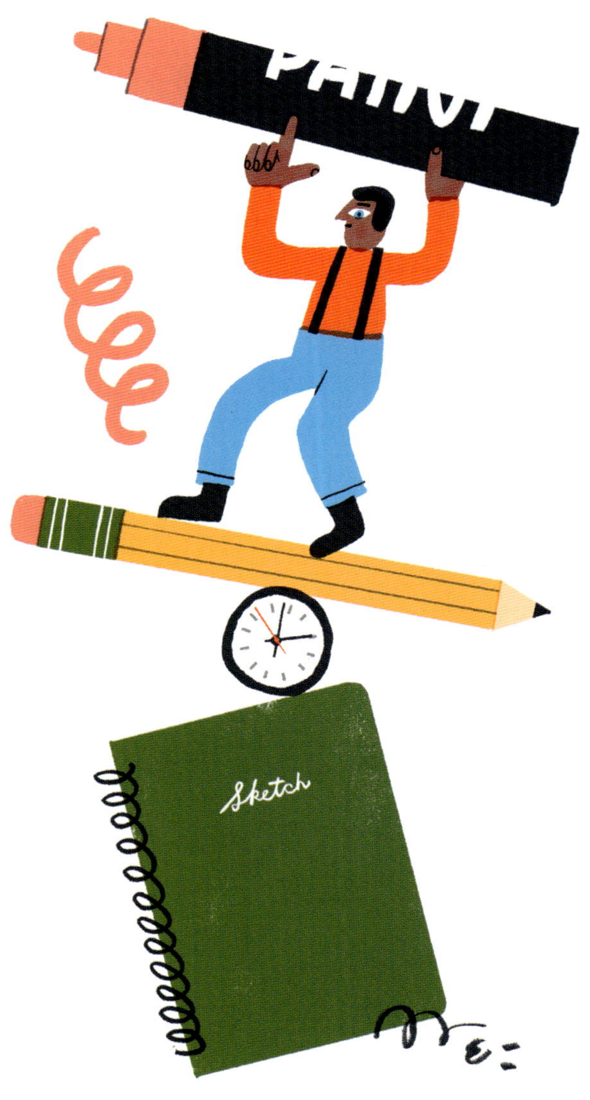

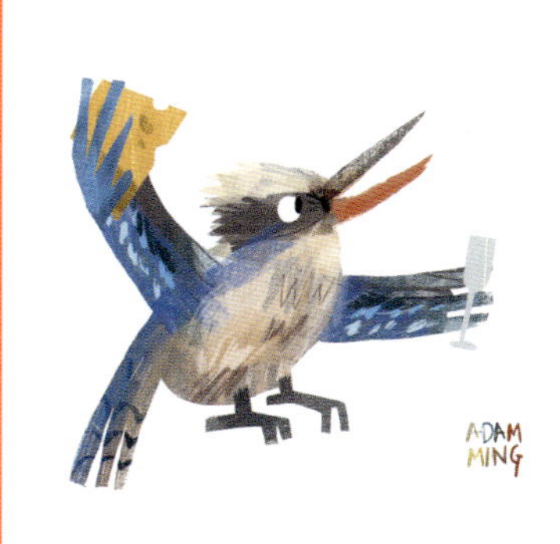

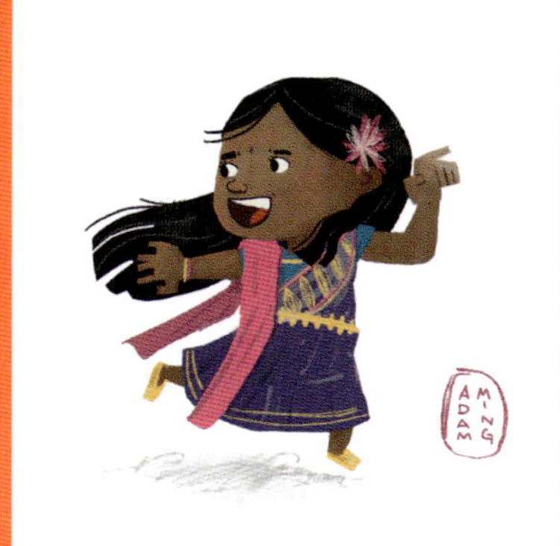

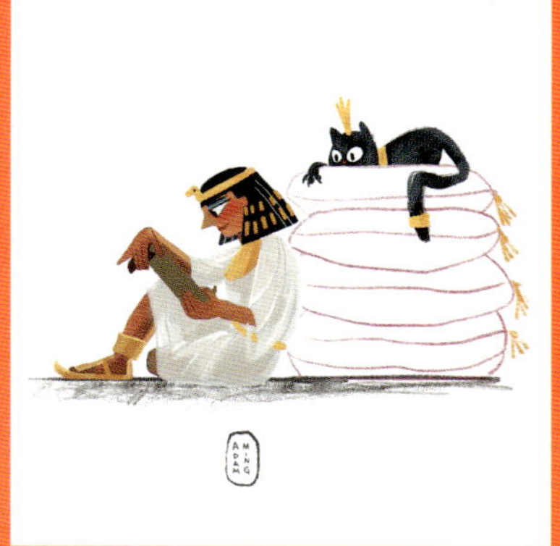

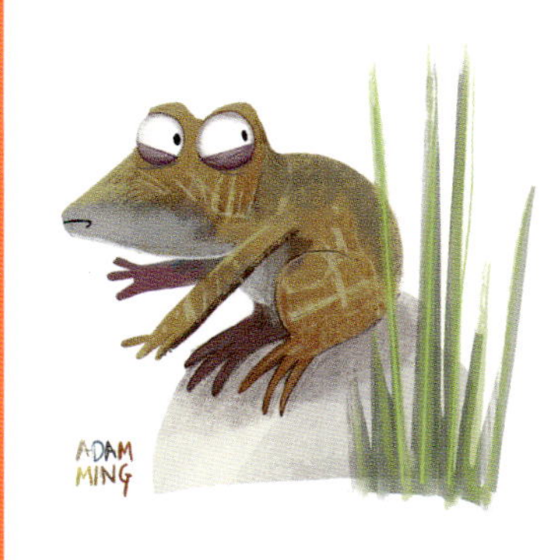

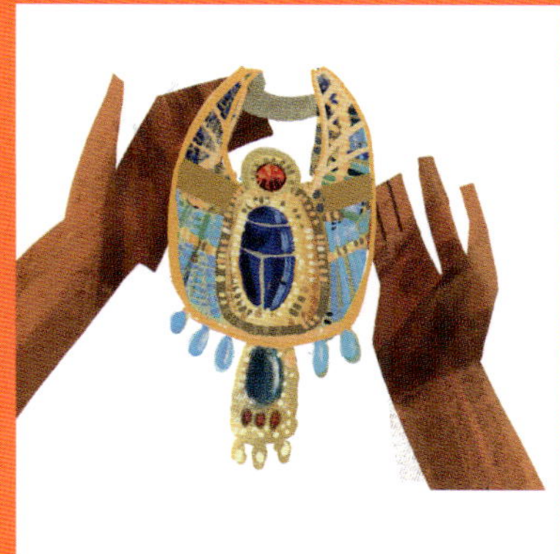

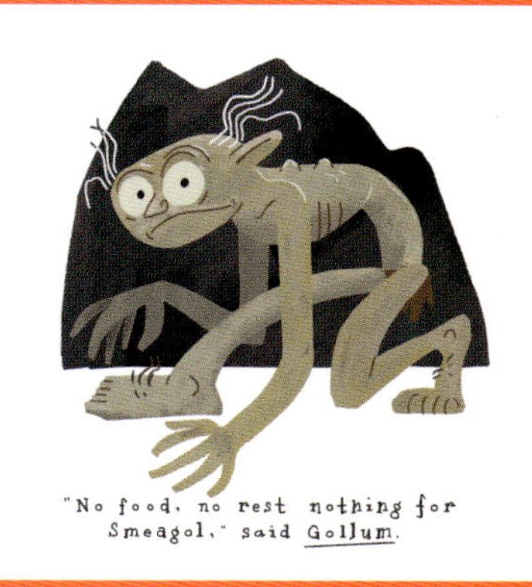

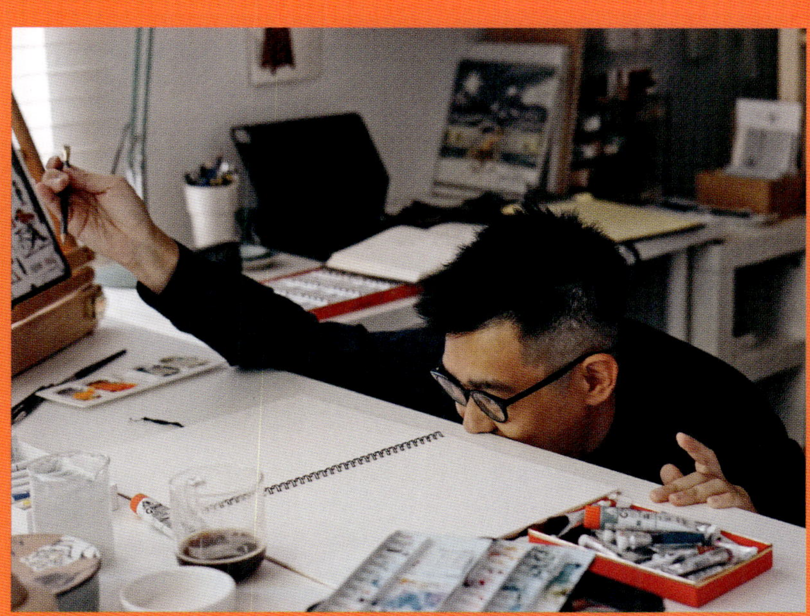

Adam Ming

adamming.com
Adam Ming makes witty and energetic illustrations with a comic sensibility. Adam runs a community of daily drawers called Ten Minute Artist, with page-a-day prompts to help new and experienced creators build their daily personal art practice.

Separate or Together?

Should you share your Daily Drawing Practice alongside your main work, or keep it separate? It might sound like a small detail, but for those who care about consistency in their brand or style, it can feel like a big deal. There's no one-size-fits-all answer—it depends on how you use social media (or wherever you share your work) and what message you want to send.

Some artists seamlessly incorporate their experiments into their public-facing image, while others feel held back by concerns about how it all fits together. If you're stuck on this, here are a few things to consider.

Keeping It Separate

One of the clearest reasons to keep your Daily Drawing Practice separate from your main work is creative freedom. When you're not concerned about how something fits your "brand," you can experiment more freely. Whether that fear of judgment is valid or not, it's real—and it can hold you back.

Think of it like beta testing. When companies release a new app or product, they often launch it quietly to a smaller group of users. These early adopters know it's still in progress, so their expectations are different. I treat my Daily Drawing Practice the same way. Sharing it in a separate space feels like testing new ideas with a smaller, more forgiving audience (at least that's how I imagine it) before bringing them to my main feed.

That's why I created a dedicated identity for my daily drawings: @drawingisimportant. It's a space where I can loosen up, play, and not worry about aligning with my commercial style. Ironically, over time, my daily drawings started influencing my professional work. For example, drawing with paint pens has changed how I build shapes in Photoshop. So even if you keep things separate, they can still cross-pollinate—naturally, over time.

Keeping It Together

On the other hand, if you're not worried about how people perceive your experiments, why not share everything in one place? The most important thing is that your Daily Practice keeps you inspired and growing. If maintaining separate accounts feels like a chore, then maybe it's not worth it.

Some artists—like Gosia Herba (*on the opposite page*)—don't need to compartmentalize because experimentation is already part of their public creative identity. But for those of us who hesitate to share our more "out there" ideas, perhaps we need to practice putting ourselves out there anyway. Challenging your assumptions—about your work and how people will respond—is part of growth.

Remember: A Daily Drawing Practice is a habit, not a straitjacket. You can always adjust how you present it—integrating it more, separating it more, or doing a little of both.

My Experience

While writing this book, I tried a "Keeping It Together" approach. I started a series of jazz-inspired daily drawings and decided to share them on my main Instagram feed. For me, this felt bold—I worried I might confuse my audience or hurt my "brand." But I'm glad I did it. It helped me take myself less seriously, and it was interesting to read what people thought in the comments. That being said, I did discover through a poll that many of my followers were unaware of the jazzy drawings at all—which I can only assume was the work of *the algorithm*.

Honestly, I don't need more reasons to second-guess what and how I share, so I ultimately decided to go back to keeping things separate.

Ultimately, there's no wrong choice. Do whatever keeps you moving forward. Whether you keep things separate or all in one place, the goal is the same: to keep your Daily Drawing Practice fun, freeing, and creatively rewarding.

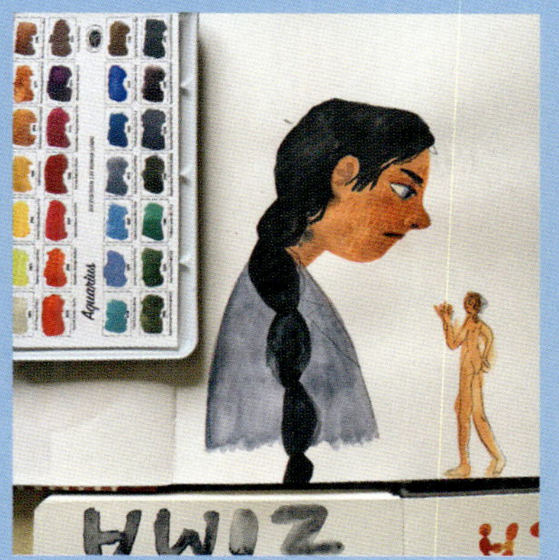

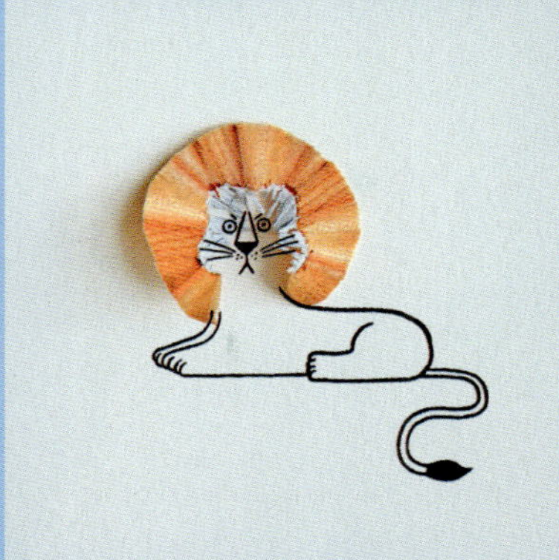

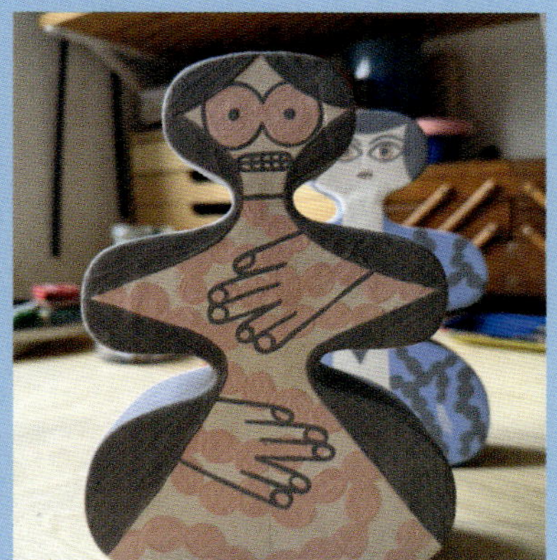

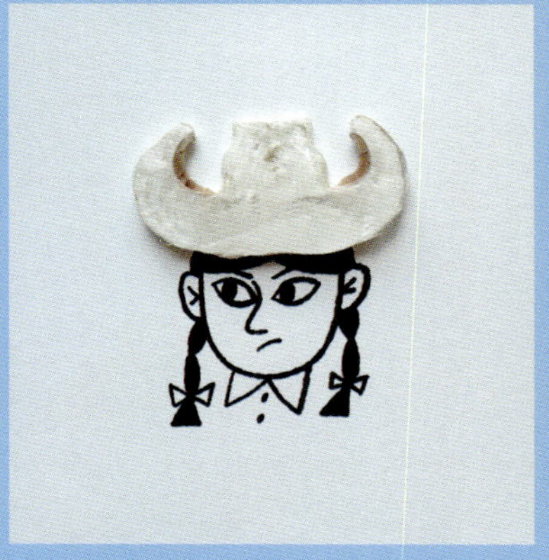

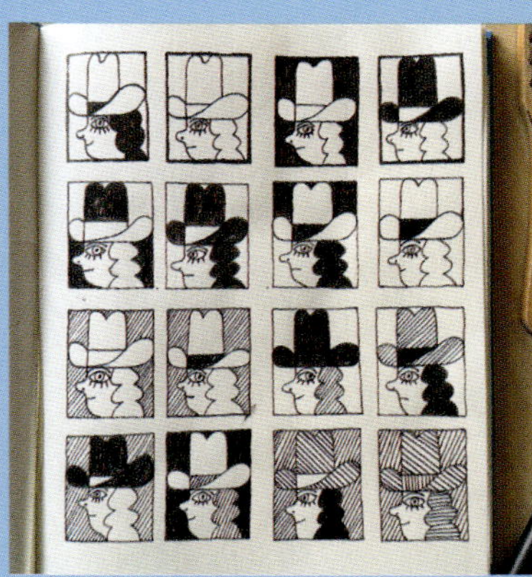

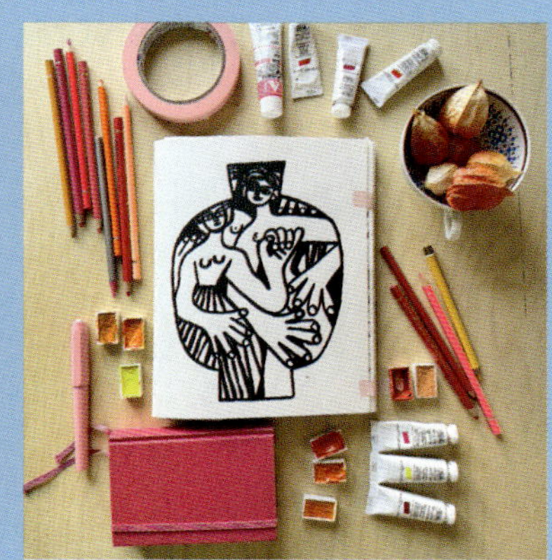

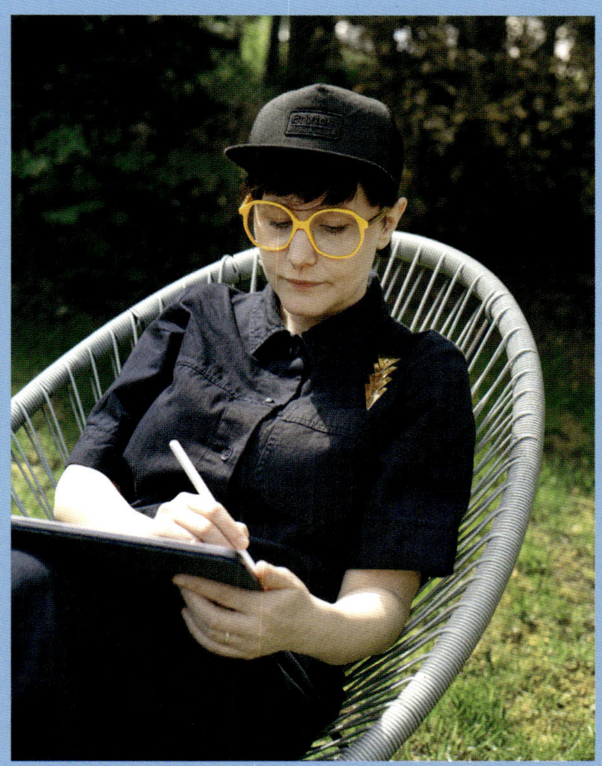

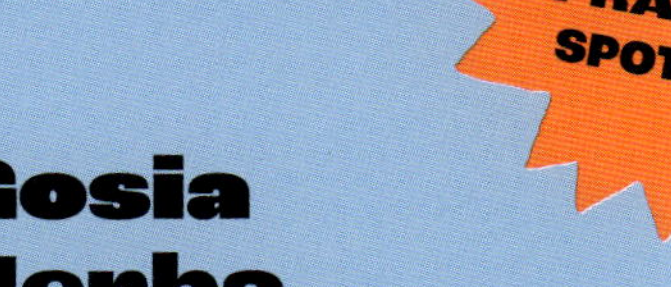

Gosia Herba

gosiaherba.com

Whether she's seeing a lion's head in a pencil shaving, working on a character study, or prototyping a porcelain figurine—or sharing a recent client project—Polish illustrator Gosia Herba shares it all together in one place. I love how she captures her daily creative life through casual but well-composed photos and simple captions.

The New Year's Resolution

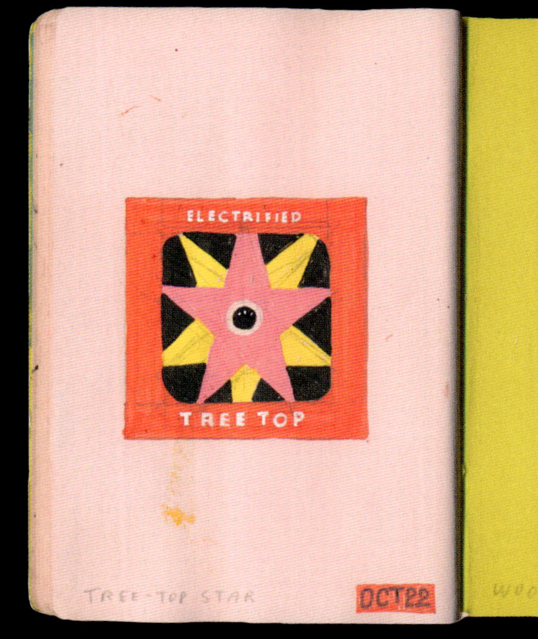

Before I had a full "thesis" on daily drawing—now a Skillshare class and the basis of this book—my own practice came and went. My "Reboot" period (*see Interlude II, page 58*) was very sporadic and didn't last long. At the time, I was busier than ever with client work, so my creative itch was already being scratched (mostly!). I often thought about drawing more, even felt like I should be, but I never felt enough of a sense of purpose to commit.

That changed one Christmas break when my then-nine-year-old daughter asked me to teach her how to draw. As we got going, I really felt out of shape, especially in drawing from observation! Given that I don't draw in a traditional or realistic way, I became self-conscious (nine-year-olds can be sticklers for detail and realism). I know it sounds ridiculous, but I couldn't shake the feeling that, because I was a professional illustrator, she expected more from me!

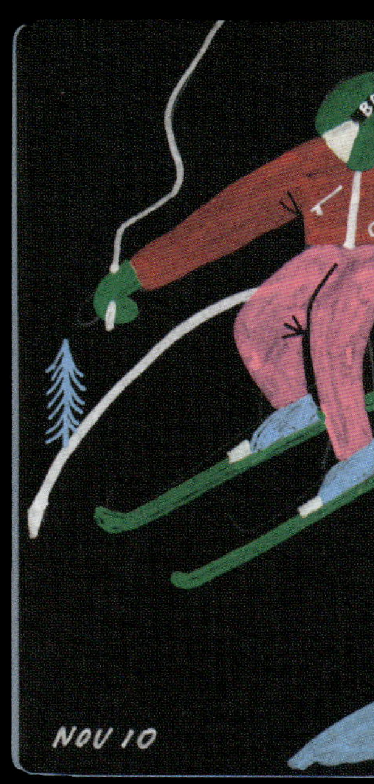

So that New Year's, I resolved to reboot my Daily Drawing Practice. This time, I set a low-pressure goal: five minutes a day, from life, using my 0.5 mm pencil and Moleskine notebook, posting on @drawingisimportant. The lessons lasted a few weeks, but my Daily Drawing Practice has been going strong ever since.

Daily drawing and sharing can plant seeds that you later discover as full-grown opportunities: Not long after that New Year's resolution, a scrappy little sketchbook brand, Uglybooks, asked if I'd try out some of their products as part of my practice. The colored pages forced me to branch out—pencil didn't show up, so I tried Sharpies, then some paint pens I had lying around. This turned out to be a highly addictive combination. Hooked, I started drawing objects from a vintage catalog I had lying around, and I've been going strong ever since.

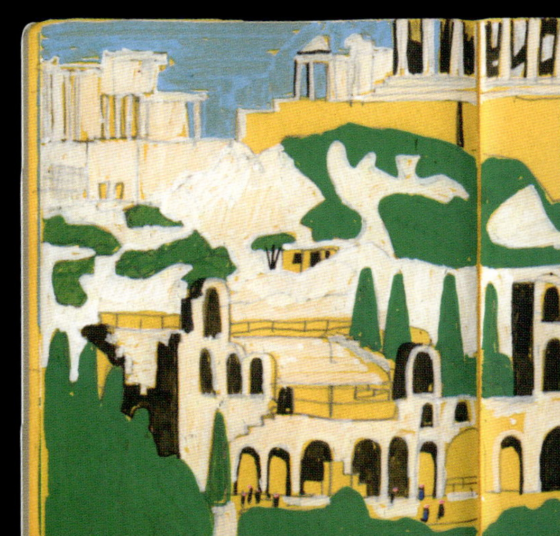

What started as a five-minute daily commitment grew a little longer over time, to the point where I can go for much longer than an hour if I don't force myself to stop!

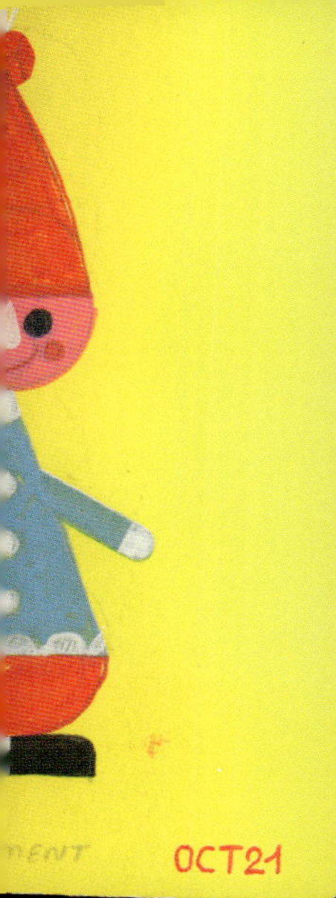
OCT21
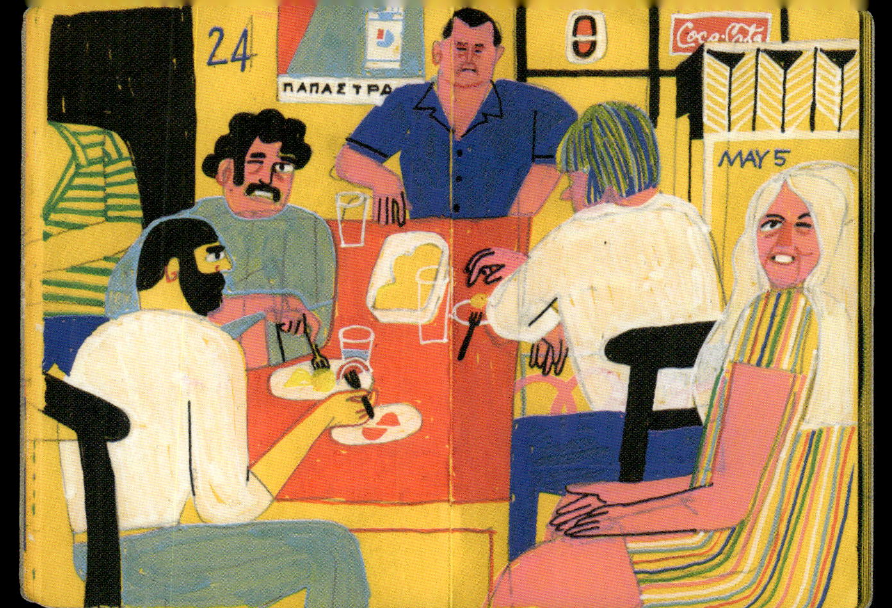
24
ΠΑΠΑΣΤΡΑ
Coca-Cola
MAY 5
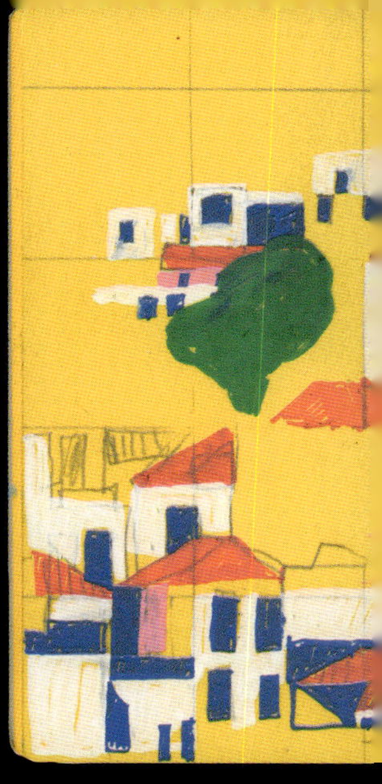
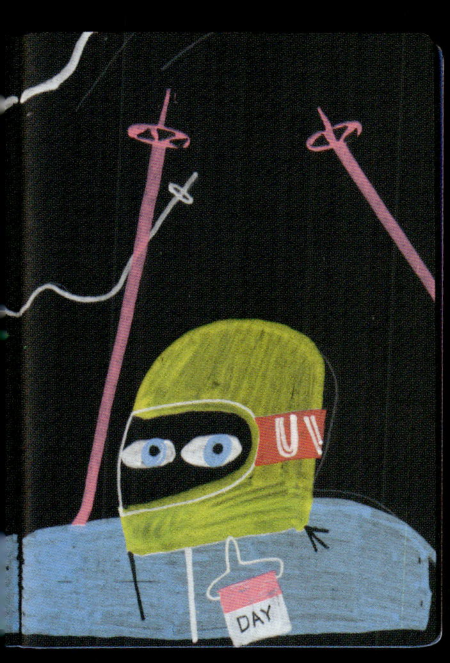
DAY
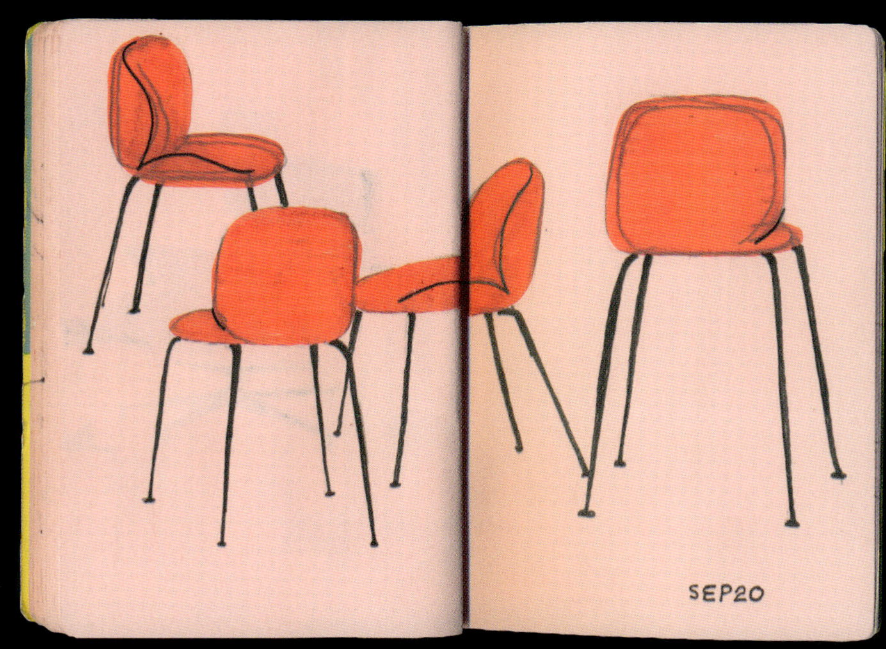
SEP20
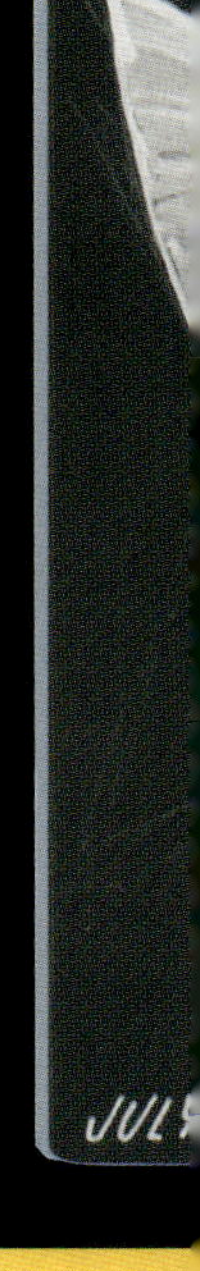
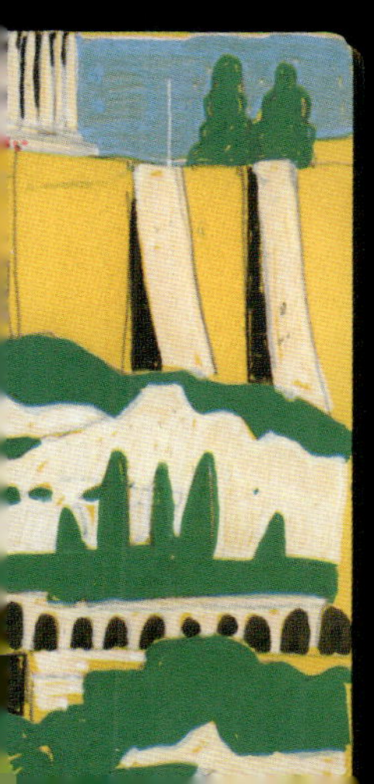
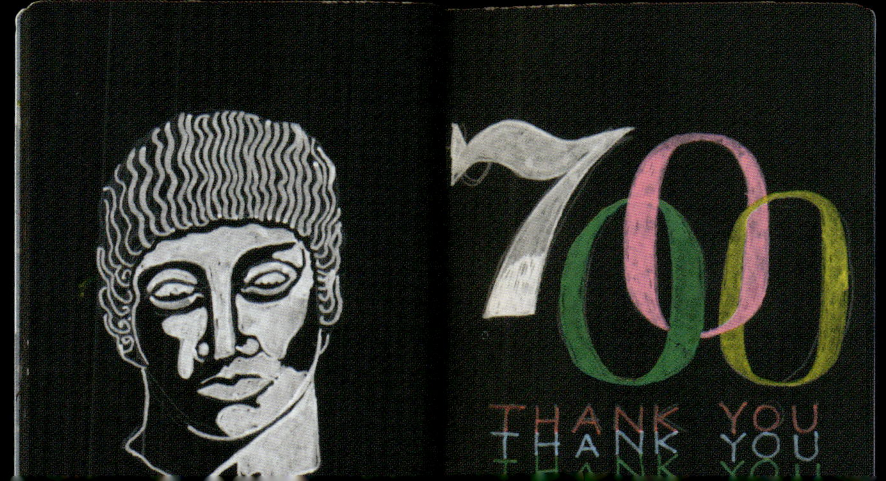
700
THANK YOU
THANK YOU
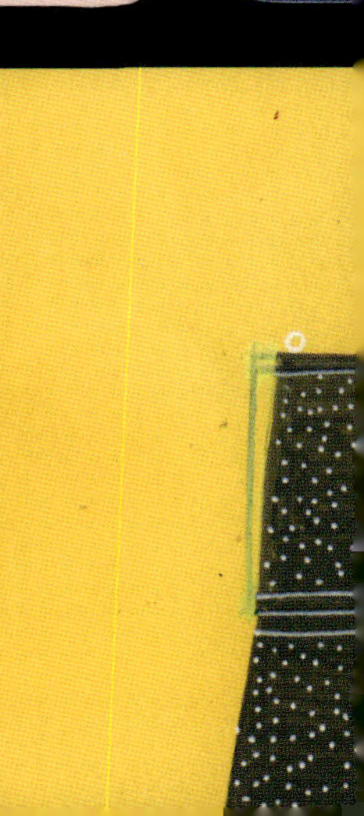

DRAWING GOALS 2022 — JUST TO STAY FRESH — TO GET BACK INTO DRAWING FROM LIFE OR REFERENCE — O-MODE.
NINA SEES ME SUCKING!
DRAWING EVERYDAY WILL HELP ME TEACH MY DAUGHTERS HOW TO DRAW. I DO NOT ENJOY TRYING TO TEACH NINA BASIC DRAWING BECAUSE I AM NOT CONFIDENT — I DON'T KNOW HOW TO TEACH DRAWING, esp. BASIC DRAWING skills. WHAT IS THE MOST IMPORTANT SKILL TO TEACH FIRST? — BUT FOR ME + THIS GOAL, WHAT DO I WANT TO IMPROVE UPON? DRAWING OBSERVATIONALLY
JAN 3 2022
5 minutes

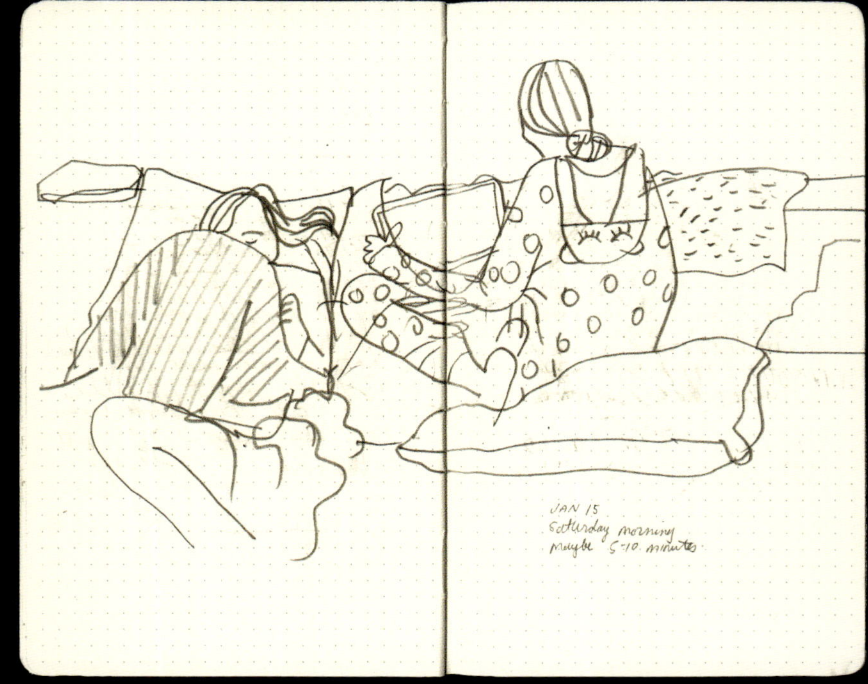
JAN 15
Saturday morning
maybe 5-10 minutes

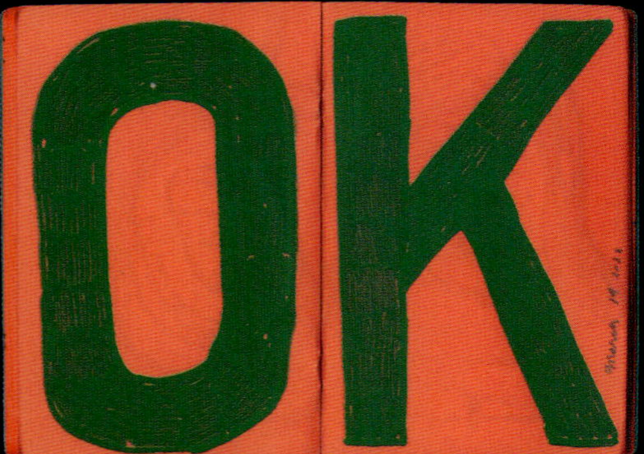
OK
March 14

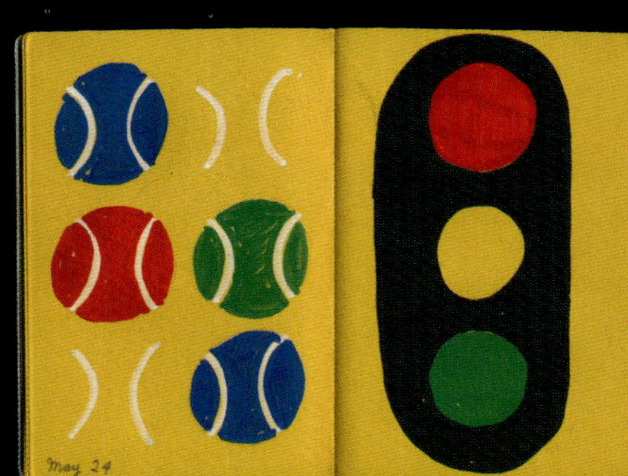
May 24

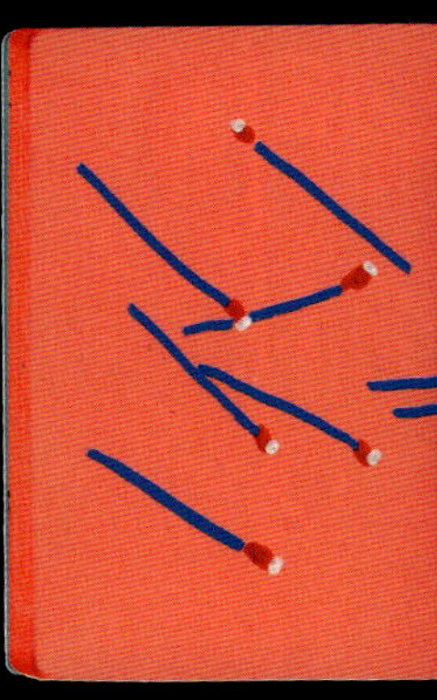

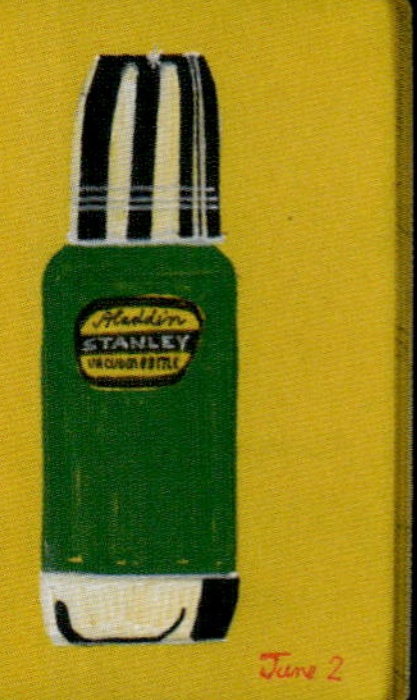
Aladdin
STANLEY
June 2

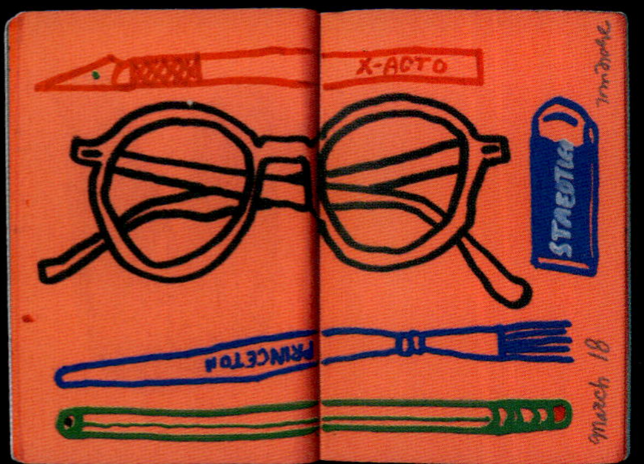
X-ACTO
STAEDTLER
PRINCETON
March 18

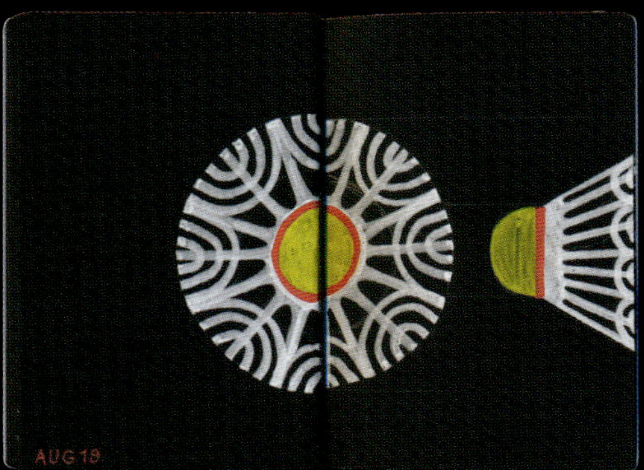
AUG 19

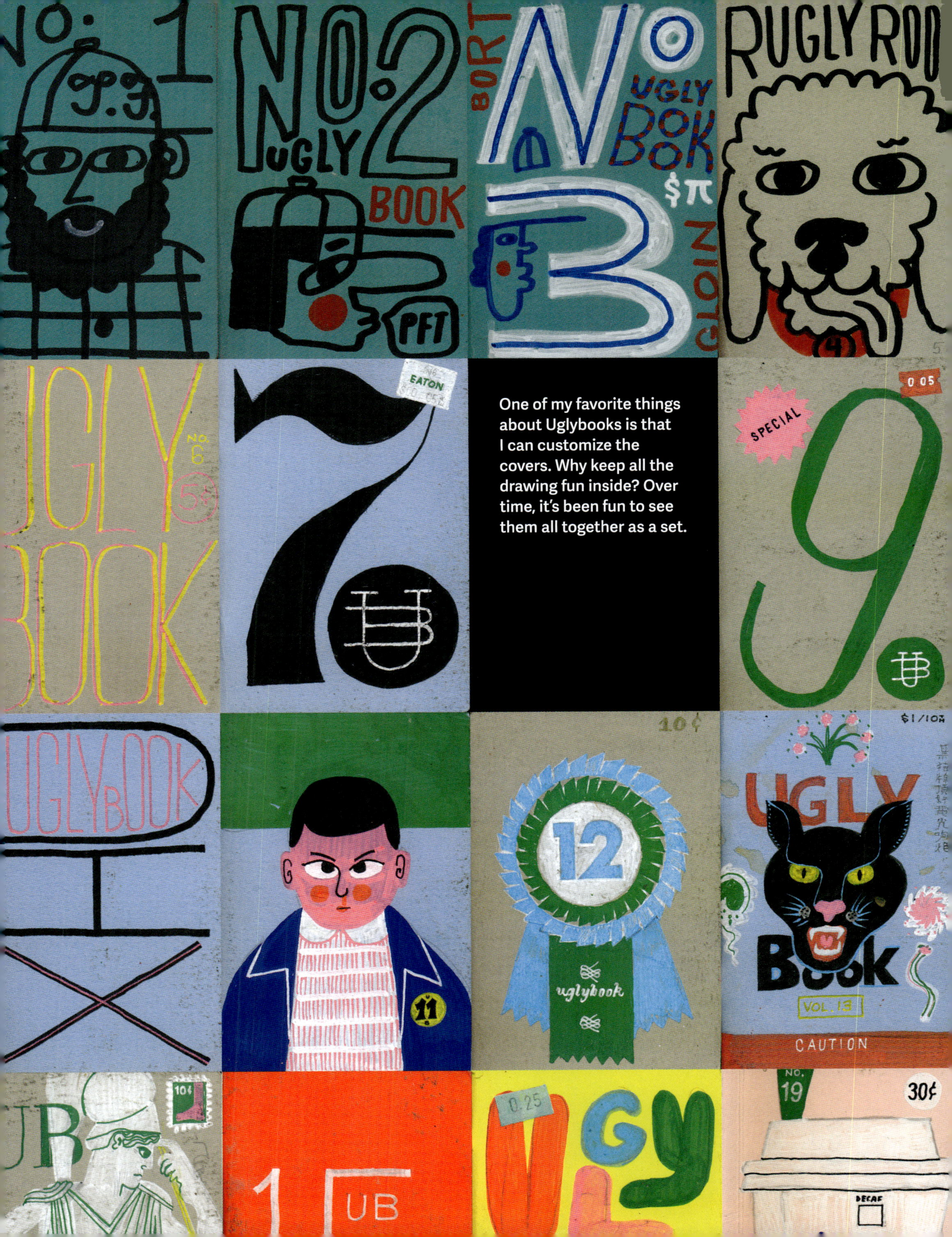

One of my favorite things about Uglybooks is that I can customize the covers. Why keep all the drawing fun inside? Over time, it's been fun to see them all together as a set.

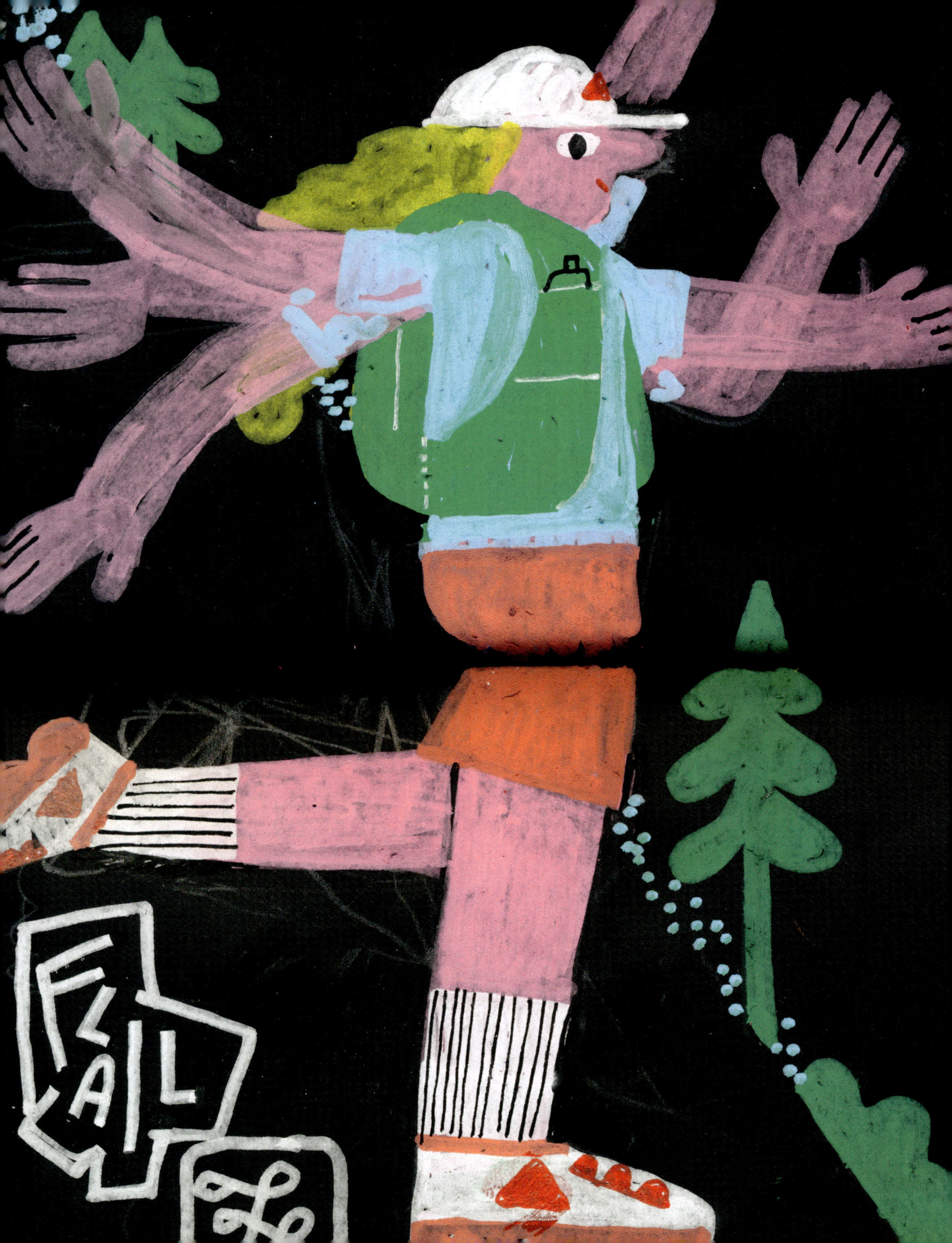
FLAIL

> "I would never hire anyone who doesn't have side projects. To me, that shows that someone has ideas, self-initiative, and can make things happen."
>
> **Tina Roth-Eisenberg, Interview on *The Great Discontent***

Chapter

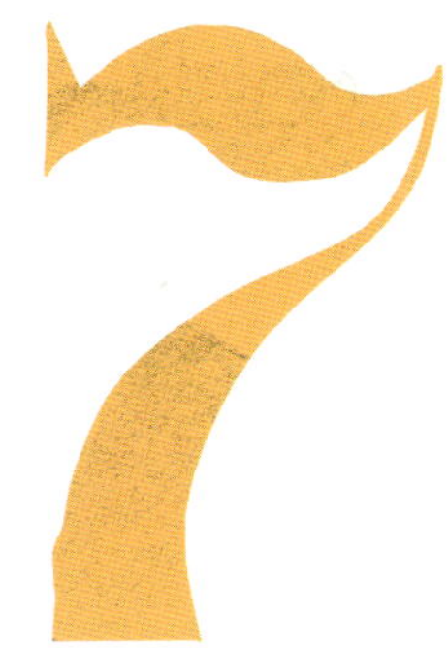

DAILY PRACTICE VS. DAILY PROJECTS

So far, we've focused on building a sustainable daily drawing habit. But what about shorter-term creative sprints? In this chapter, we'll explore the difference between a Daily Practice and Daily Projects—and how both can serve your growth in different ways. I'll show how projects can spark breakthroughs, help you develop specific skills, or reinvigorate your practice when it starts to feel stale. You'll also see real-world examples of how combining both approaches can keep your creativity flexible, focused, and fun.

Daily Projects Are Important Too

Throughout this book, I've focused on what I call the Daily Drawing Practice. But there's another closely related concept: the Daily Project. While they share many similarities, the biggest difference is that practice is ongoing, while projects are temporary. In fact, the starter kits I introduced earlier in the book are technically Daily Projects, not practices. Whatever you stick with over time, that becomes your practice. Another key difference lies in intensity. While a Daily Practice is meant to be sustainable—looser, more forgiving, lower pressure—a Daily Project can be the opposite. It's often a focused, high-energy push toward a specific goal. Daily Projects also tend to go beyond simple drawing exercises. While they can involve traditional tools and techniques, they're also a great opportunity to explore larger creative processes. Personally, I often use Daily Projects to experiment with blending analog and digital techniques—integrating hand-drawn elements into my digital illustration workflow.

Training vs. Maintenance

As a runner, I think in terms of training cycles. When I'm preparing for a race, I follow a structured plan with clear, ambitious goals. But between races, I'm not pushing as hard—I'm simply maintaining my base level of fitness so I don't fall out of shape.

In this analogy, a Daily Project is like race training: You choose a big goal, make a plan, and follow it step-by-step. A Daily Practice, on the other hand, is like maintenance mode. It's how you stay creatively fit between projects so you're always ready for the next challenge.

A lot of time and effort go into building up your creative "fitness," just like it does in running. If you don't use it, you lose it! A Daily Drawing Practice helps you keep your skills sharp, your ideas flowing, and your creative confidence intact.

Of course, we need both. You can't train hard all the time or you'll burn out, but if you never set bigger, more challenging goals, you risk losing motivation and direction. Thus, maintenance (Practice) and training (Projects) are both important parts of your overall creative "training cycle."

You might wonder if you need to keep your Daily Practice going while you're doing a Daily Project, and the answer is no! Just like I can't be in training and maintenance mode at the same time while running, you can give yourself permission to switch from practice mode to project mode for a while when drawing. Each has its time—and both are vital.

Projects vs. Practice

Projects
- Like training for a big race
- More intensive and high-effort
- More focused goal
- More substantial or complete works
- More finite period
- A shorter-term routine

Practice
- Like maintaining fitness
- More relaxed, sustainable effort
- More general purpose
- More sketches or incomplete works
- Indefinite period
- More of a habit or routine

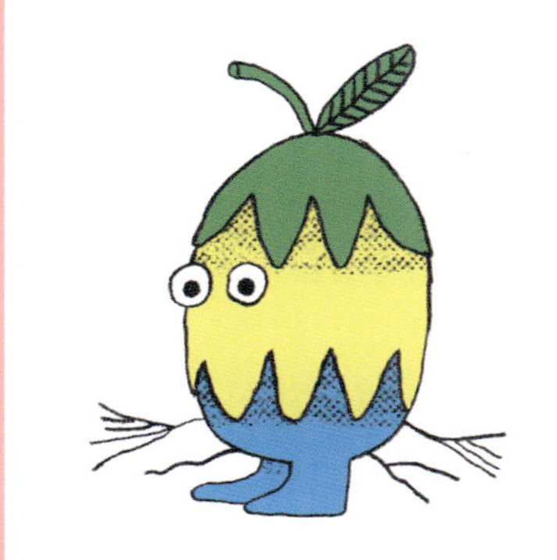
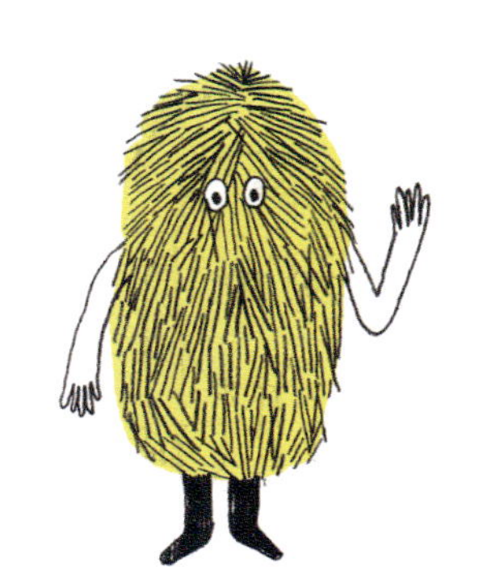
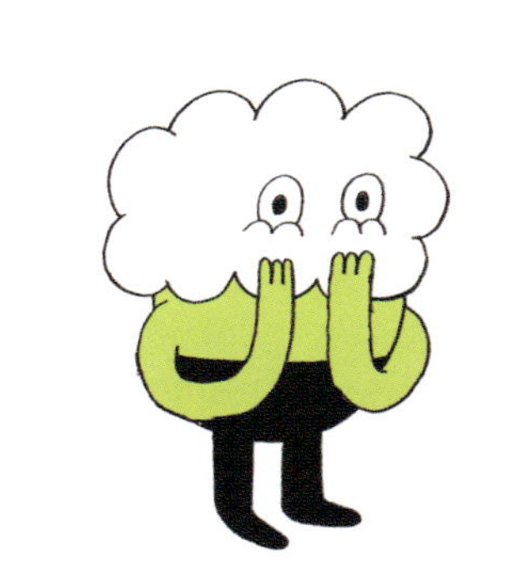
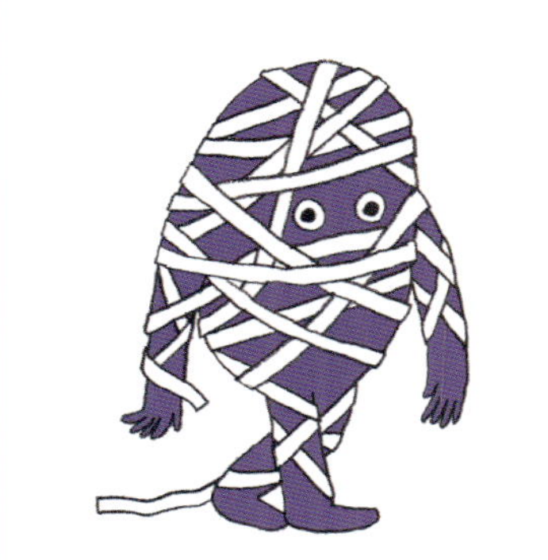
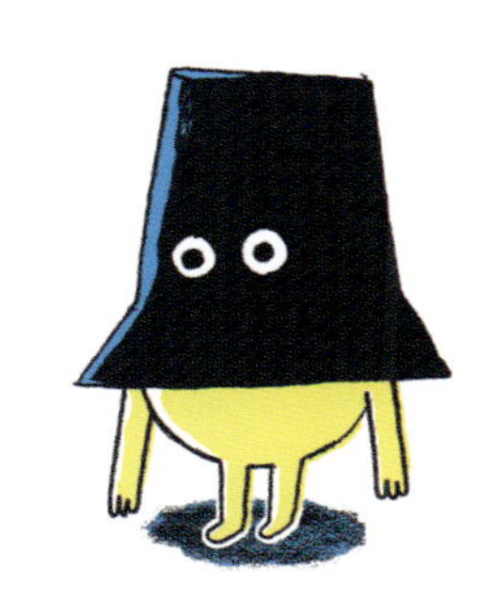
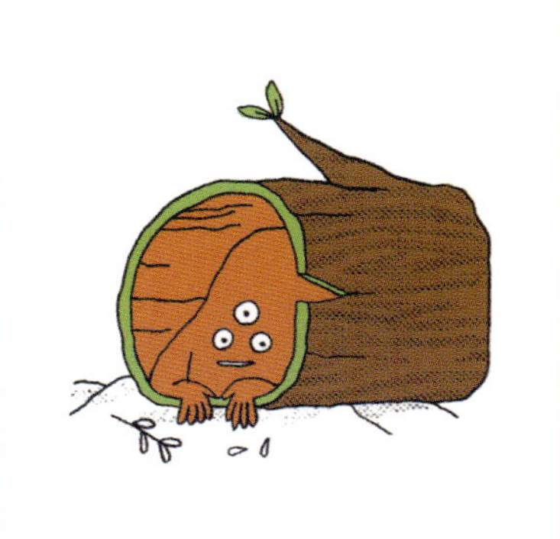

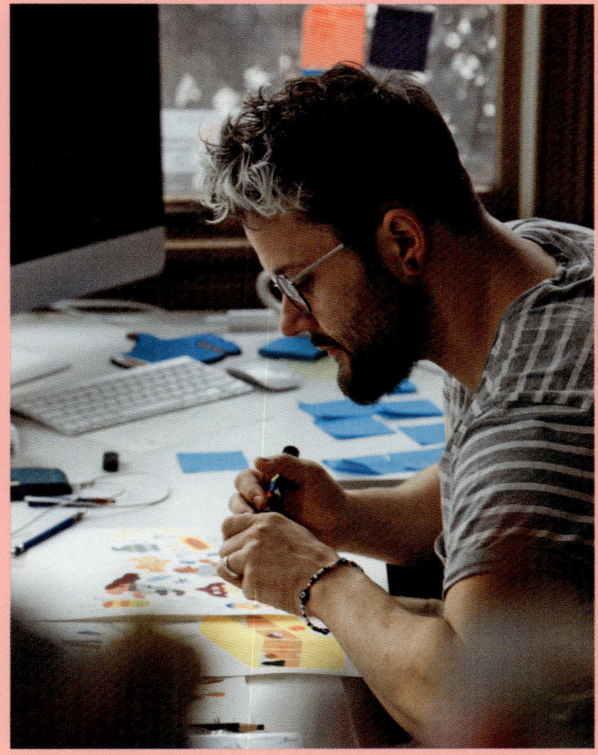

Andy J. Pizza

andyjpizza.com

Andy J. Pizza may be best known today as the host of the *Creative Pep Talk* podcast. But way back in 2011, Andy kick-started his illustration career with a year-long Daily Project he called Day-After-Day in NOD. Andy created and shared 260 characters in this imaginary universe. Years later these would resurface in a more refined iteration called *Invisible Things*, which became a *New York Times* best-selling picture book.

Why Do Daily Projects?

Keeping a Daily Drawing Practice is a great way to stay in shape as a creative, but every now and then, you might want to push yourself a little harder to accelerate growth in a more focused area, such as:

- Developing a specific artistic technique
- Learning a new tool or app
- Building your illustration portfolio
- Creating a series of characters
- Developing a line of products (such as greeting cards)
- Improving your skills, such as drawing hands or conceptual illustration

As with a Daily Drawing Practice, I recommend starting out with a plan that includes the same five elements: Purpose, Media, Schedule, Source, and Sharing. The main difference is that you're more likely to emphasize quality over quantity in a Daily Project. That may even mean leaning a bit more into a bit of *healthy* perfectionism! While not always the case, Daily Project sessions will tend to be more intensive—which is why they're not as sustainable as a Daily Practice.

It's Going to Be Worth It!

Whatever your goal, be prepared to put in some serious time and effort! It's going to be worth it: Done well, Daily Projects can lead to outcomes you might never have dreamed of down the road. Focus and consistency over time are the surest way to success.

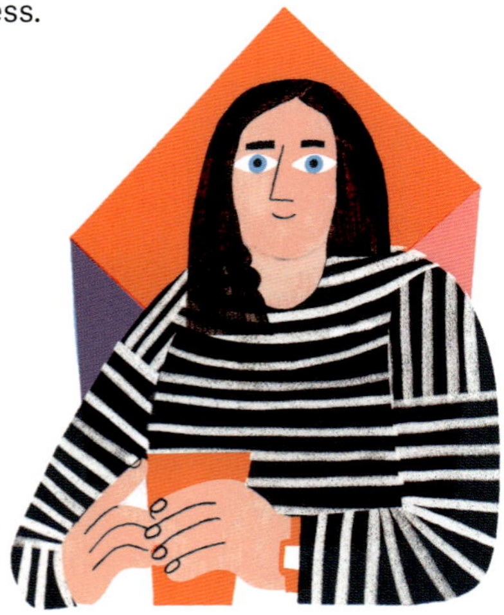

Should You Switch to a Daily Project?

You'll know when you're ready for a more intensive Daily Project when you feel like you're hitting a creative wall in you practice. When I grew bored of my all-digital process for client work, I knew it was time to start experimenting with physical media. I shifted out of Daily Drawing Practice mode and began a thirty-day #Inktober project experimenting with bringing more analog elements into my process. By that November, I was so inspired that I started a new Daily Project combining my new techniques with my love of jazz (*see page 113*). I got that out of my system and was able to fall back into my usual routine. This is the beauty of having a long-established Daily Drawing Practice: It's not that hard to get back into it after taking some time away.

Turning Side Projects into Start-ups

The magic of Daily Projects isn't just a drawing thing. Tina Roth-Eisenberg (@swissmiss) is a Swiss-born graphic designer, longtime blogger, and entrepreneur living in New York City. As the founder of many well-known and successful projects, including CreativeMornings, Tattly, and TeuxDeux, she says that all of these started as side projects. When asked for advice for other creatives starting out, she speaks unusually highly about side projects: See below.

"Believe in side projects. Tattly was a side project; swissmiss was a side project; CreativeMornings was a side project; TeuxDeux was a side project. These are all things that turned into revenue streams for me and made it possible not to have clients. I would never hire anyone who doesn't have side projects. To me, that shows that someone has ideas, self-initiative, and can make things happen."
—Tina Roth-Eisenberg

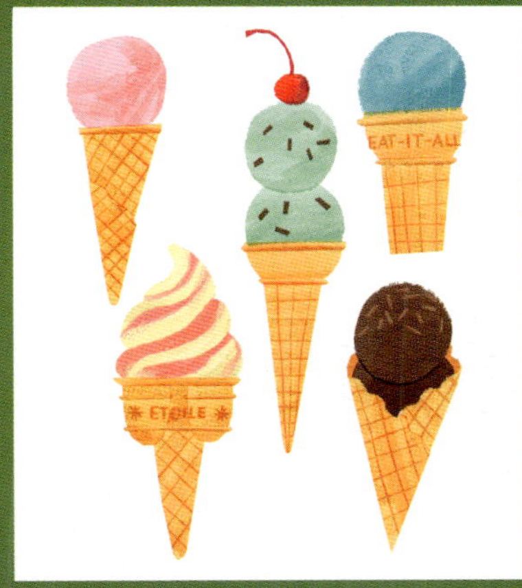

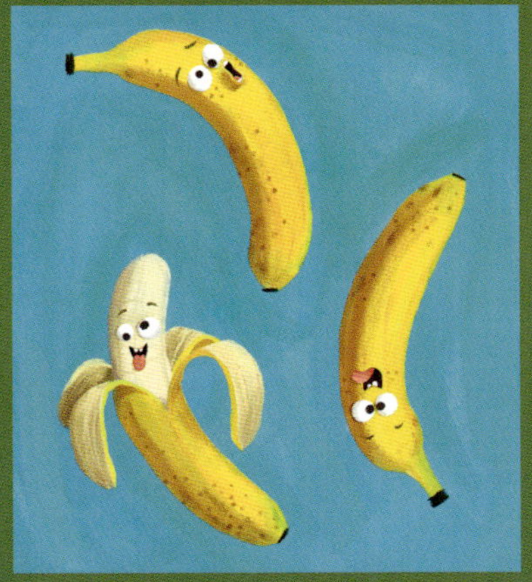

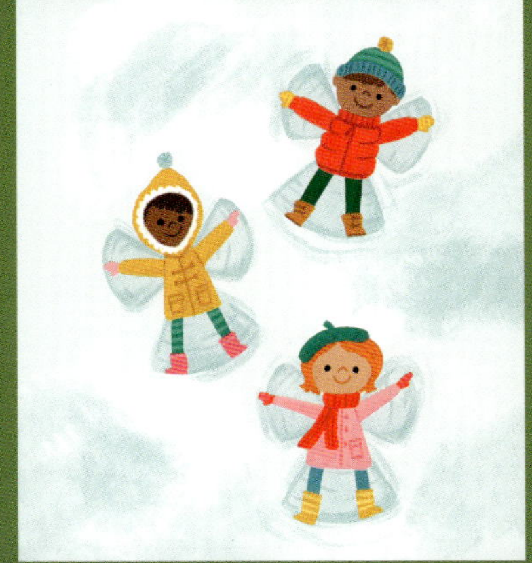

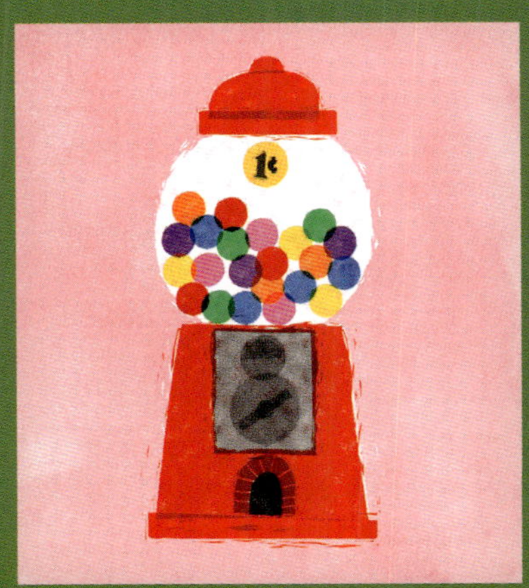

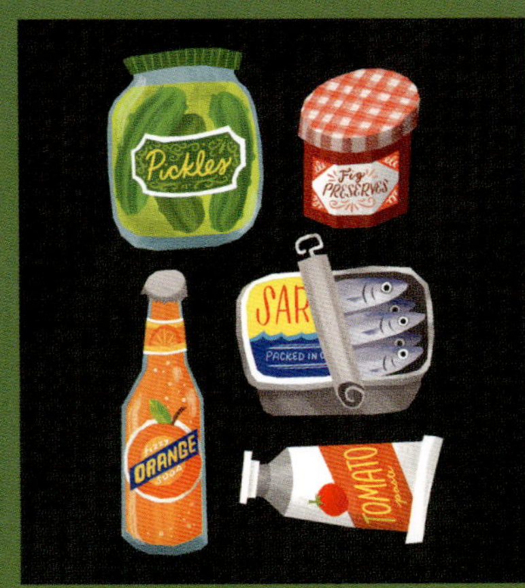

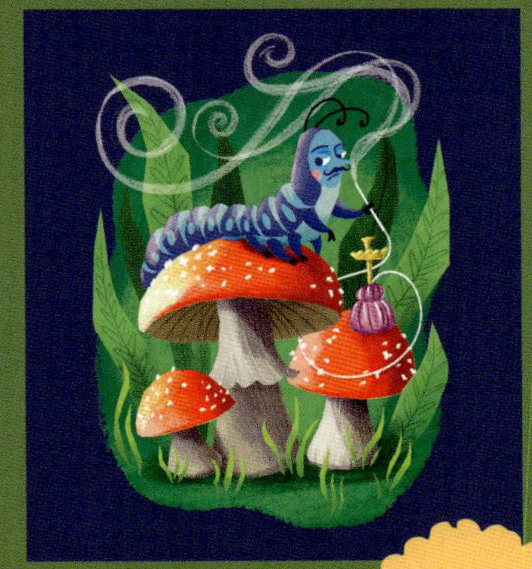

DAILY PROJECT SPOTLIGHT

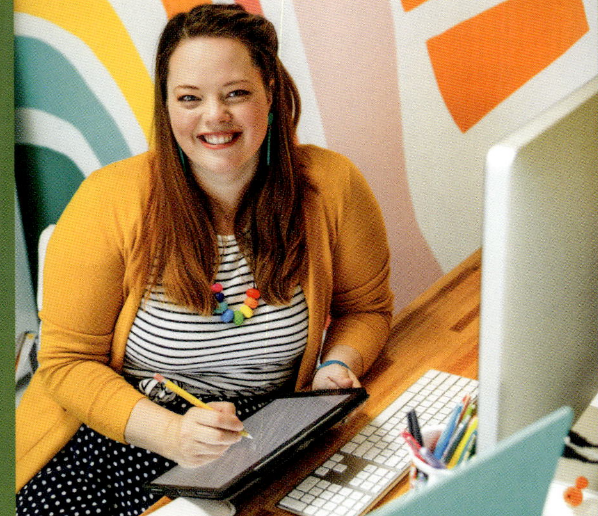

Lisa Bardot

@lisabardot
Based in Sacramento, California, Lisa Bardot is an illustrator, educator, creative explorer, and Procreate brush designer. After the birth of her first child, she sought a way to stay connected to her creativity amid the new demands of parenthood and running a business. Procreate turned out to be the perfect fit: portable, accessible, and easy to pick up during naptime. In 2016, she challenged herself to draw something every day, a personal project that reignited her creative spark and set her on a new path. That journey led to the 2019 launch of Making Art Everyday, a daily drawing challenge that has since inspired thousands of people to build their own creative habits. Today, Lisa continues to support artists of all skill levels through free daily prompts and her vibrant community, Art Maker's Club.

Setting Goals and Accelerating Breakthroughs

Chipping away at creative goals over time is a great way to grow without pressure. But sometimes we want to grow in a more specific direction—and see progress more quickly. That's when we need a clear target and a plan to reach it. This is where Daily Projects come in. Like workshops or classes, they help us focus our efforts and accelerate our growth.

This principle has played out clearly in my running life. At one point, I wanted to break twenty minutes in a 5k race. My personal best at the time was twenty-one minutes—a time that already felt like a massive achievement. Going faster seemed almost impossible. But I knew if I wanted to reach that next level, I'd need a plan. As I searched for one, I wondered: Am I being too ambitious? Do I have any hope of success here?

Thankfully, most training plans offer guidelines—benchmarks to help you assess whether your goal is within reach. The one I found suggested that, yes, I was in the "hope zone." That sense of possibility was key. It gave me the confidence to start, the belief that the goal was hard but not out of reach. It also helped me avoid aiming too high and burning out in the process. I followed the plan, put in the work, and crossed the finish line in 19:25—my first sub-twenty. That kind of breakthrough can only happen when you set a goal that's just beyond your current limits.

So how does this relate to creative projects?

Set Realistic Goals
Start by asking: Is this actually doable? A Daily Project should be challenging but within reach. Look at where you're at now, and where you want to be by the end. How long might it take? How likely is it that you'll get there? These questions can help you set the right level of ambition and avoid setting yourself up for frustration.

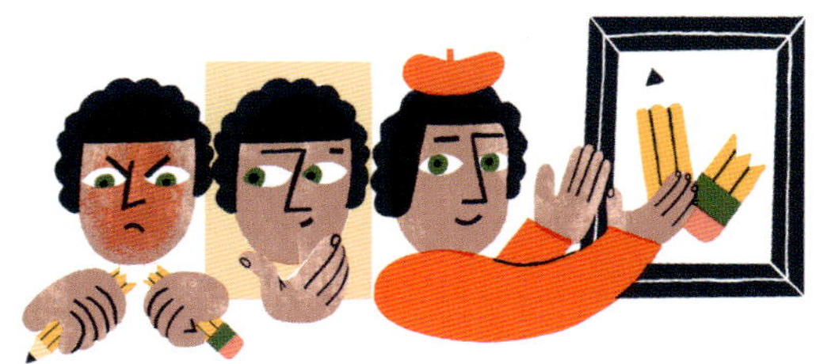

Set Measurable Goals
Unlike running times, creative growth isn't always easy to measure. But the more concrete your goals, the easier it is to stay motivated. That's why quantity-based goals—like making 260 characters in 260 days, as Andy J. Pizza did in his NOD project (*page 89*)—are so helpful. They give you something you can count and track. Even vague goals like "develop a series" or "find my voice" can be broken into measurable steps: number of drawings completed, hours invested, techniques explored.

Learn From Failure
Of course, not every goal will be met. You might aim too high—or not high enough. And when you fall short, it's easy to get discouraged. But failure isn't the enemy. In fact, when you've set specific goals, failure becomes a powerful feedback tool. It gives you something to evaluate, adjust, and try again. The worst kind of failure is the kind you can't name—the result of having no direction at all. A clear goal, even one you miss, teaches you something. No matter the outcome, the effort moves you forward.

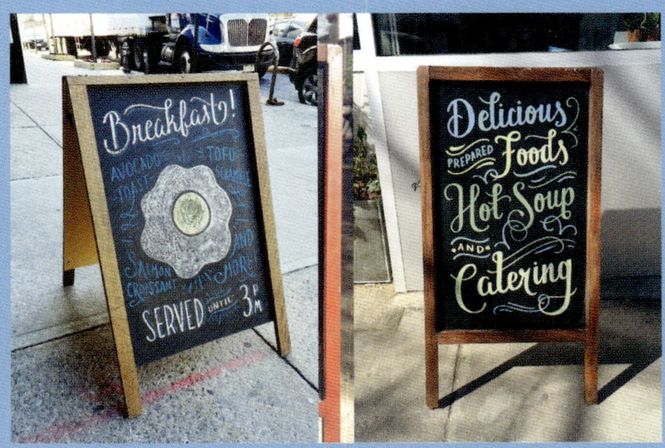

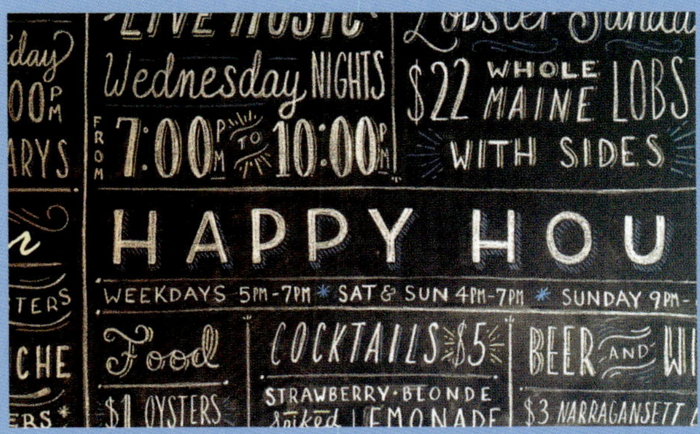

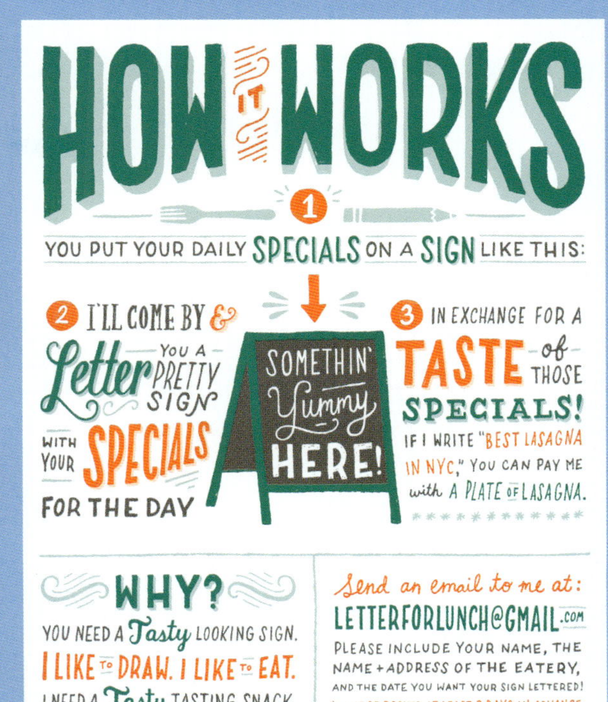

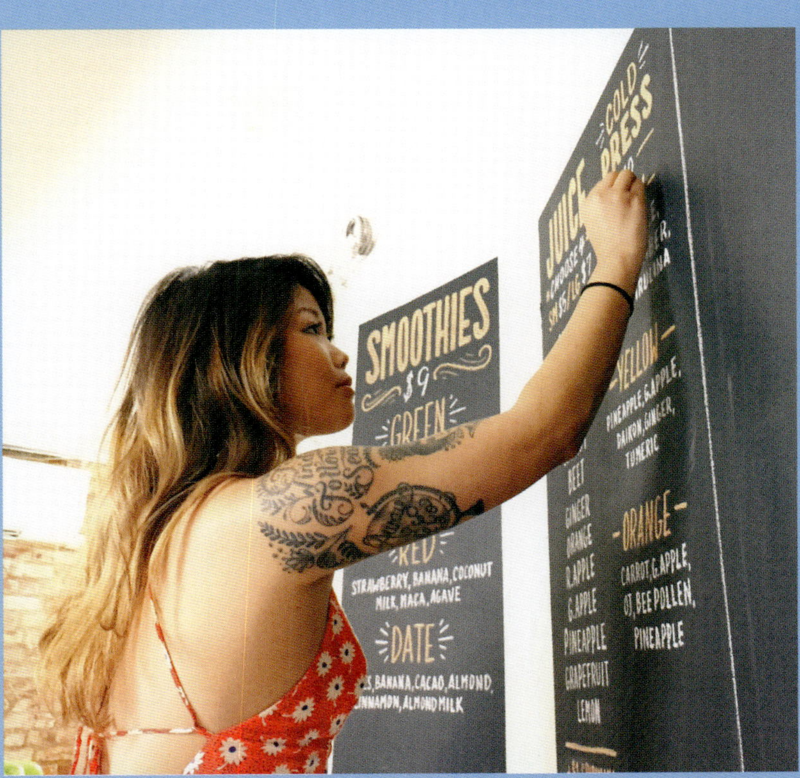

DAILY PROJECT SPOTLIGHT

Lauren Hom

homsweethom.com
Lauren Hom is an American designer and lettering artist who truly believes in passion projects. She launched her own career with a Daily Project called Will Letter for Lunch, where she literally learned to letter on the job—and was paid with lunch. Another popular project of hers was *Daily Dishonesty*, where she shared lies, lovingly hand-lettered. Today she teaches an entire class about side projects called From Passion to Paid.

Student Projects Showcase

In the next few pages, I invite you to feast your eyes on these inspiring student projects, all taken from my class, The Style Class: Work Out Your Illustration Style in a Daily Project. In the class, students take measurable steps toward discovering their illustration style.

People often speak of "finding" one's style, suggesting that it's already "out there," and that if you just keep plugging away you'll eventually find it. The reality is that you need to set specific goals and make a plan to work toward them. For illustrators developing a unique, marketable style, that means learning how we use our creative skills to communicate visual ideas. One of the best ways to do this? A Daily Project!

Students in The Style Class create their own Daily Project, starting with a plan that includes their particular goals and ending with twenty-six completed illustrations. Those who make it to the end of the project are rewarded with the experience of testing their ideas and their skills to the limit—and some even figure out the keys to their own artistic style. These are just a snapshot of the many and diverse projects. If you'd like to see more, they can be found on Skillshare.

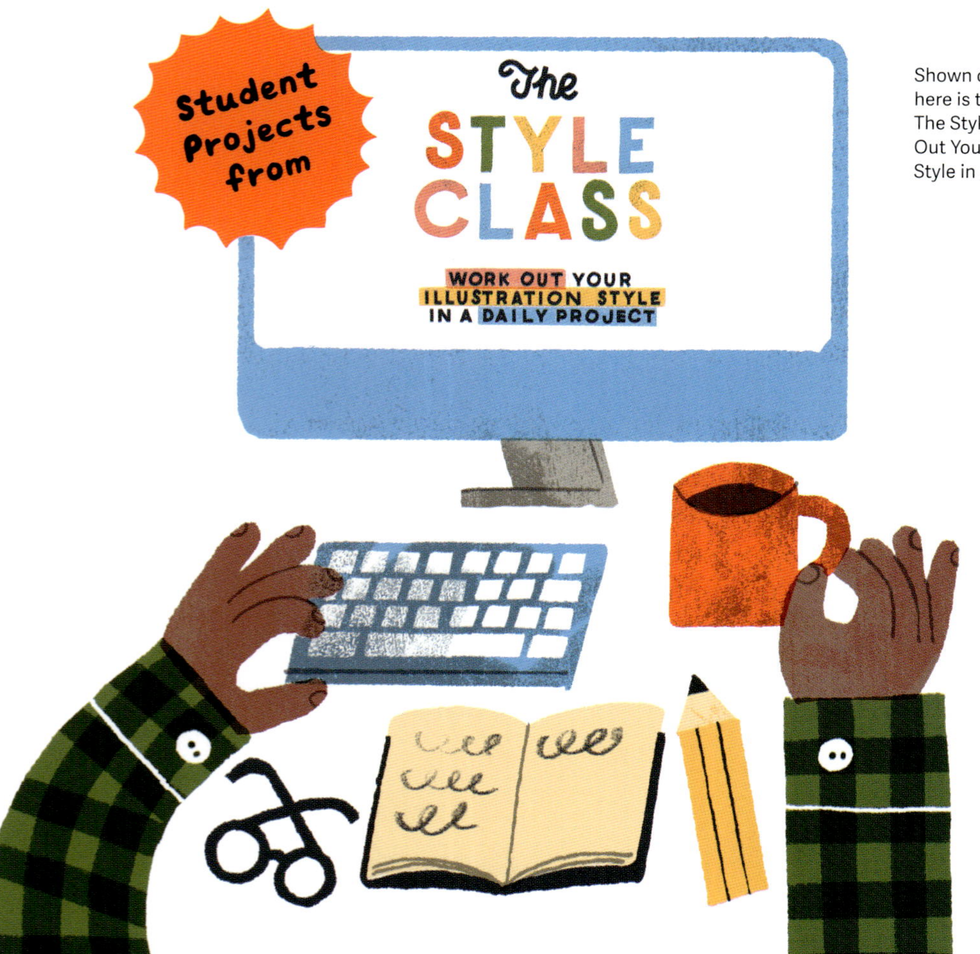

Shown on the screen here is the logo for The Style Class: Work Out Your Illustration Style in a Daily Project.

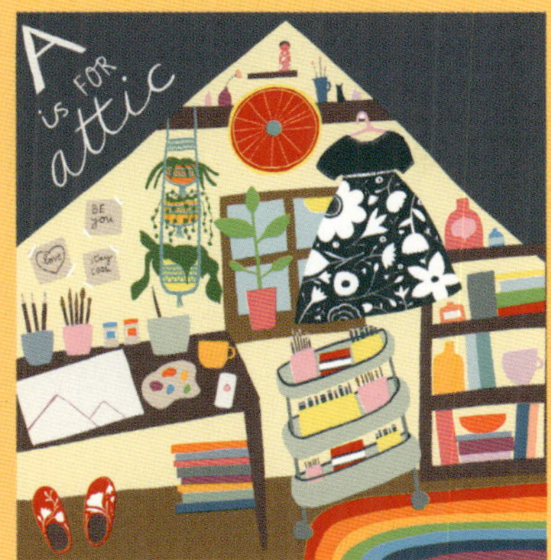

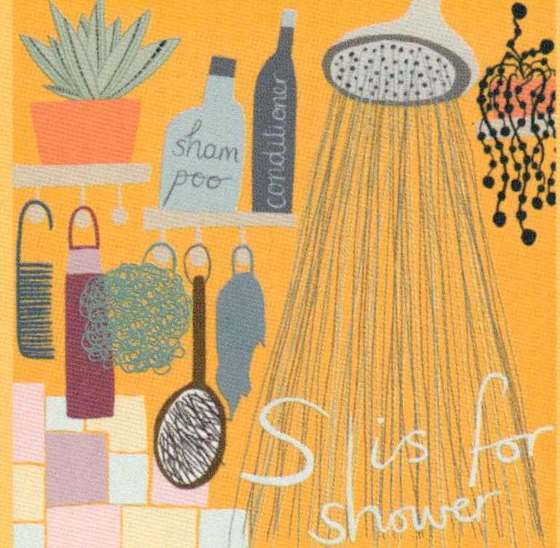

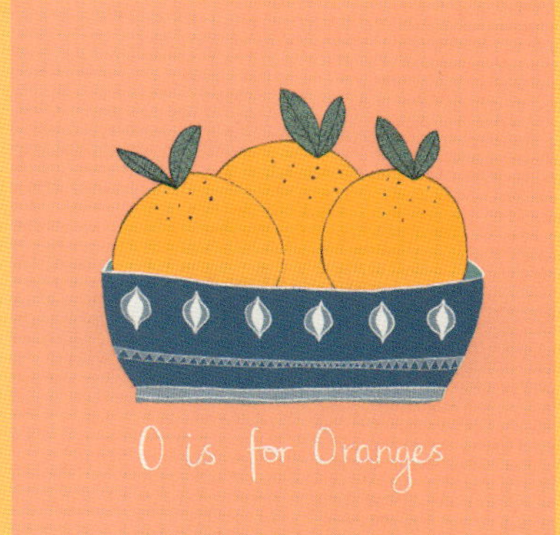

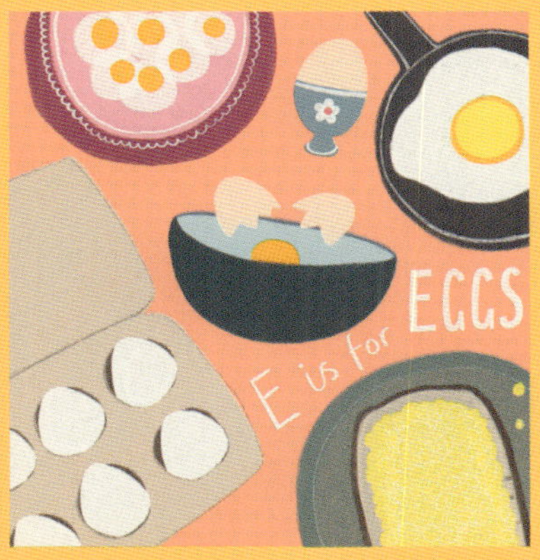

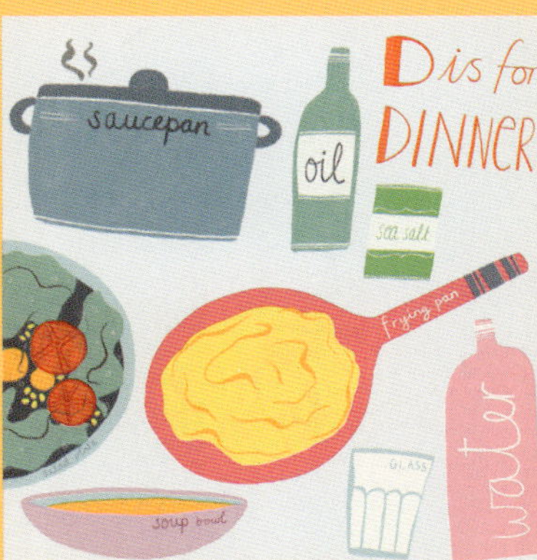

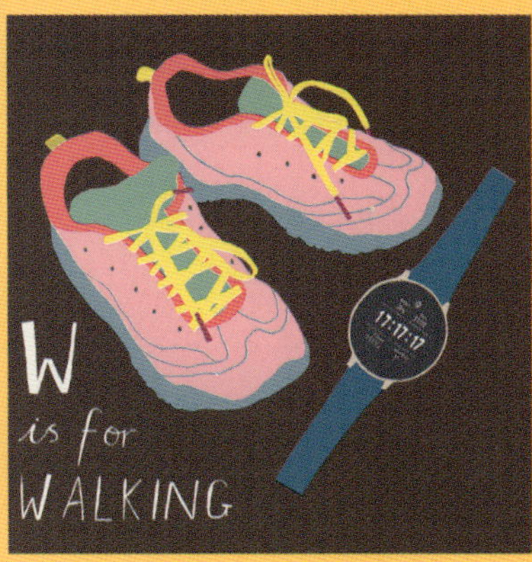

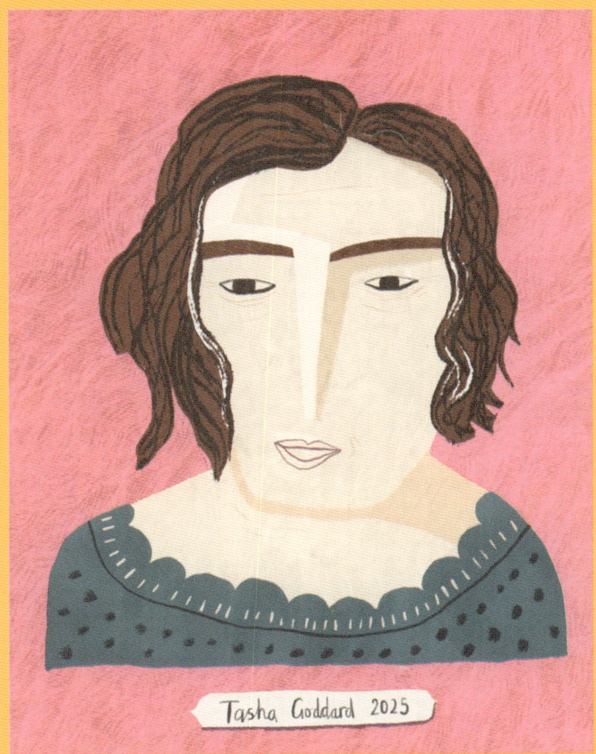

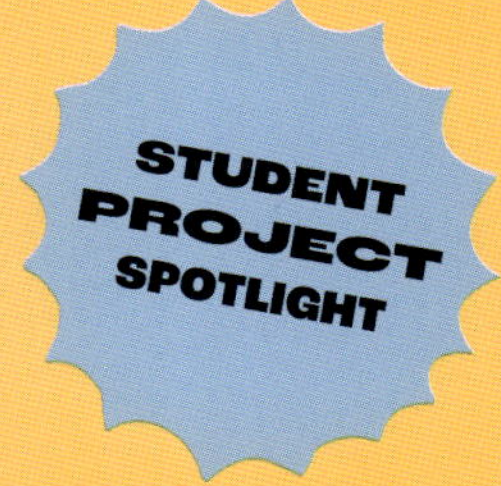

Tasha Goddard

tashagoddard.com

Tasha Goddard used The Style Class project to develop her skills using Procreate to emulate physical painting media like gouache. She started by illustrating an alphabetical list of things from everyday life. She says that she found it so useful and enjoyable that she followed it with an A to Z list of fruits and vegetables, and then an A to Z list of animals.

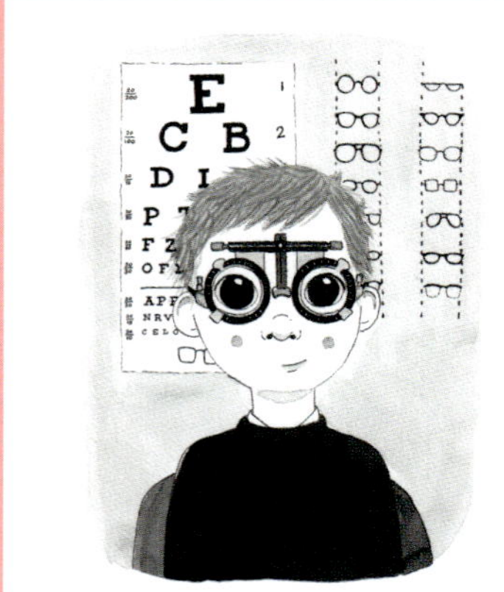

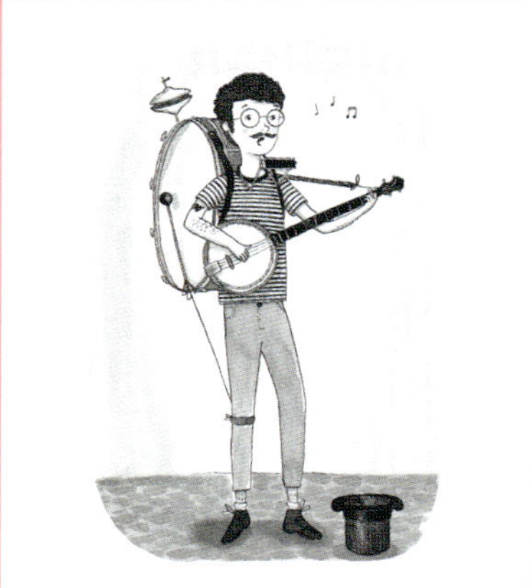

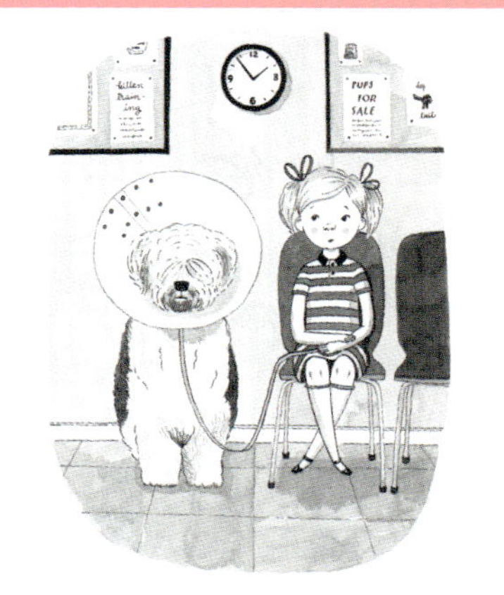

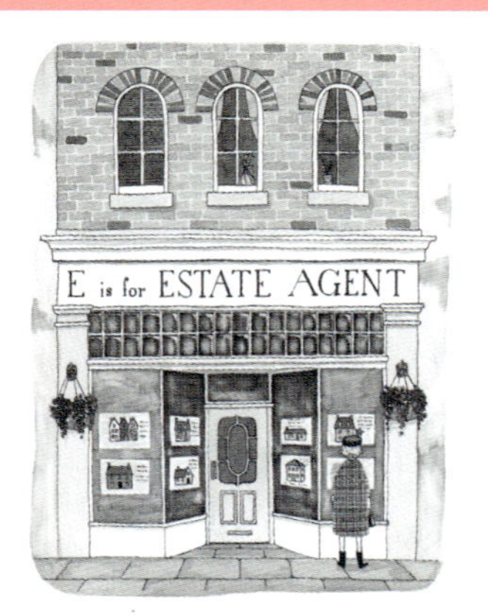

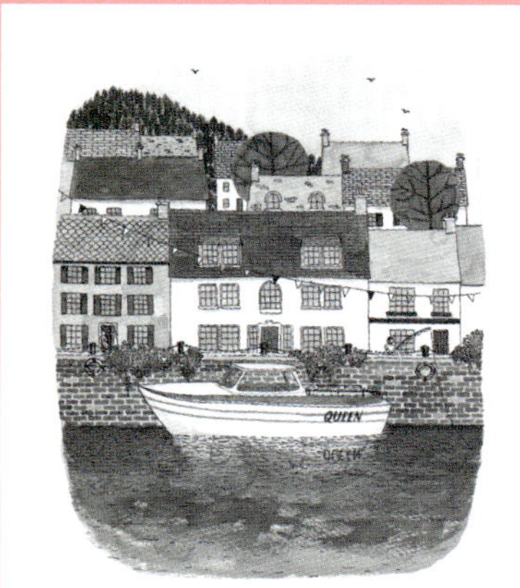

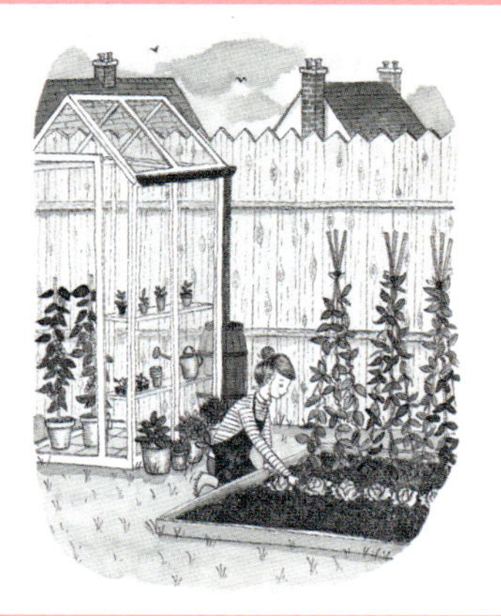

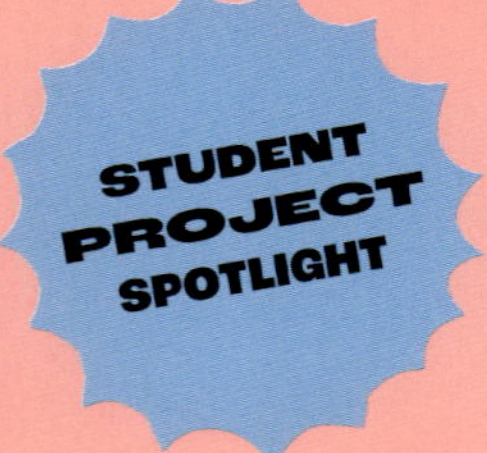

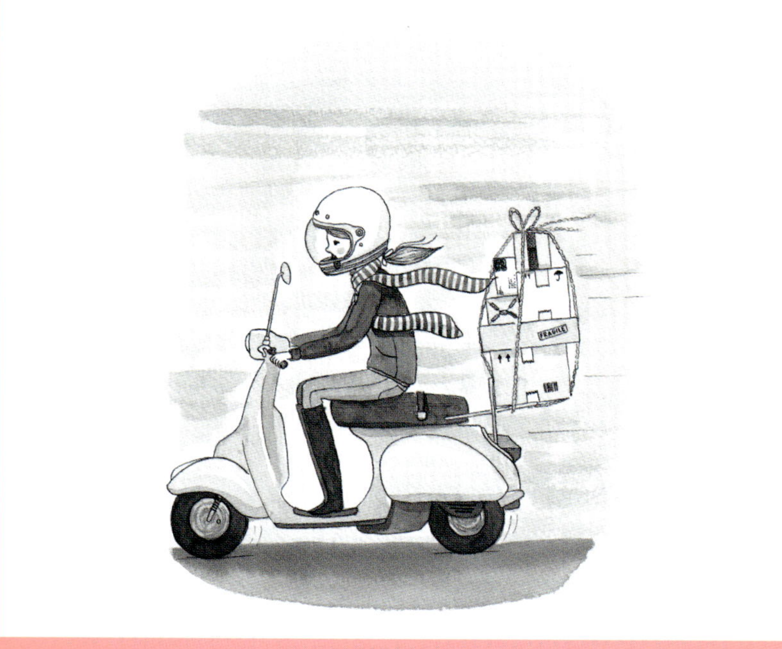

Laura Fuller

laurafuller illustration.com

Laura Fuller's gorgeous black-and-white illustrations are based on the theme "small town." Envisioning these in picture books, she lovingly made them using an ink and wash (a pen and ink technique).

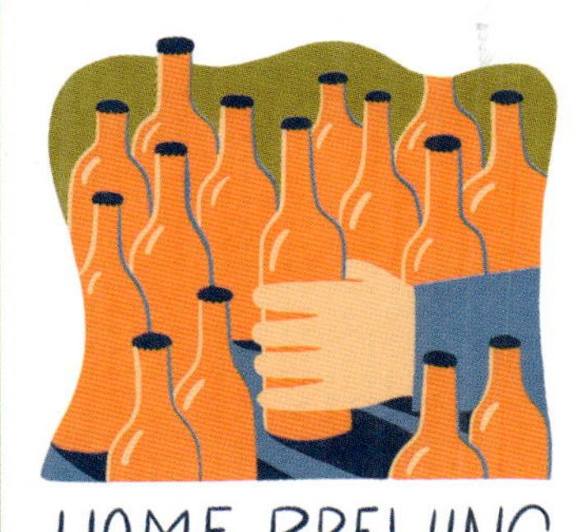

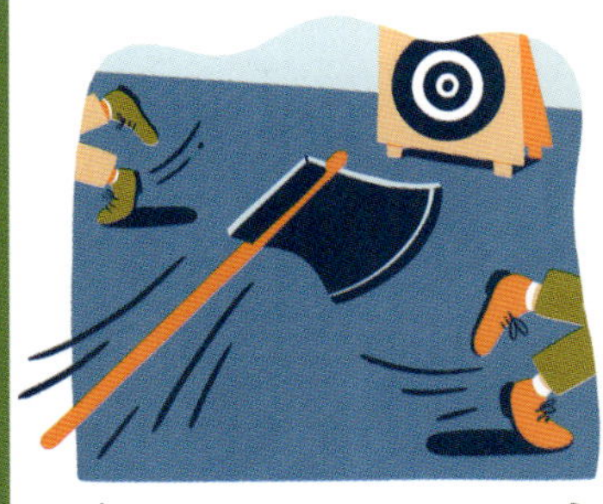

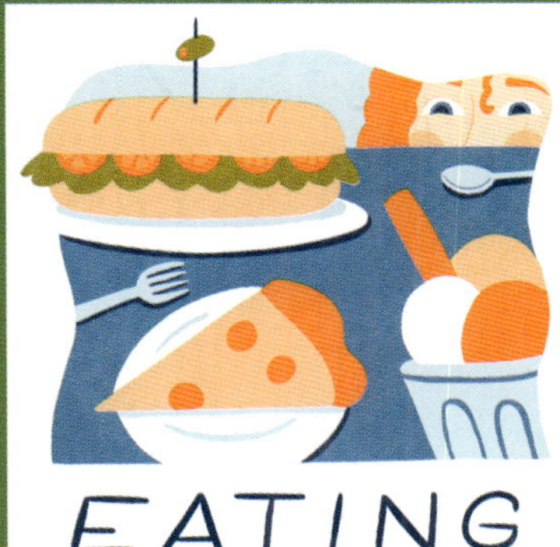

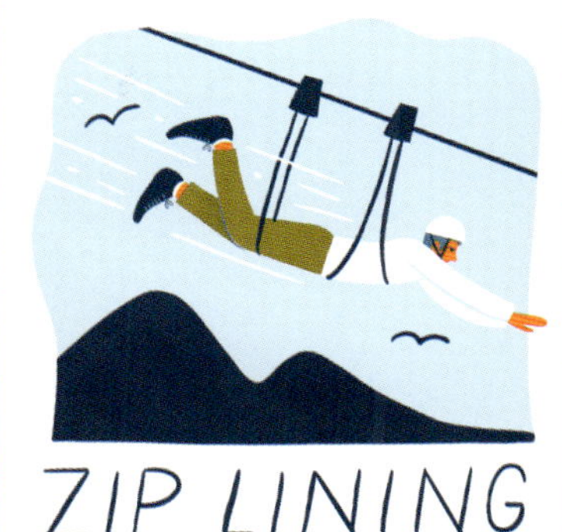

BIKE RIDING

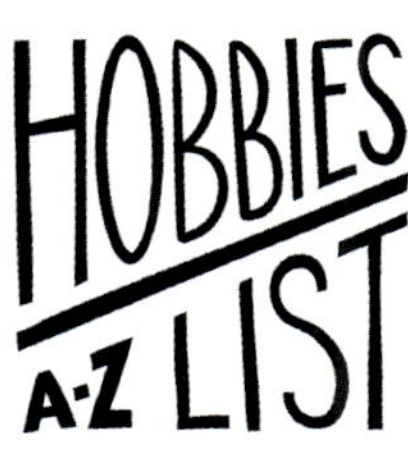

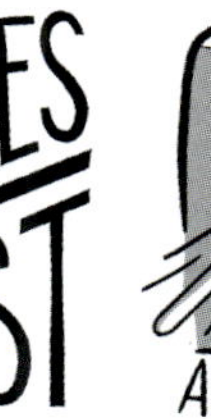

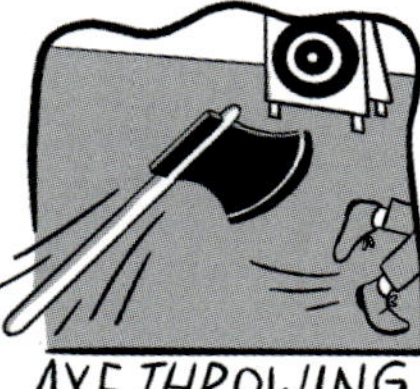

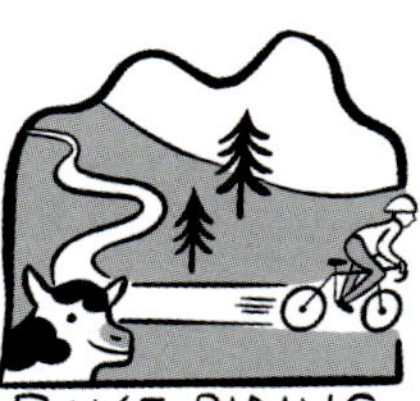

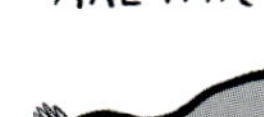

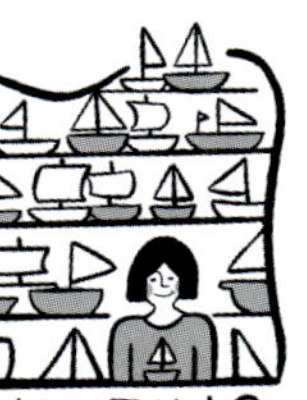

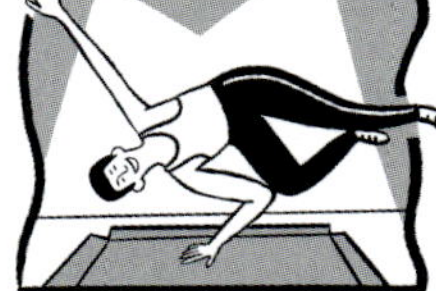

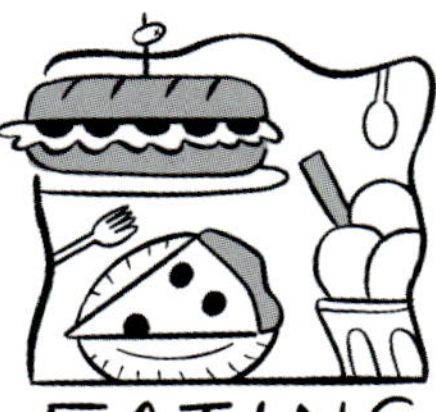

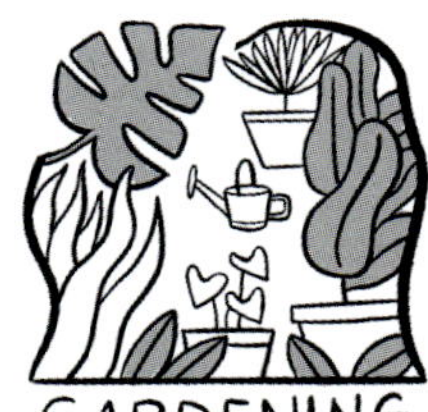

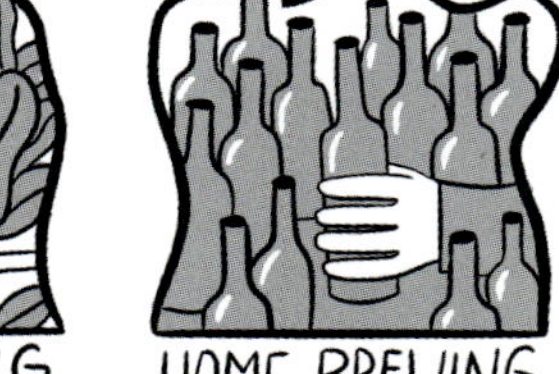

Kimberly Carpenter

kimberlycarpenter.com
For her Style Class project, Kimberly Carpenter chose the theme "hobbies" and then set out to create these beautifully simple, graphic-style illustrations.

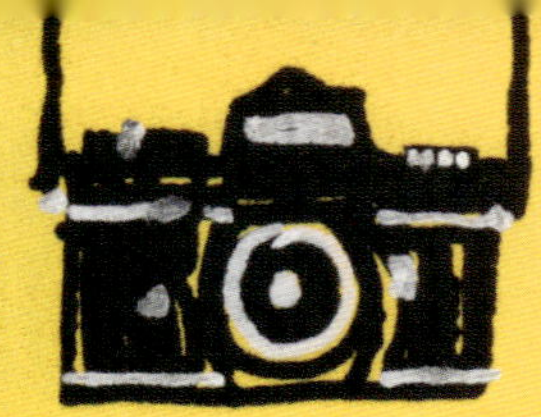

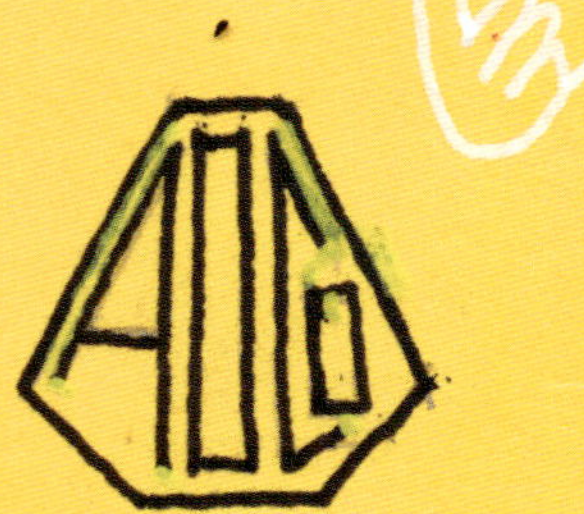

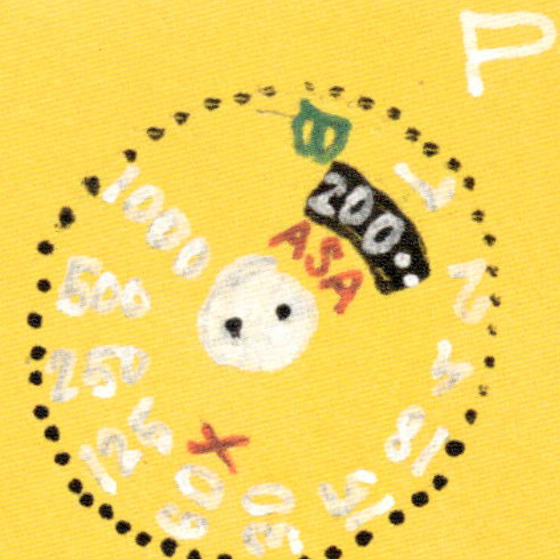

PENTA
SP

ADCO

1:1.4/50

R
EMPTY

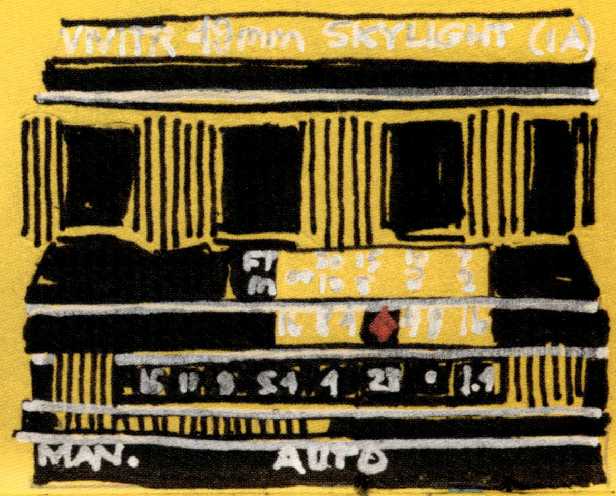

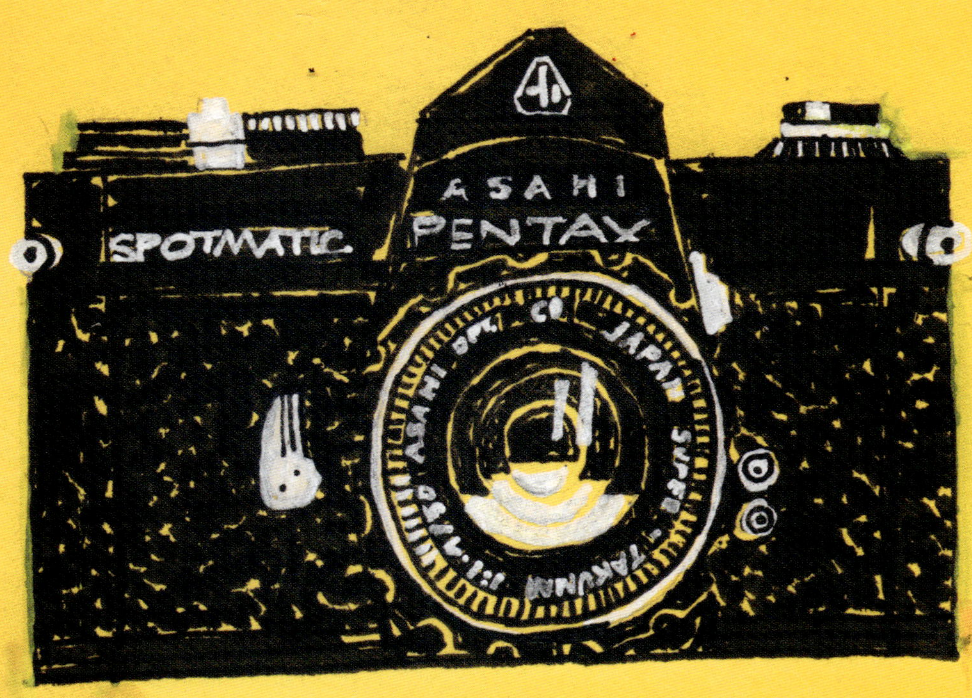

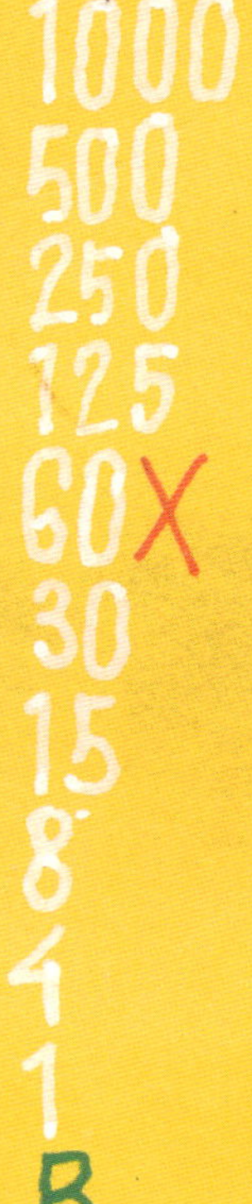

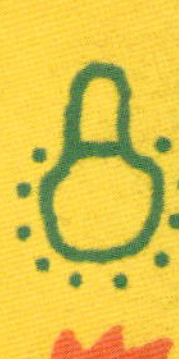

MAY11

Chapter

8

SHARING IS IMPORTANT

"If you wait until you're ready, you'll be waiting the rest of your life."

Violet Baudelaire, in *The Ersatz Elevator* by Lemony Snicket

Drawing is a deeply personal act—but art is ultimately meant to be shared with others. In this chapter, we'll look at the role of sharing in a Daily Drawing Practice: what it means, why it matters, and how to do it in a way that feels good. I'll offer options for sharing beyond social media, and tips for finding the audience that matters most to you. Whether or not you consider yourself a natural "sharer," this chapter will help you connect with others through your work—and maybe even reconnect with yourself.

Why Is Sharing Important?

What is visual art unless it's shared with others? As kids, we naturally showed our drawings to our parents or teachers, beaming with pride. They'd say "Good job!" and maybe post it on the fridge. That instinct to share doesn't go away—as grown-ups, we just reframe it as "showing our work" or "building a portfolio." If you're a visual artist, you're a communicator. While you might not feel ready to share it all, it's hard to imagine never sharing any of it.

Sharing is a key part of the Daily Drawing Practice because it keeps us accountable. It gives us a sense of audience—real or imagined—that helps us follow through. And it allows our work to be reflected back to us, not just in likes or comments, but in how others engage with and respond to what we've made. For anyone working in or aspiring to a creative field, sharing is the best way to get discovered and plant seeds for future opportunities.

Sharing Yesterday, Today, and Tomorrow

These days, sharing often means social media—and for many of us, that brings mixed feelings. It's hard to separate the act of sharing from the anxiety and pressures that come with it: Am I good enough? Am I being seen? Is this helping or hurting me?

I might be romanticizing things, but I remember a time when online sharing felt more personal, less strategic. In the early blogging days, I'd check in each morning to see what my favorite illustrators were posting. I had a blog too—part sketchbook, part journal—and sharing felt natural, like something I did for myself, not just for validation or growth. While blogging had many of the same features we see on today's platforms—commenting, reposting, following—the experience felt slower and more intentional. And because you *visited* an artist's blog (not scrolled past individual posts), you'd actually spend time with their work and thoughts. There was more of a connection between artist and audience.

When Instagram first came out, it felt like the best parts of blogging, but more focused (and portable). You followed people and actually saw what they posted. There were no ads or algorithm, just people sharing and having fun. Today it feels like it's more about staying on top than sharing from the heart. Many of us now feel stuck in a loop of chasing engagement rather than creative expression and connection.

Creative Babies in the Bathwater

Still, I'm grateful for how easy it's become to share with the world. It takes minutes or even seconds to do what used to take me a good half hour or more. But the downside is that your work competes in a much louder, more crowded space. Audiences are bigger but often less engaged.

Despite this, I believe sharing remains one of the most meaningful things we can do as artists. It's how we connect, build trust, and find our people. If social media feels too noisy, find another way—newsletters, zines, live meetups, small group chats. Sharing can still be joyful. It's not about chasing virality. It's about finding your people and being seen by them.

Sharing is the final part of the plan because it gives your work a greater sense of purpose. Once you find your audience, your Daily Drawing Practice will feel less like screaming into the void and more like a conversation.

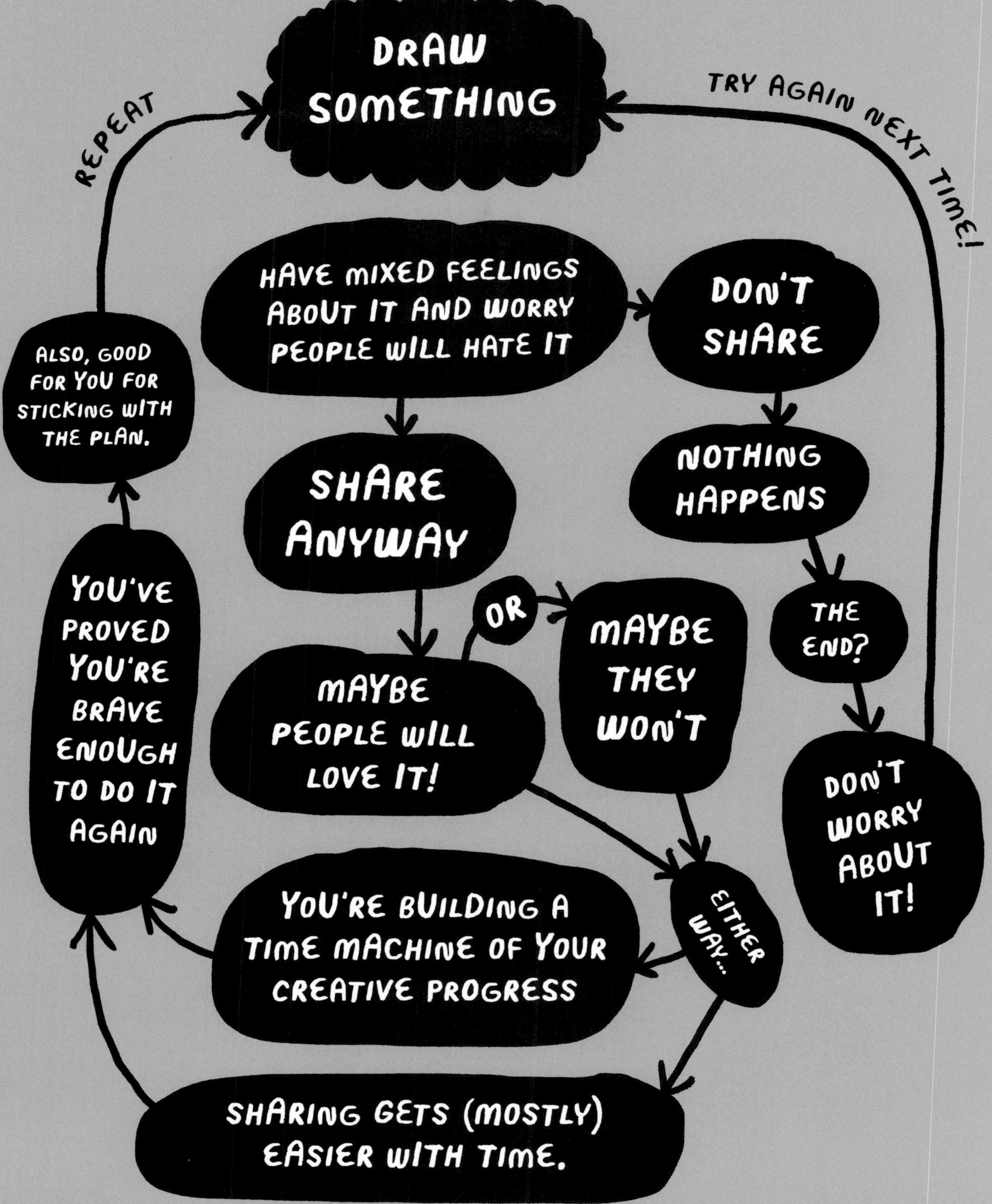

DRAW SOMETHING

REPEAT

TRY AGAIN NEXT TIME!

HAVE MIXED FEELINGS ABOUT IT AND WORRY PEOPLE WILL HATE IT

DON'T SHARE

NOTHING HAPPENS

THE END?

DON'T WORRY ABOUT IT!

SHARE ANYWAY

MAYBE PEOPLE WILL LOVE IT!

OR

MAYBE THEY WON'T

EITHER WAY...

YOU'RE BUILDING A TIME MACHINE OF YOUR CREATIVE PROGRESS

SHARING GETS (MOSTLY) EASIER WITH TIME.

YOU'VE PROVED YOU'RE BRAVE ENOUGH TO DO IT AGAIN

ALSO, GOOD FOR YOU FOR STICKING WITH THE PLAN.

10 Evergreen Sharing Principles

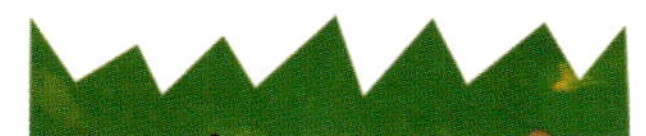

Writing about technology in a book is tricky—it can become outdated before the ink is dry. But the principles behind sharing your creative work with a global audience have held true for decades, regardless of trends and technology.

These are evergreen ideas: simple, lasting truths that will serve you no matter what platform you use or when you happen to be using them. If you've ever felt unsure about putting yourself out there—or like everyone else has figured something out that you haven't—these tips are for you. They're here to help you share with more ease, joy, and confidence.

1. Start Before You're Ready
Your inner perfectionist will always want more time. But showing up imperfectly is how all creative journeys begin—even for the pros. Don't wait. Begin.

2. Don't Be So Precious
A Daily Practice thrives on looseness and imperfection. If you overthink every post, you'll wear yourself out. Let it be a little messy. Let it breathe.

3. Have a Sharing Mindset
Instead of posting to perform, share to connect. Share because the process brought you joy—and you want to pass a bit of that joy along.

4. Think Quality of Engagement, Not Quantity
The number of likes doesn't measure your worth. What matters is genuine response. One thoughtful comment can mean more than a hundred hearts.

5. Be Relatable
Being relatable isn't about oversharing. It's about sharing something that helps others feel seen—or helps them see something in a new way.

6. Go Where Your People Are
Don't try to be everywhere. Focus on the platform or space where you feel most at home—and where you're most likely to find the kind of community you want to connect with.

7. Scratch Your Own Itch
Make what lights you up. Follow your curiosity. If it excites you, chances are it will speak to someone else too.

8. Don't Be a Tool!
Digital platforms are just tools. They should serve your creativity—not control it. If it's draining you, step back. You're the one in charge.

9. Caption Your Work
A little context can turn a good post into a meaningful one. Let people in—just a little. What were you feeling, thinking, wondering?

10. Try the Happiness Algorithm
Post what you want. Post when you want. Post as often as you want. And don't worry about it!

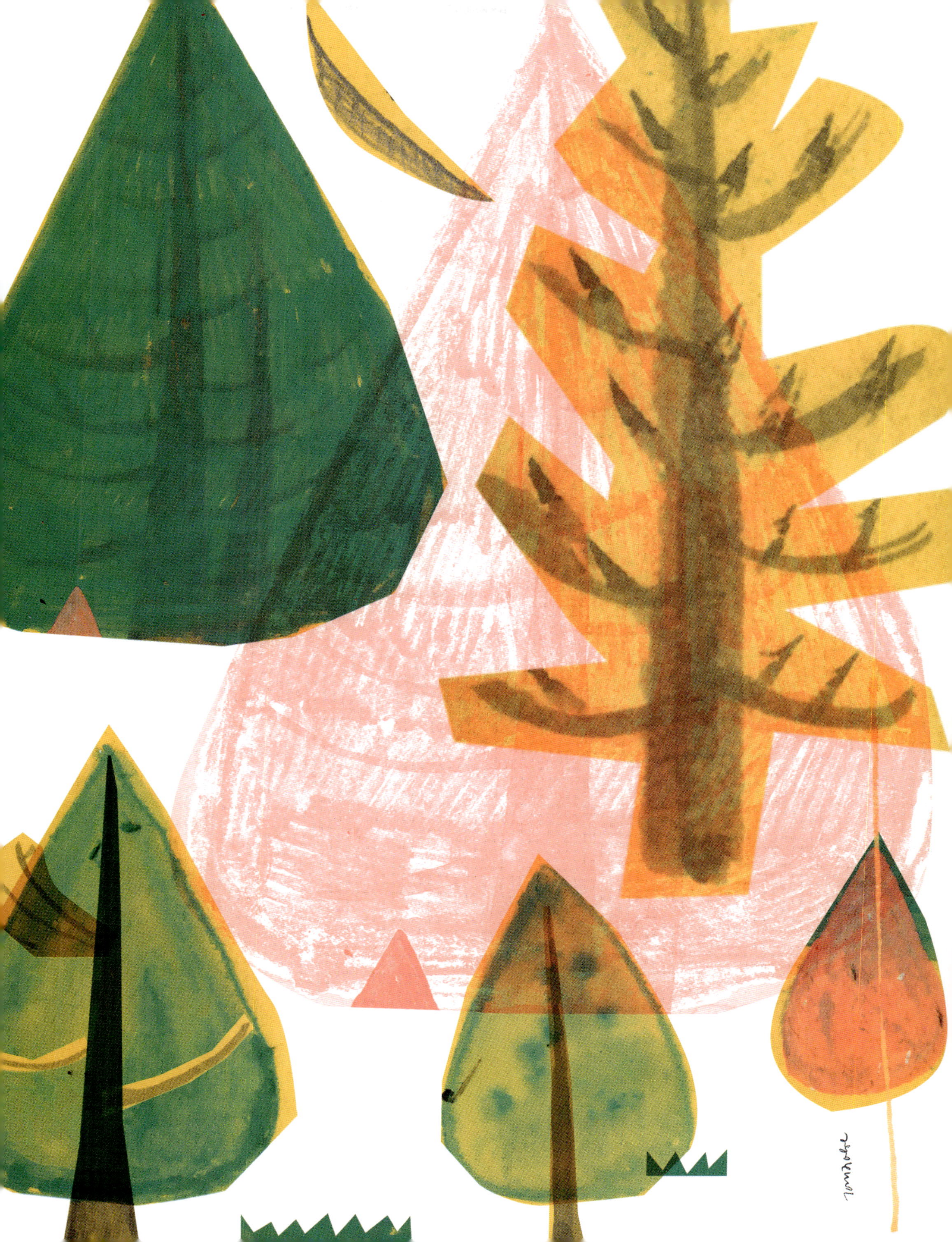

Best Practices for Sharing Your Practice

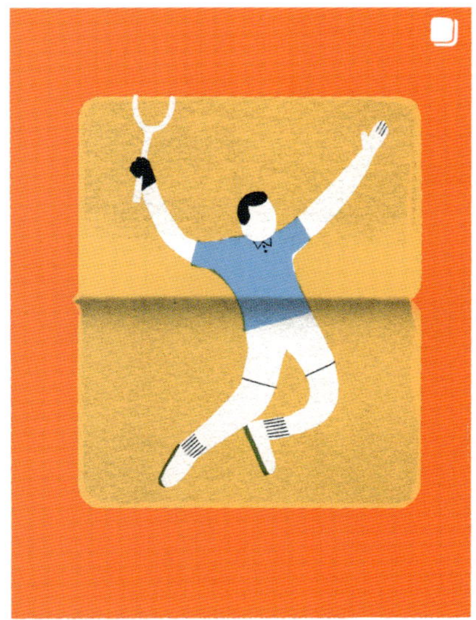

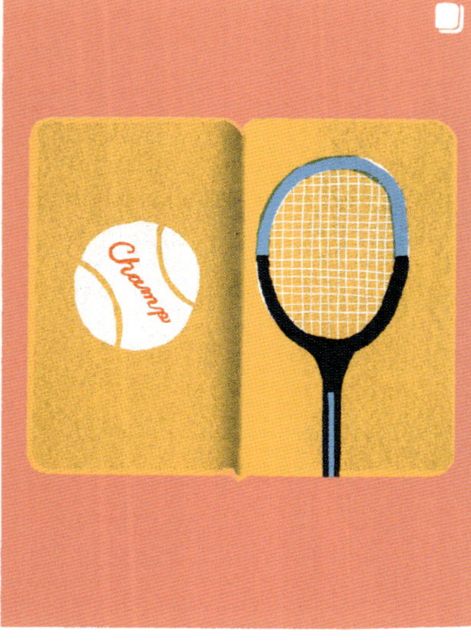

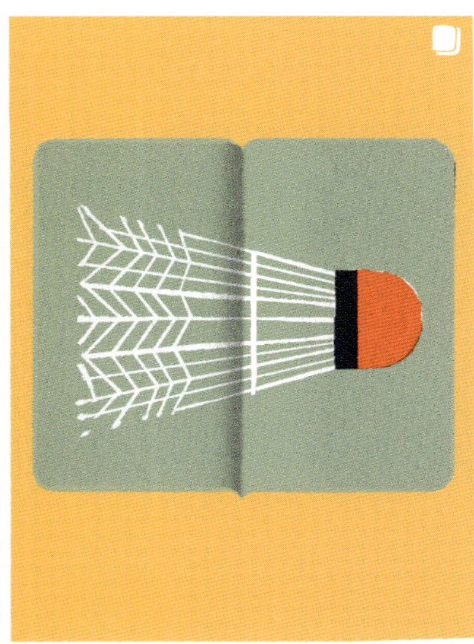

Strengthen your look with a consistent presentation style.

Presentation matters when sharing your work. This is not about whether your work is perfect or not, but simply making it easier for others to pick up what you're putting down! This is an opportunity to shine as an online artist. As more people share today than ever, the bar for how it is presented is being raised. Fortunately, you can exceed that bar with just a few simple tips. A little extra effort and thoughtful presentation go a long way in making your work look its best while growing your audience.

Use the following nine tips to help your work shine online, from planning to posting. While some are a bit technical, I've focused on things anyone, regardless of their apps or gear, can access. Where I do suggest adding to your kit, I believe those tools will make sharing easier for you.

Tip No. 1:
Have a Consistent Presentation Style.
In a world where everyone is sharing something, it's important to stand out. It helps to be instantly recognizable in the crowd. This is branding 101: Over time, work out a consistent "look" or style for your images. I'm not talking about the style of your drawings, but how you present them. There are many ways to do this, but the top three on my list include:

1. **Use the same sketchbook.** In chapters 3 and 4, I encouraged you to find your go-to media and stick with it. Not only does this make it easier for you to enter into your daily sessions, but it also makes how they look more consistent, especially if you use a visually distinctive kind of sketchbook (such as Moleskine or Uglybooks).

2. **Use a consistent background.** If you're sharing full pages or spreads of your sketchbook, chances are you'll also be sharing what's around them. Your background could just be the table under your sketchbook (perhaps with some of

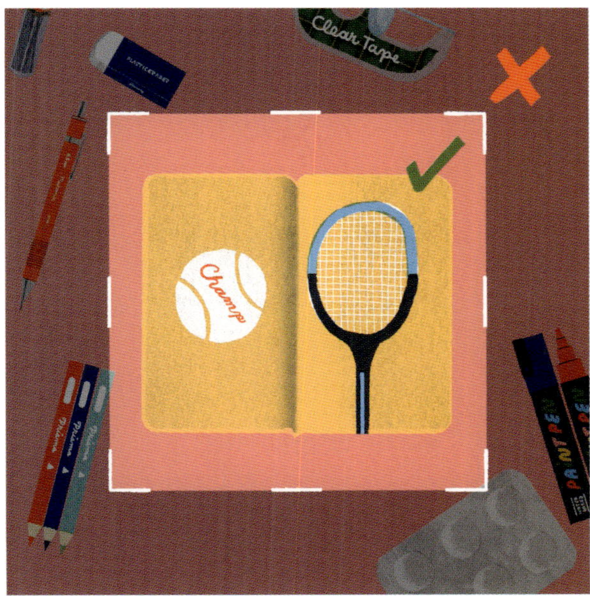

Focus on the art by cropping out distractions.

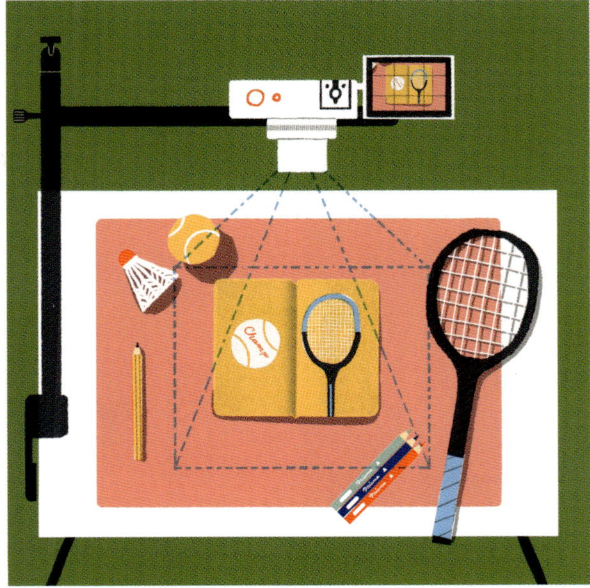

Use an overhead mount to keep your camera steady.

your drawing tools in the shot), or a colored piece of paper. If you're always travelling, you can hold your sketchbook up and include a bit of your current location in the background. Whatever you choose, the more consistent it is, the more identifiable it will be out in the wild.

3. **Shoot straight-on, not from an angle.** While it's a matter of preference, if your drawing is the hero of the shot, it should be shown as it was drawn: flat on the page. Angled shots will distort your drawings and possibly add distracting elements to the scene.

Tip No. 2: Focus on the Art.

Remember, your drawing is the hero of the shot, so keep these three tips in mind:

1. **Avoid distracting backgrounds.** Whatever you choose to include around your drawing, it should complement rather than compete with it. If you choose to include your tools somewhere in the shot, focus on the one or two that are most relevant to the drawing itself. Use tools as more of an accent than a tell-all of how the image was made. Give your art the space it deserves!

2. **Crop it tight.** When you crop an image, you are choosing an area to focus on and "cropping out" everything else beyond the edges. Cropping includes choosing a particular aspect ratio, whether a square, a vertical box, or a horizontal one. Keep as much of the drawing or spread in the frame as possible within your desired aspect ratio (*see Tip No. 6 for more on aspect ratios*).

3. **Keep it flat.** Most sketchbooks have the annoying tendency to spring shut unless you're holding them down. That makes shooting straight-on (as recommended previously) a challenge. To remedy this, you can just accept that your one hand will always be in the shot. You could also weigh the pages down with a well-placed drawing tool. Some use bulldog clips. I've even seen one person use a tiny hand on a stick as their go-to keeper-flatter.

Tip No. 3: Hold It Steady.

Be sure to hold your camera steady while you shoot. While most cameras today are fast enough to make tripods unnecessary in most lighting conditions, you'll still get the best quality if you use an overhead mount. There are many affordable options out there; just be sure to find one that has a phone clip (if using your phone), or a mount that fits your dedicated camera.

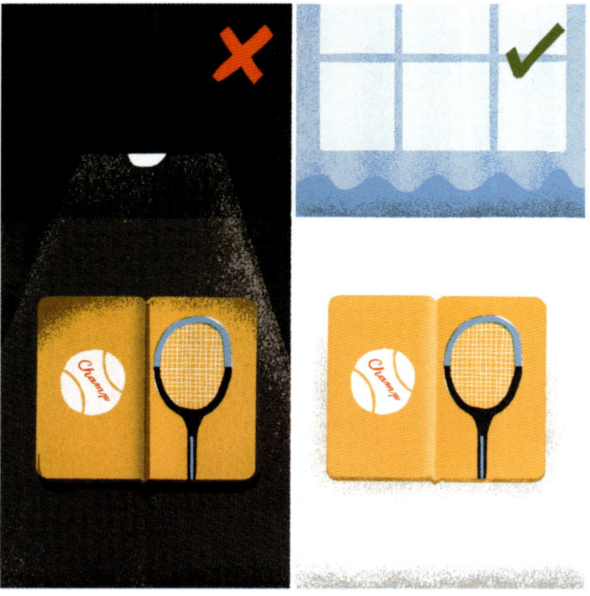

Use bright, even light when shooting your work.

Tip No. 4:
Light It Well.

Shoot your work in bright, even lighting. Professional indoor setups try to reproduce the same quality of light you'd find outdoors on an overcast day. If it's available, indirect daylight from a nearby window will work just as well. Find the sweet spot for shooting: a bit away from the window, where the light is even and no shadows are being cast on the drawing itself. Alternatively, try a cheap ring light, which casts light on your subject without your camera getting in the way.

PRO TIP

If you're using auto mode on your camera or phone, tap your drawing on the screen before you take the photo. This tells the camera to adjust the brightness for that part of the image, making your artwork look nice and clear.

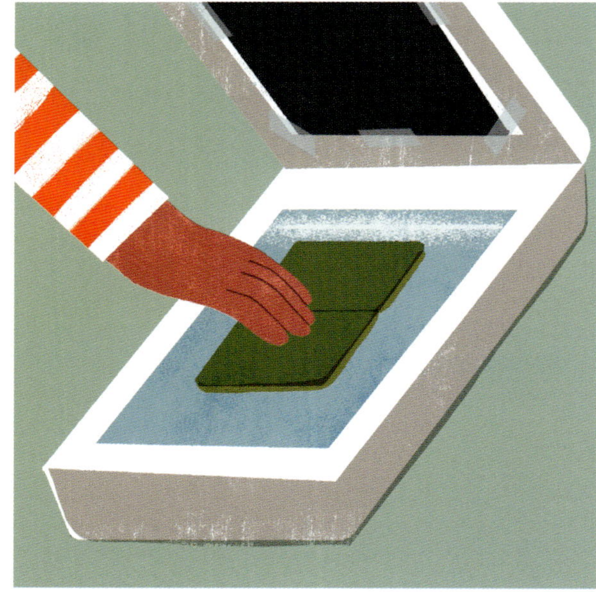

Simplify sharing with a scanner.

Tip No. 5:
Just Use a Scanner!

While most phone cameras today make shooting a breeze, it's still possible to struggle with taking good shots of your work, especially with lighting and keeping your darn sketchbook flat! You can sidestep all of these frustrating details by using a flatbed scanner. Whether it's old or new, attached to a printer or standalone, any scanner that can give you 300 dpi or more will do.

But there's a catch: First, your sketchbook will have to be smaller than the scanner's maximum scanning area. Second, if you're scanning your entire sketchbook, you'll need to consider what's around it. My work-around: I taped a piece of black Bristol board to the underside of the lid, and this has become part of my presentation style when I share.

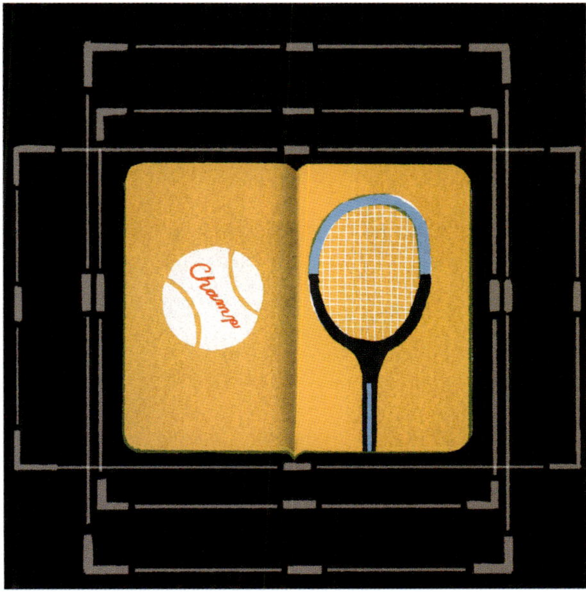

Leave room around your sketch to account for different aspect ratios.

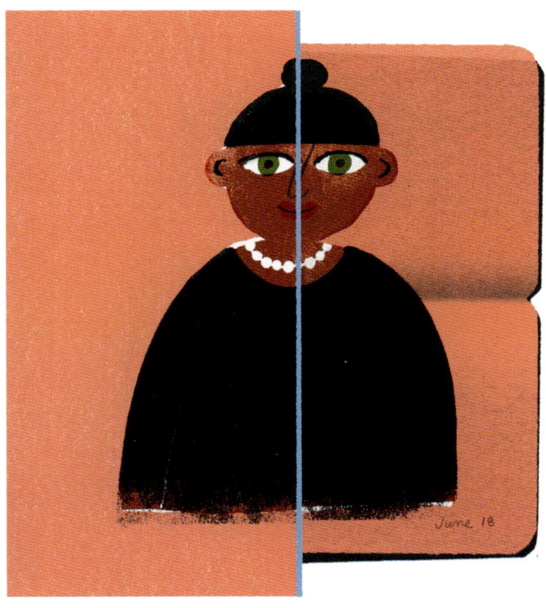

Showing the sketchbook context keeps the focus on practice over perfection.

Tip No. 6:
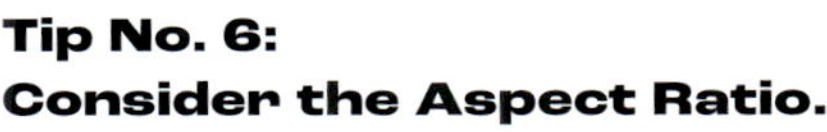
Consider the Aspect Ratio.

Sharing platforms often have a preferred aspect ratio that might not match the proportions of your sketchbook. For example, my preferred sketchbooks have an aspect ratio of 2:3 (vertical) when closed, and 4:3 (horizontal) when opened. Meanwhile, my current platform favors a 4:5 format. Other platforms variously prefer square, tall, or wide formats. Wherever there's a mismatch, the platform will decide how to crop your images, and you may not like the results. The more intentional you are about how you compose and crop your images, the more control you will have over how they are seen.

Tip No. 7:
Show the Context.

People need a frame of reference to understand what they're looking at. If you're posting small daily drawings without context, they might seem random or insignificant. But when you show them inside your sketchbook, they instantly read as sketches—part of a larger, ongoing practice. This simple context makes them easier to appreciate and takes the pressure off each drawing to be "finished" or meaningful. If you're not showing the sketchbook itself, at least include a caption and date (*see Tip No. 9*).

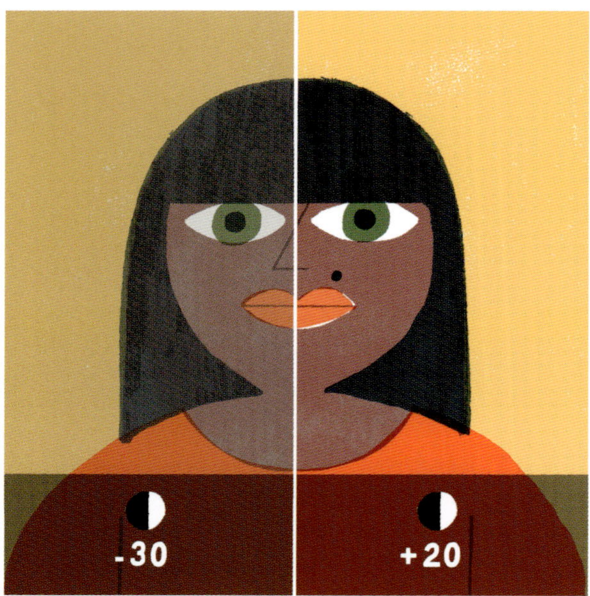

Bump the contrast a bit to make images punchier.

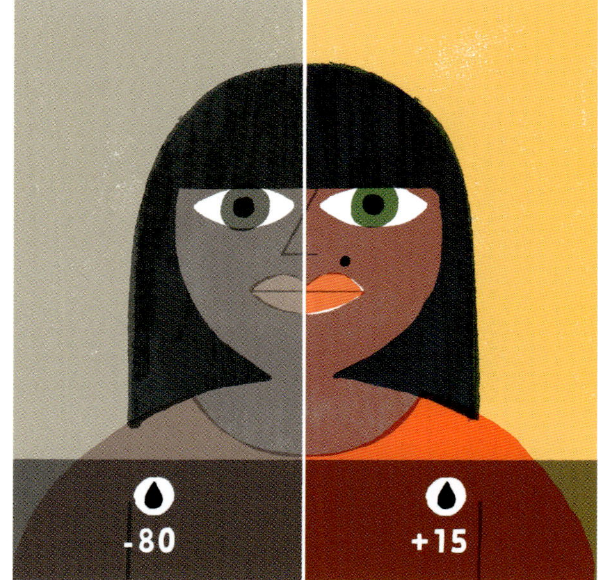

Bump the saturation to make colors pop.

Tip No. 8:
Make Your Images Pop.

After shooting or scanning, your images may still appear a little dull. Fortunately, making them pop is easy using your phone's built-in photo editor, Instagram's editing tools, or an app like Photoshop.

1. **Increase the contrast:** To make your drawings stand out more against the paper, increase the contrast by a small amount, maybe up to 20 points (on a scale of 100).

2. **Increase the saturation:** If your colors don't pop the way they do in real life, or you want them to pop a bit more on the screen, you can increase the saturation by a small amount, again, anywhere up to 20 points.

Remember, a little bit goes a long way: Don't overdo these adjustments. As a rule of thumb, your edits should enhance your images but not be so obvious that your viewers know you made them.

Tip No. 9:
Sign and Date Your Work!

Signing your work is like putting a name tag on your luggage. It's more likely to come back to you if someone else finds it. Sign your work in a tasteful way so that it's always clear who made it—and that there is a real "who" behind the art. And while a signature won't prevent others from stealing your art, it's a great way to signal to yourself that you're done. When I need to get on with my day but have a hard time pulling away from my drawing, I sign and date it.

Conclusion

There's no single right way to capture and share your drawings. Every setup is different, and there's no one-size-fits-all preset. The goal is to keep things simple and keep the focus on the drawing itself—ideally within the context of your sketchbook, to remind both you and your audience that this is about practice, not perfection.

Drawing is the main thing. Sharing is just what comes after. As with drawing, you'll improve with experience. You'll fumble a bit at first, but you'll figure out what works, what doesn't, and what feels right for you. So don't overthink it—just get in there, make the work, share it, and see where it leads. Most of all, enjoy the process.

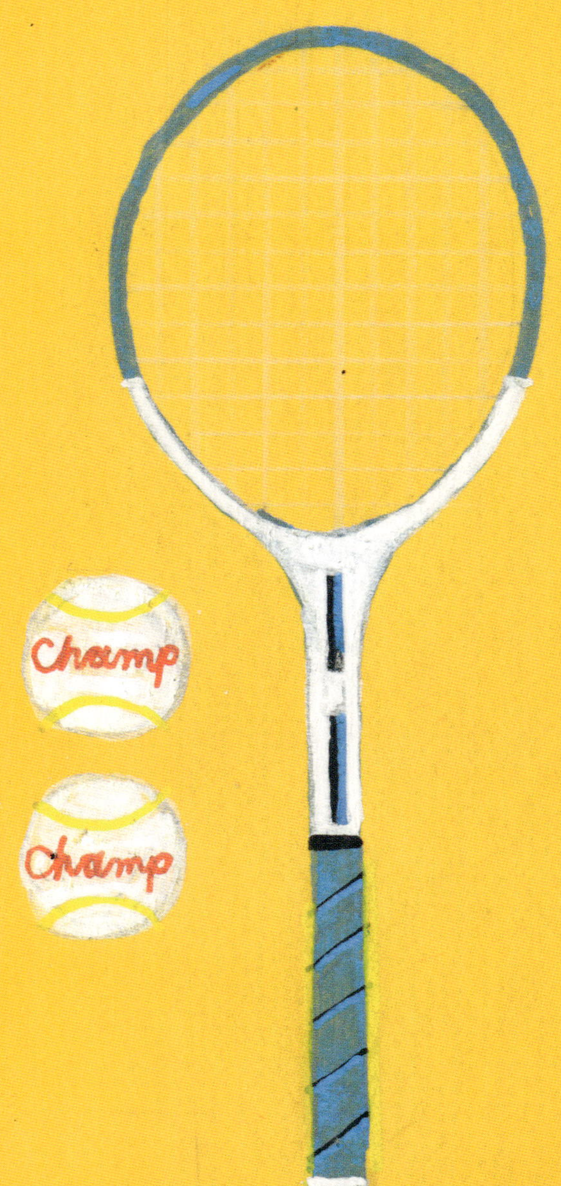

Tom Froese
13 JUN

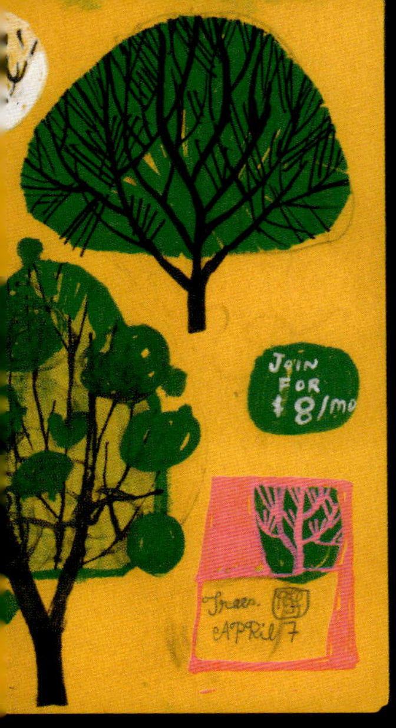
Join FOR $8/mo
Trees. APRIL 7
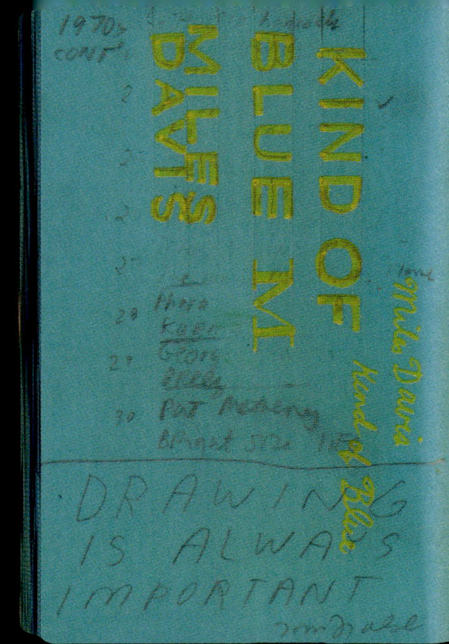
KIND OF BLUE
MILES DAVIS
Miles Davis Kind of Blue
DRAWING IS ALWAYS IMPORTANT
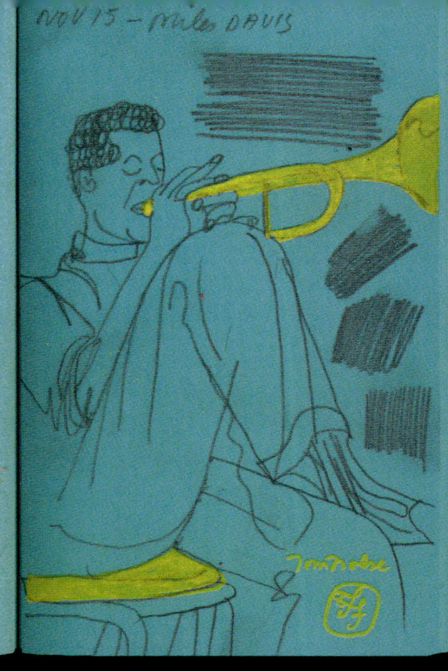
NOV 15 – Miles DAVIS
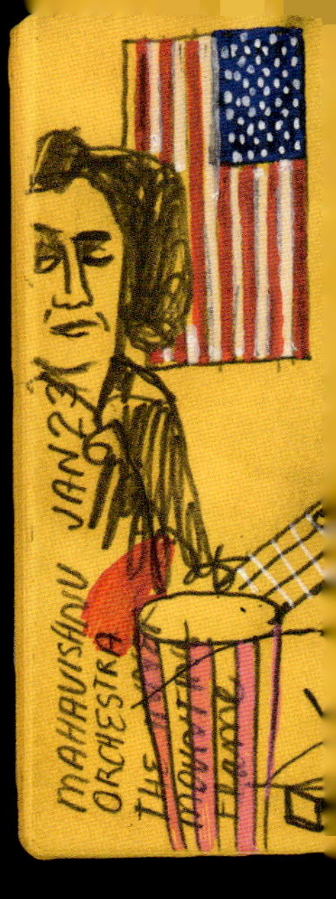
MAHAVISHNU ORCHESTRA
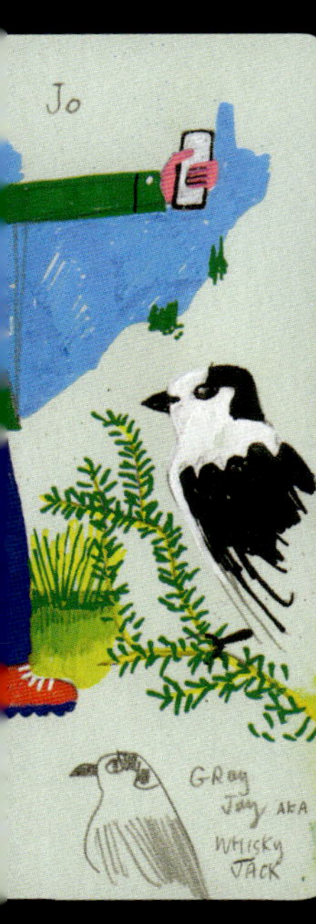
Jo
GRay Jay AKA WHisky JACK
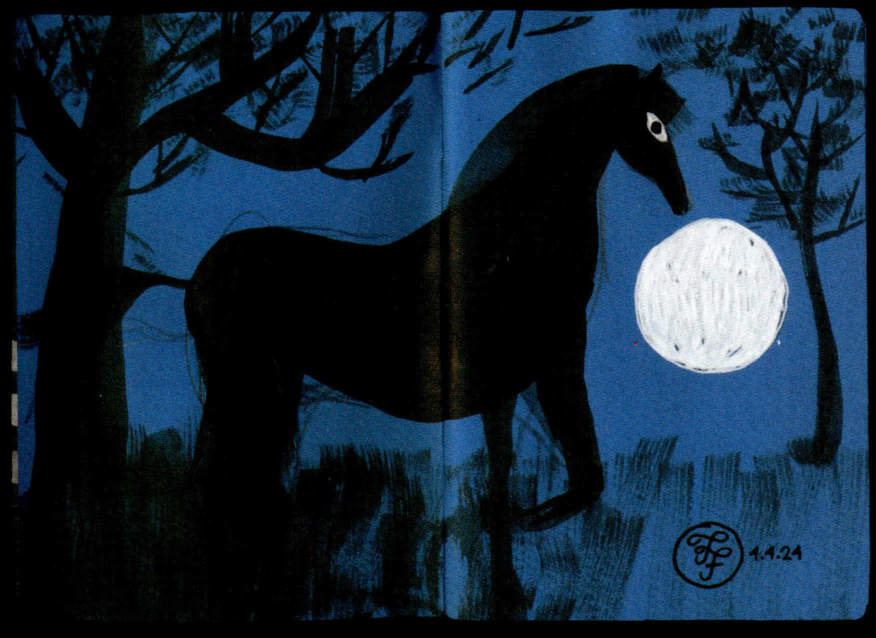
1.4.24
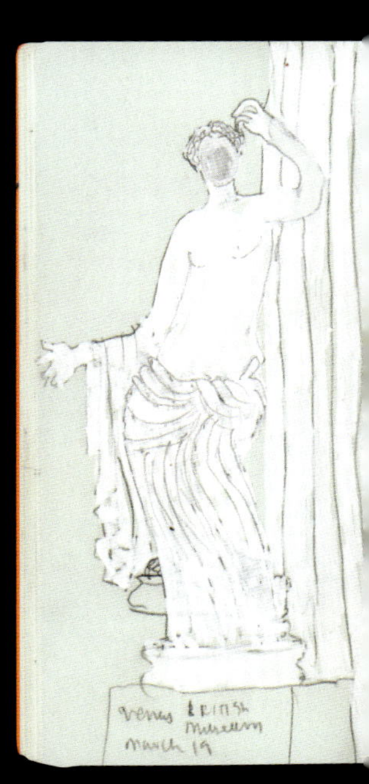
Venus British Museum
March 19

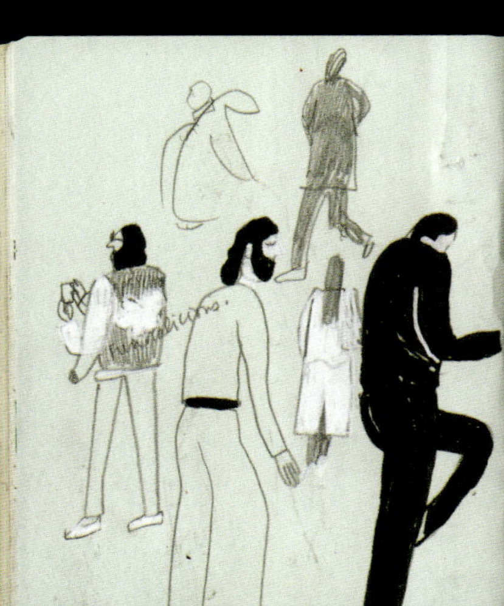
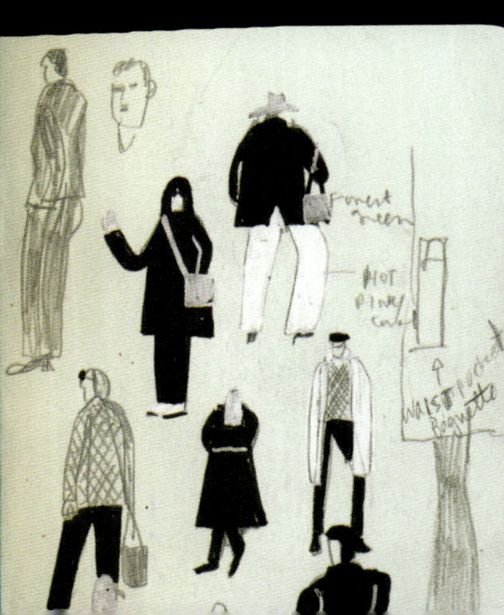
Forest Green
Hot Pink
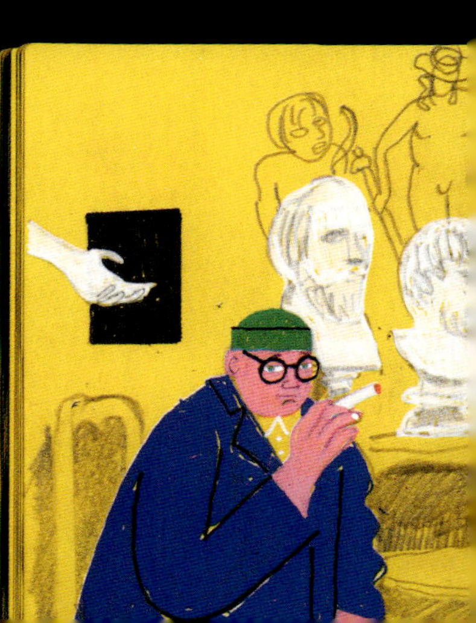

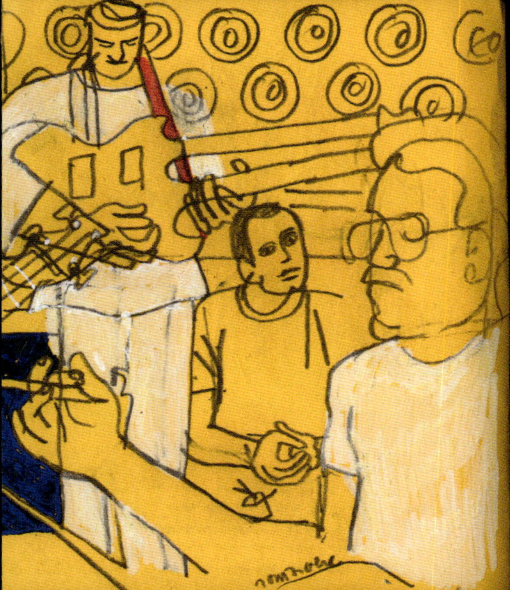

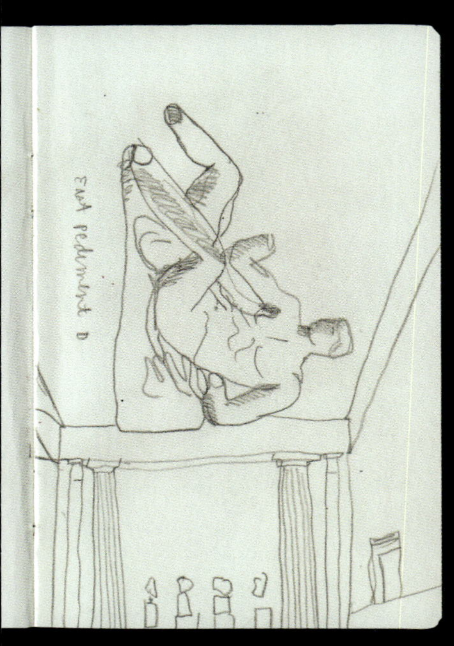

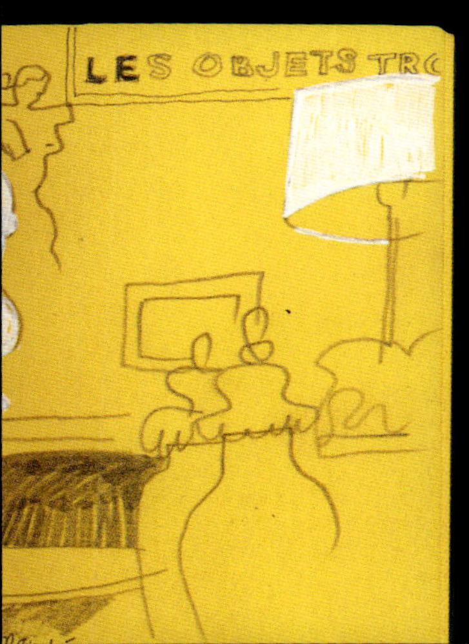

Interlude IV

Getting Back to Inky

As a professional illustrator, I've always craved a process that feels hands-on and open to happy accidents—results that surprise me in ways I couldn't have planned. For me, that has usually meant bringing in off-screen, analog elements like ink splatters, pencil smudges, and rough paper textures—marks that digital tools can't fully replicate.

Over the years, though, my commercial process drifted almost entirely into the digital realm. Tools like the iPad, Apple Pencil, and a reliable set of digital brushes made it easy—almost too easy—to leave behind the tactile materials I built my early career on. In chasing efficiency, I had unknowingly made my process too predictable. It started to feel lifeless to me.

Then, over the holidays one year, I heard Andy J. Pizza say on *Creative Pep Talk*: "All art is self-expression. How can you love your art if you hate what it's expressing?" That hit me hard. I didn't hate myself—but I was bored with my process. I had stripped out the very things that made it joyful and meaningful.

Not long after that, I was starting a major picture book project. I knew I'd struggle to love the process unless something changed. So I made a choice: This book would be a turning point. I brought back analog tools—ink, paint pens, real paper—and allowed chaos back into the mix. I experimented daily to loosen up, and it changed everything. I'm deeply proud of the final work, and my publisher was thrilled with it too.

Since then, I've continued leaning into more handmade, analog-influenced techniques in both my Daily Practice and client work. Reconnecting with physical materials has helped me reconnect with my creativity—and with myself.

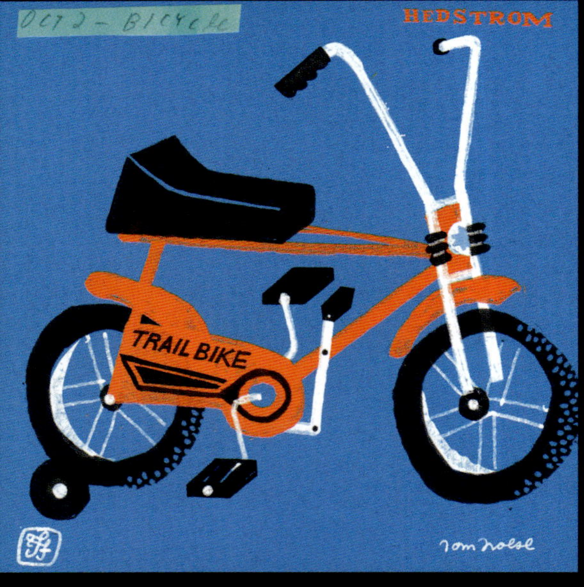

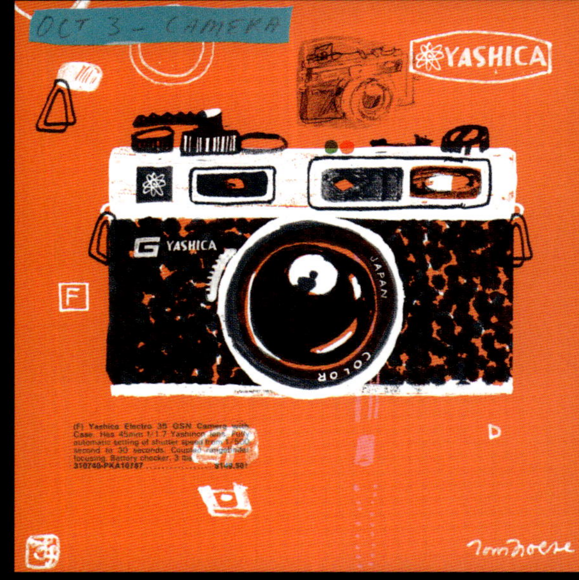

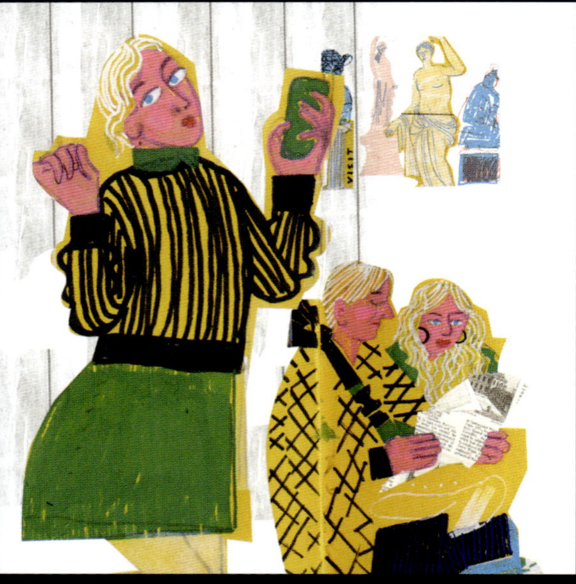

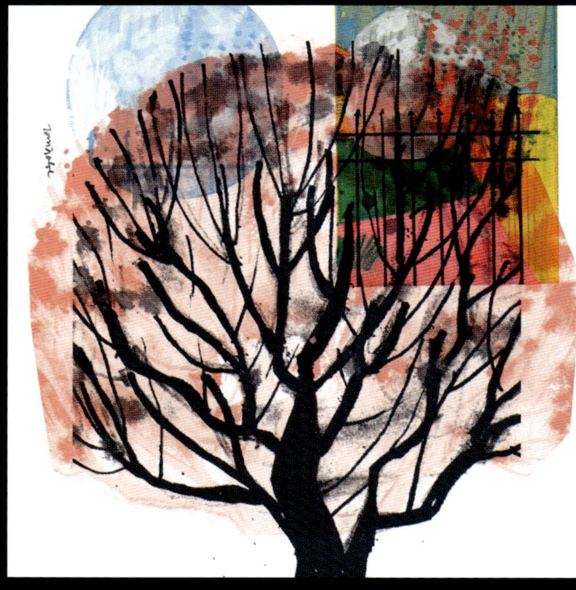

The pain of feeling estranged from my illustration process jettisoned me into an analog renaissance. I declared 2024 “the year of breaking things,” and through the cracks flowed more joy in the process.

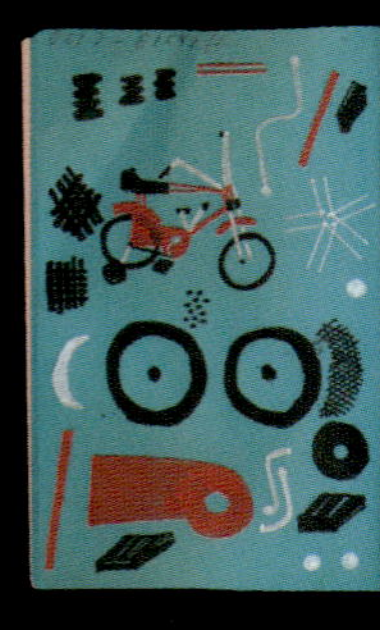

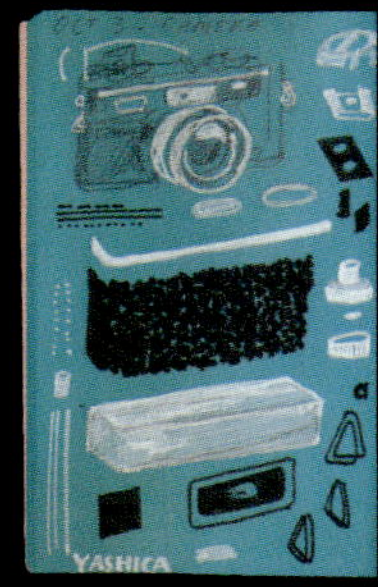

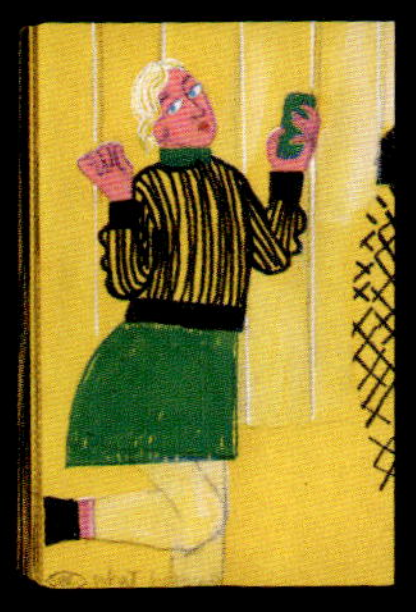

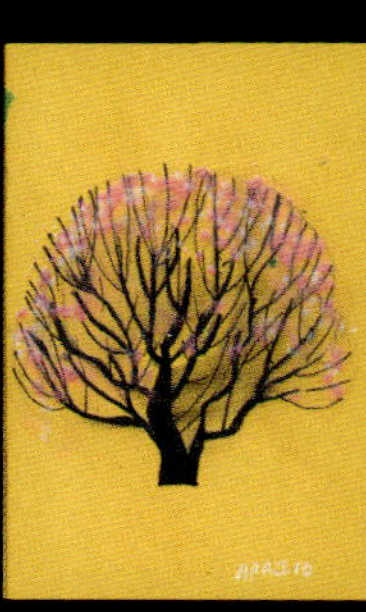

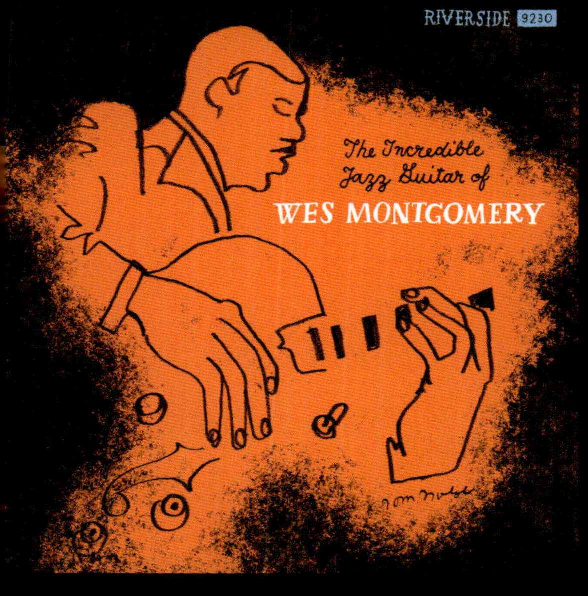
RIVERSIDE 9230
The Incredible Jazz Guitar of
WES MONTGOMERY

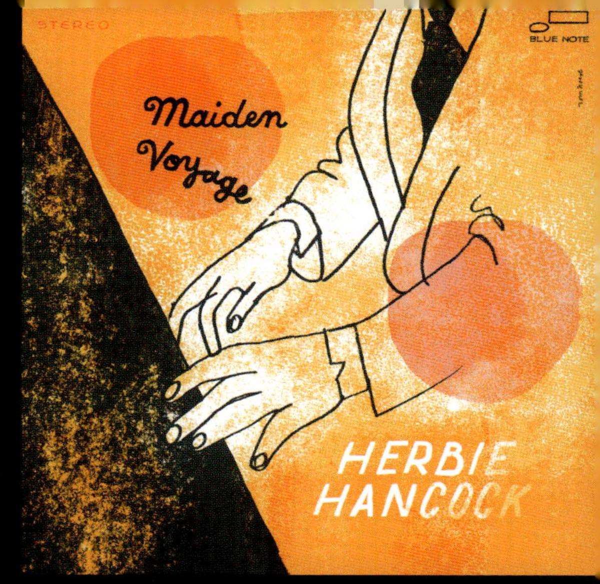
STEREO
BLUE NOTE
Maiden Voyage
HERBIE HANCOCK

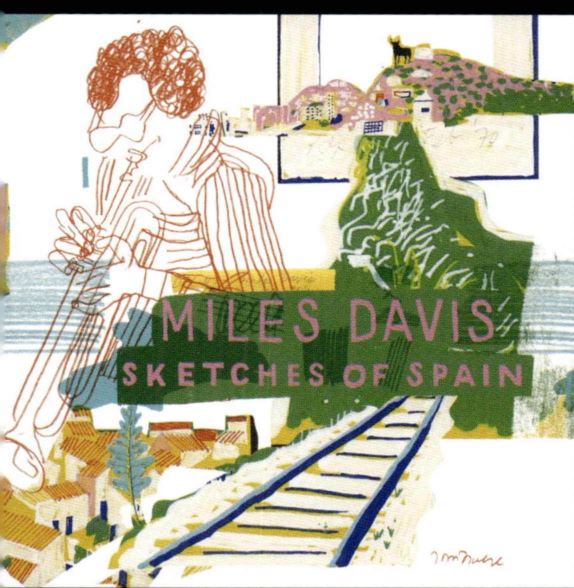
MILES DAVIS
SKETCHES OF SPAIN

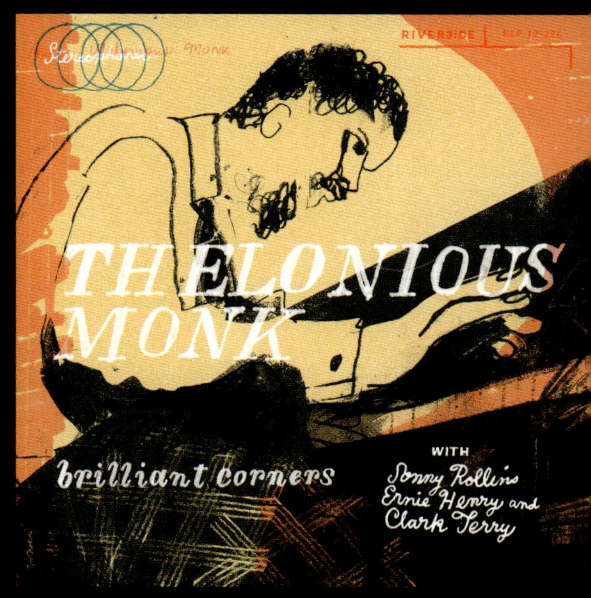
RIVERSIDE
THELONIOUS MONK
brilliant corners
WITH
Sonny Rollins
Ernie Henry and
Clark Terry

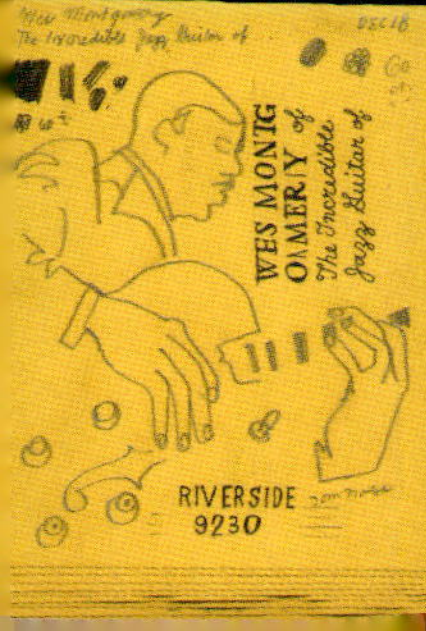
WES MONTG OMERY
The Incredible Jazz Guitar of
RIVERSIDE
9230

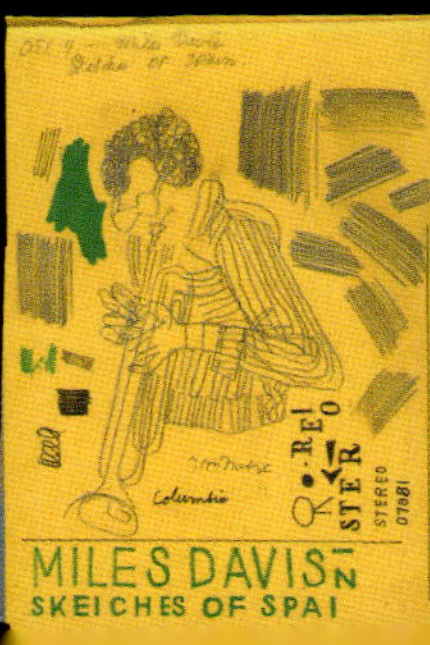
MILES DAVIS

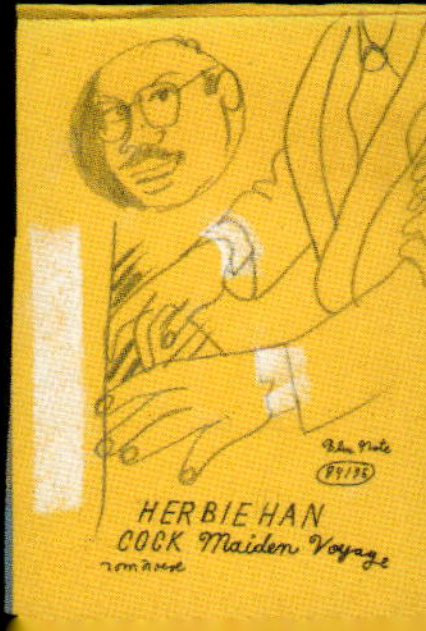
HERBIE HAN
COCK Maiden Voyage

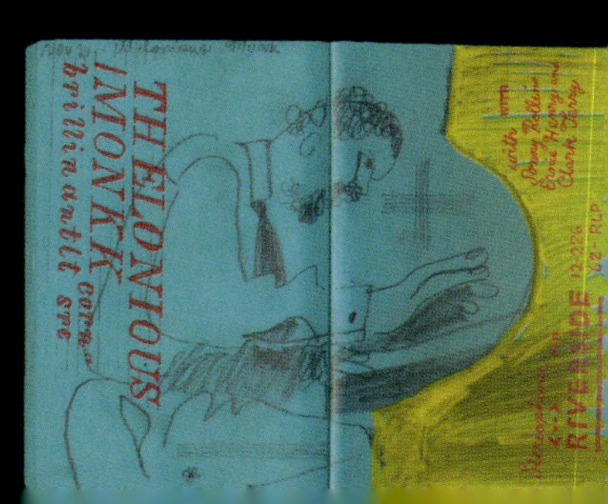
THELONIOUS
MONK
RIVERSIDE

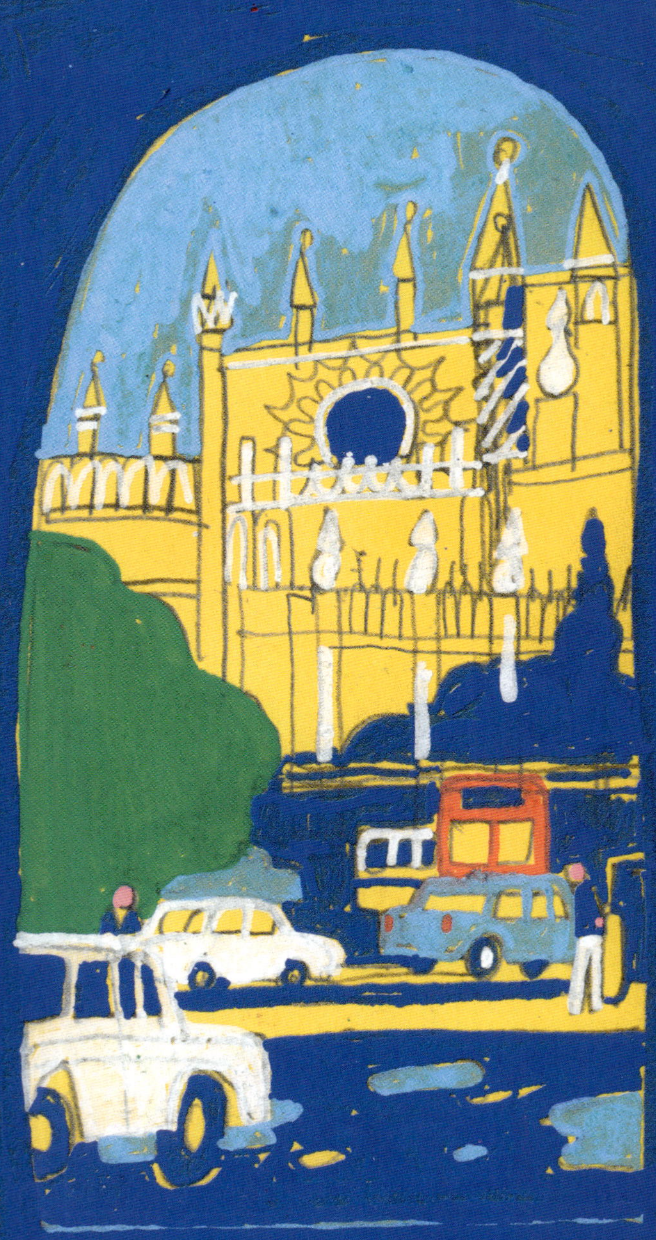

APR26

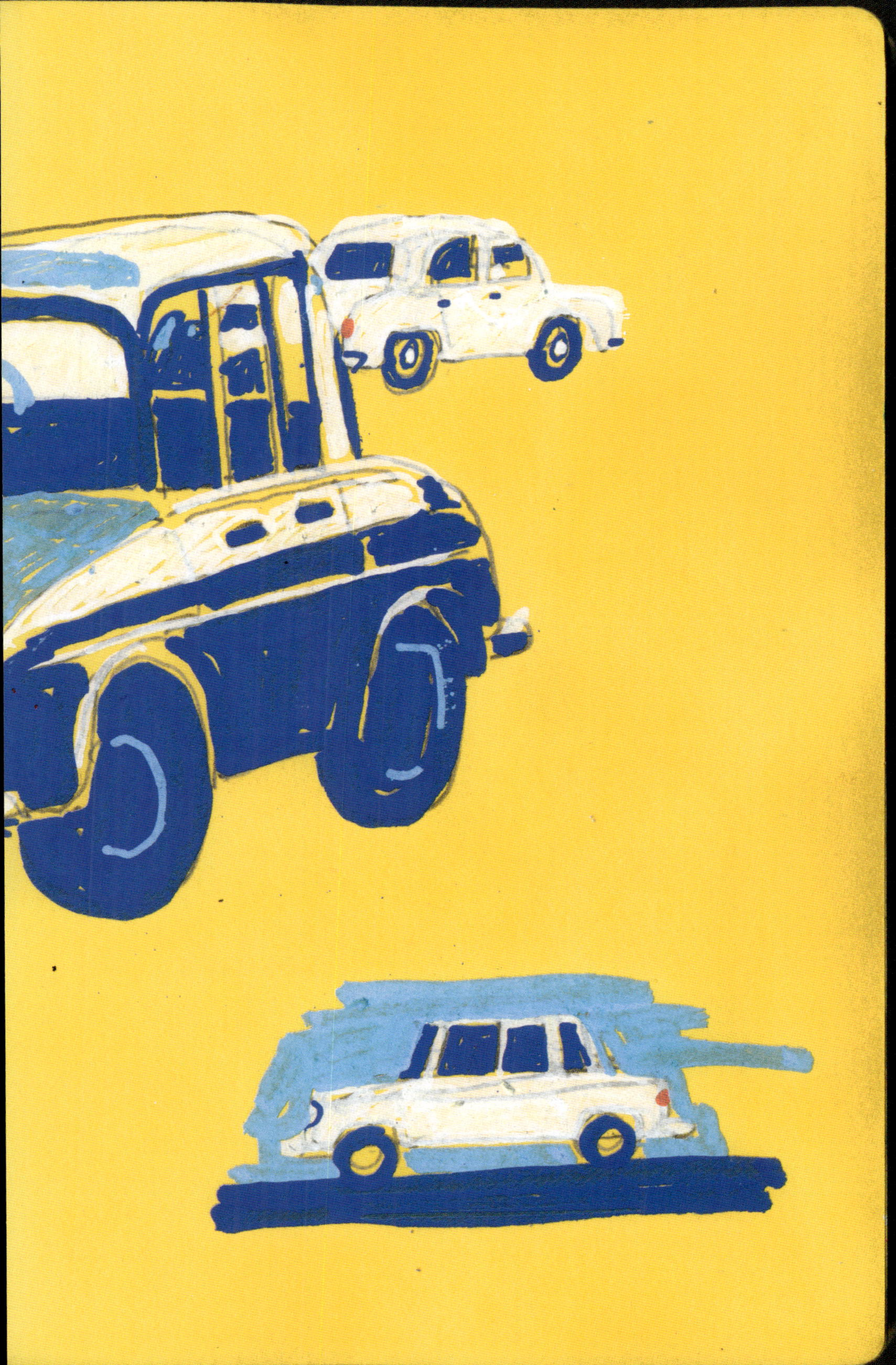

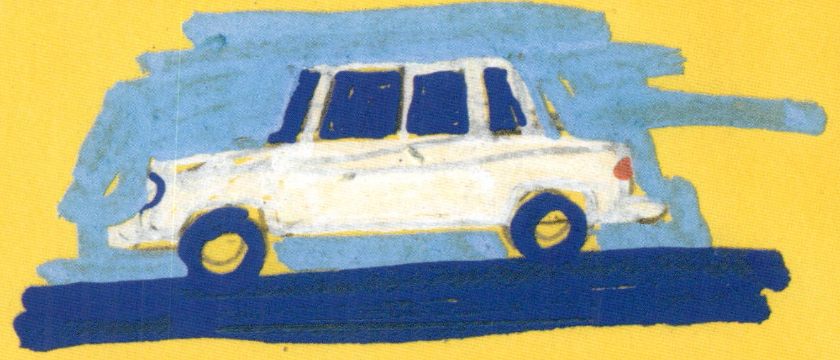

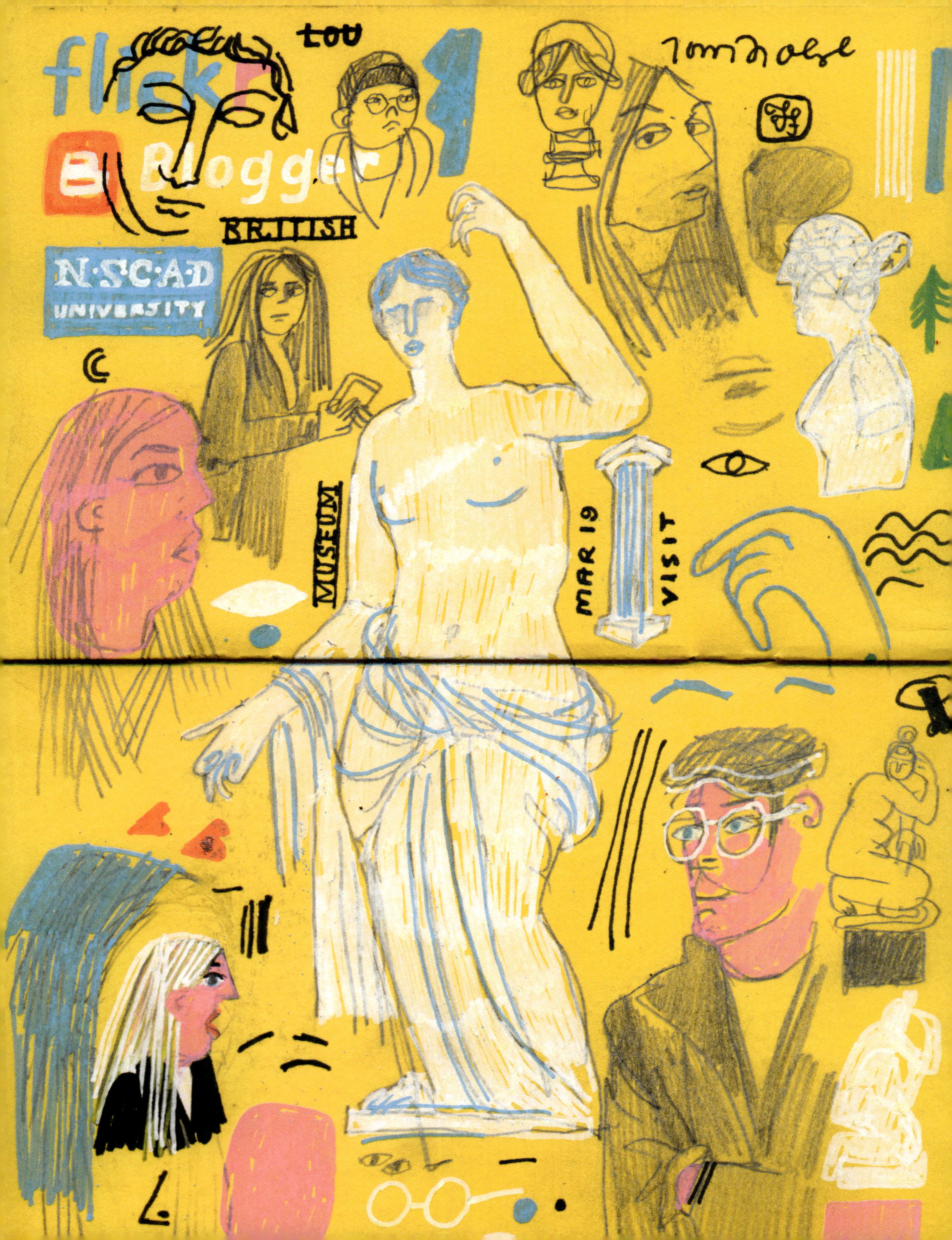
flickr
Blogger
BRITISH
N·SC·AD
UNIVERSITY
MUSEUM
MAR 19
VISIT

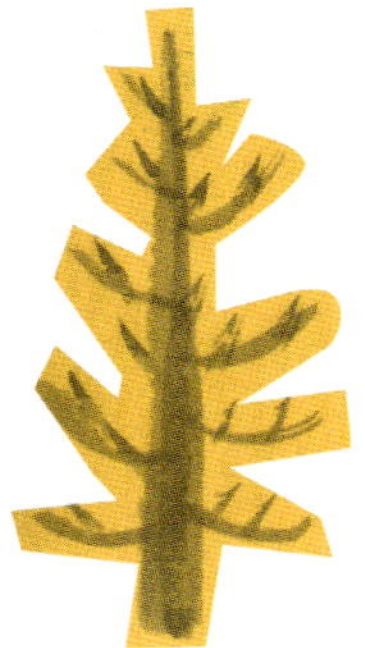

EVOLVING WITH YOUR PRACTICE

> You never arrive at your dream; the moment you do, if that's how you feel, well I guess that means you've stopped dreaming.
>
> Me

As your life changes, your drawing practice should change with it. In this final chapter, we'll talk about the tension between consistency and evolution—why both are necessary and how to balance them over time. Whether you struggle with sticking to a routine or feel boxed in by your current style, you'll find ways to make your practice more sustainable, joyful, and true to who you are. This chapter is about playing the long game—learning to adapt, take breaks when needed, and keep drawing with purpose.

Consistency vs. Evolution

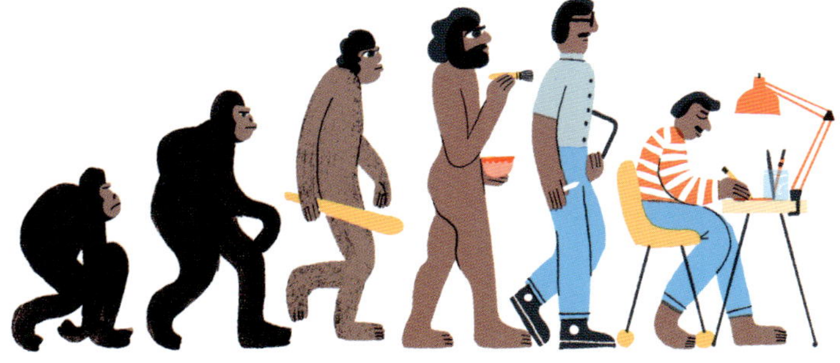

For better or for worse, sharing my daily drawings online makes me self-conscious about consistency. Is today's drawing too different from yesterday's? Will people think it's too different? Will they even know it's mine? Of course, that is not the point of a Daily Drawing Practice; it's to creatively experiment and evolve. At the same time, we need to be consistent enough to learn something from it. When I see my own progress, and that of others, mastery can only come through a repetitive, focused effort.

You might have great ideas in your head, but without consistent effort, working them out on the page, you'll never find their true potential. Whether it happens in just a few drawings, a few days, or a few months, you'll never know until you try, with some level of consistency.

At the same time, you are not a time capsule. You're constantly growing, learning, and changing, and your Daily Drawing Practice should be where you feel most free to do that!

There's a tension here: consistency vs. evolution. On the one hand, I'm saying you should be disciplined and constrained in your practice. But on the other, I'm saying you should feel totally free to evolve and experiment. So—which is it? It's both, sometimes in balance and sometimes to one extreme or the other. Which is right for you will always depend on where you're at right now.

Are You Resisting Change?

If you're like me—a little bit reserved and very audience-focused—you might feel overly beholden to your current "thing." You opt for consistency at the expense of creative growth. If you wish you could be more bold and experimental in your drawings, but you're afraid of what people (or algorithms) think, here is my advice:

Go in Stealth Mode. Don't let self-consciousness or self-doubt stop you from trying new things! The best way to sidestep this is to try new things on the down-low for a while and see what happens. As you do this, wonderful things may happen that you can't help but share.

Do It Anyway. When you're not sure what others will think, there's only one way to find out. Who knows what people really think about your current work anyway? Perhaps getting feedback, one way or the other, can help you know whether your work is landing well on your audience. This is similar to the way comedians "write on stage," testing their jokes in front of a live audience. The risk is that they will bomb, but they don't let fear hold them back. Both boos and laughter give them the feedback they need to get funnier.

Are You Avoiding Commitment?

On the other hand, you might resist consistency with every bone in your body. Perhaps it's fear of missing out: How can you lock into just one way of drawing, or one kind of media, or just one focused subject? It can also be hard to commit when you just don't even know why you'd choose one path or the other. Instead, we try to do it all, all at once. The passion and curiosity behind this are wonderful, but if we try to push it all out at once, it will bottleneck. Trying to do everything at once can keep any one idea from growing to its full potential. If you're having a hard time finding your focus, here is my advice:

My Daily Drawing Practice has gone through many different phases. Consistency in showing up is important. Change over time is good too—it means you're growing and still having adventures.

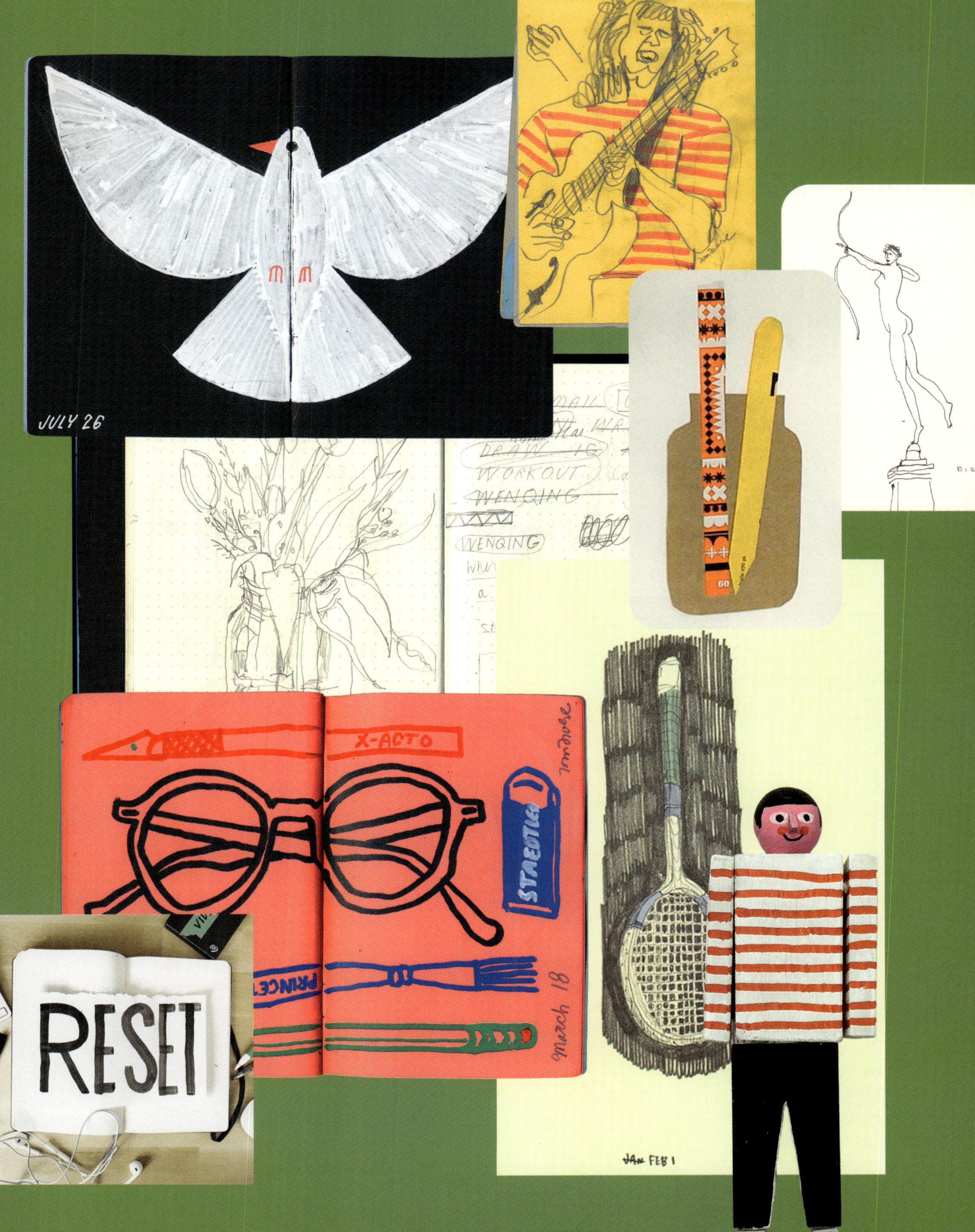

JULY 26
WORKOUT
WENQING
WENQING
X-ACTO
STAEDTLER
March 18
RESET
FEB 1

Do a Trial Run. When setting the schedule for your Daily Drawing Plan (see *chapter 3*), you get to set the duration—how long you intend to commit to showing up. While I usually recommend thirty days as a minimum, you can always try a shorter stint to see how you like it. "Try before you buy" exists for a reason. Set a shorter duration—long enough to get a feel for it, but short enough to calm your FOMO.

Commit to Non-commitment! If you simply must try all the things, then give yourself permission to try all the things—with one condition: Give it a purpose and some structure. In your Daily Drawing Plan, make your purpose about trying different things. For example, it could be trying a new drawing or media type every day for thirty days, and then write those out as daily prompts for your source.

Know What You Want—and Do It. Perhaps consistency is not your thing. The worst thing would be to dread your daily drawing sessions, or feel stuck or bored with them. Daily drawing is about staying inspired. If constant change is what really fires you up, lean into it. The catch is that you might not truly know this about yourself unless you try commitment for a time. In a twisted sort of way, this might be the mind trick to getting you to commit!

Rhythms and Seasons

Some people run every single day. Others run three days a week. Over time, runners figure out a schedule that works for them. What are their goals? How much time do they have? What can their body sustain? Likewise, in drawing, we all have to find a schedule that works best for us.

Now, I get it. This whole book is about starting a lifelong **Daily** Drawing Practice. While daily is the ideal, it's not necessarily going to be your ideal today.

Currently, I am busy writing this book, among my other roles and responsibilities as an illustrator, educator, podcaster, husband, father, and so on. I have to confess, my Daily Drawing Practice has taken a back seat lately, and I feel a little guilty about it. Does this make me a hypocrite? Of course not. The reality is that there are seasons in life when we must shift our focus for a while.

By consistently showing up to my Daily Drawing Practice over time, it's become an ingrained habit. The advantage of a habit is that, compared to starting from zero, it's easier to get back into after taking a break. It's a bit like skiing for me—I try to go as much as I can when it's winter, and the more I go, the stronger I get. But when the season ends, I have no choice but to put my gear away and do other things for a while. Thanks to muscle memory, I'm always glad to find that I'm able to pick back up from where I left off the last season.

Like any habit, keeping a Daily Drawing Practice is like building muscle memory. Drawing is important to you, so do it as frequently as you can, as consistently as you can, for as long as you can keep the streak going. Then, when a season seems to be wrapping up, listen to your intuitions.

Perhaps you're wondering if such "intuitions" are just resistance or laziness. Knowing the difference is simple: It's time to take a break from your Daily Drawing Practice when you stop enjoying it. If you find that, most days, it just feels like a chore, it's time to rest, recover, and reflect on how to find your way back into it. Ultimately, drawing should give you joy!

No Pain, No Gain

Don't get me wrong—I'm not letting you off easy. There's no question that perseverance is required to keep a lifelong Daily Drawing Practice. Most people don't do it, even though they want to—it's not always easy. Creative fitness requires that you work those creative muscles, and sometimes those muscles are going to burn!

Above all, keep your eyes on your purpose. What do you want and need as an artist, and how can your drawing practice help you achieve it? Whether you're going through a funk or a frenzy, knowing what you're aiming at and keeping your eyes on it will help you keep pushing forward with purpose and joy.

TAKE THE "SHOWING UP" PLEDGE!

I, the undersigned, pledge to show up to draw and share as planned, no matter what (and not to worry about it if I can't sometimes), and to prioritize joy and growth over everything else. And if I'm not having a good time, I'll take a break, but I won't give up forever. Because Drawing is Important!

SIGN HERE

SIGNATURE

DATE

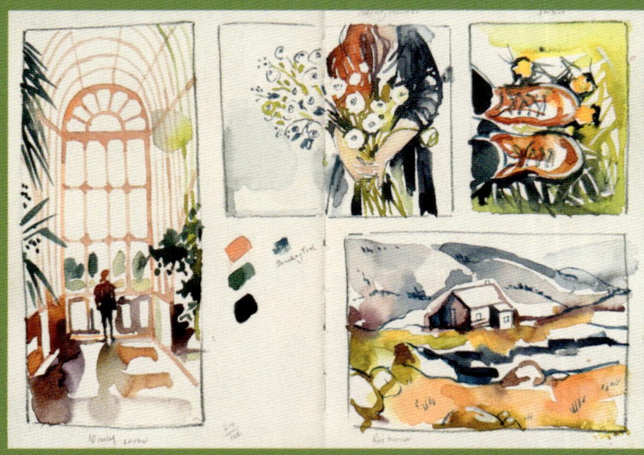

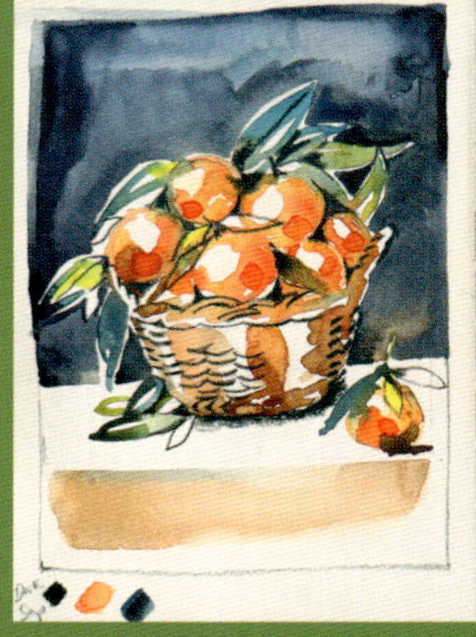

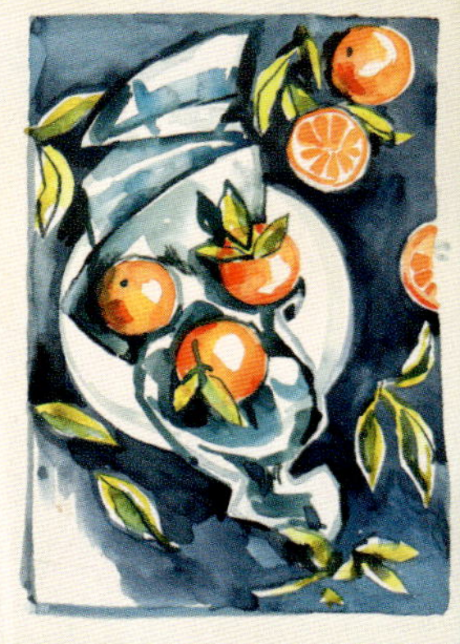

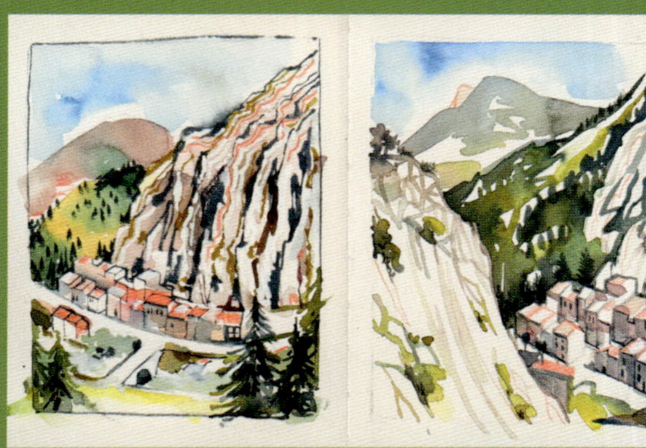

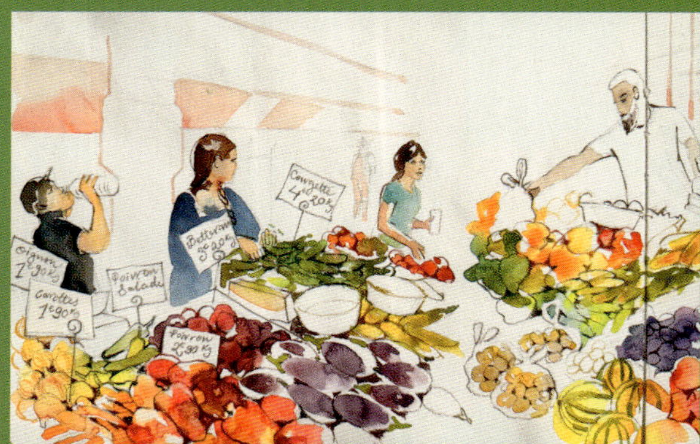

DAILY DRAWING PRACTICE SPOTLIGHT

Ohn Mar Win

artwithohnmarwin.com

Ohn Mar Win is an illustrator, designer, teacher, and author based in England. She has sixty-five-plus sketchbooks serving as a record of her creative journey (of the last ten years) as a self-taught, highly successful commercial watercolorist. She didn't have a website, a style, social media, or even sketchbooks until 2015. All she had was a mission statement that she wrote for herself: "I use my creativity and intuition to support and inspire myself and then help others do the same."

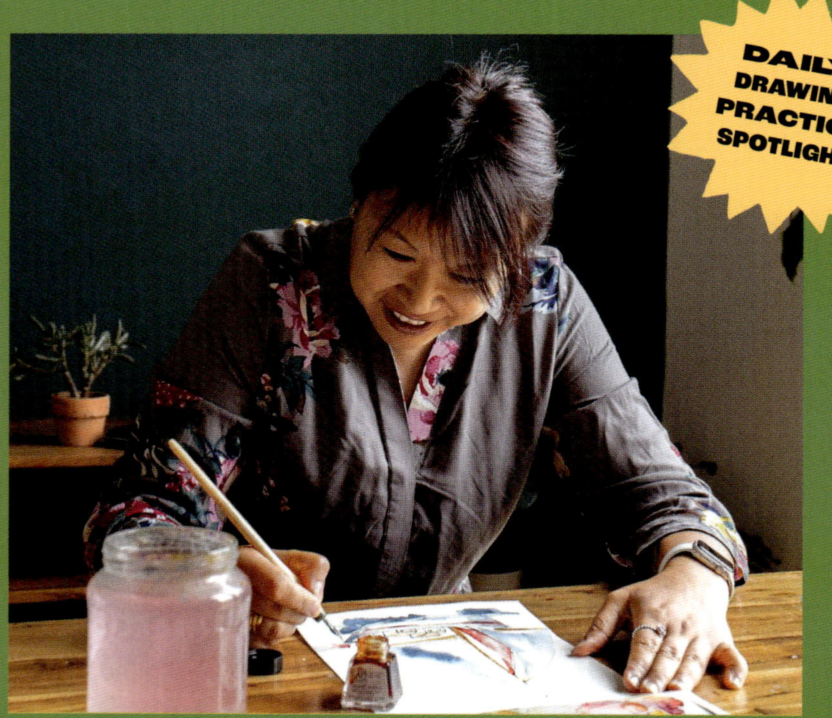

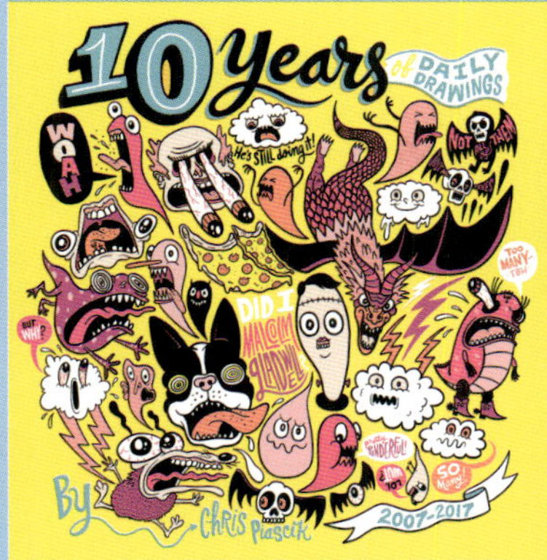

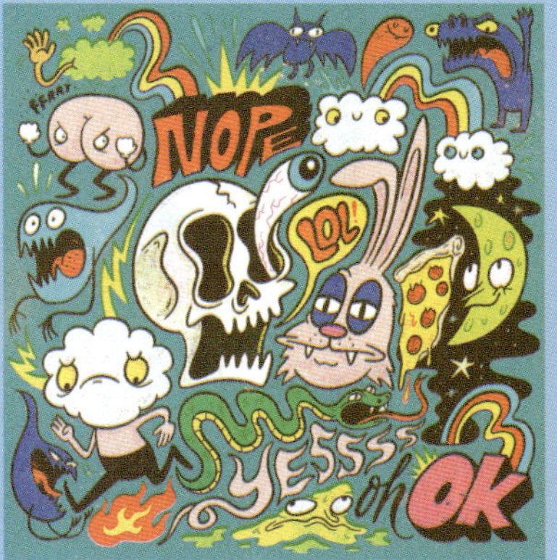

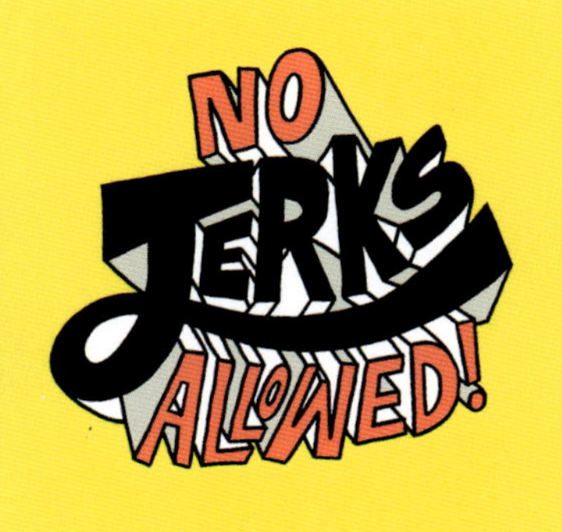

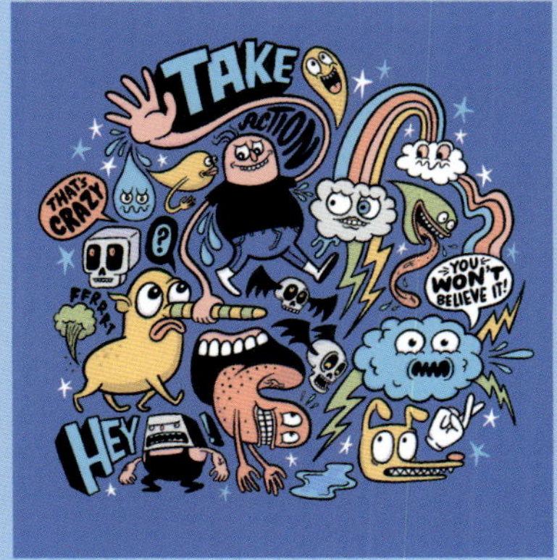

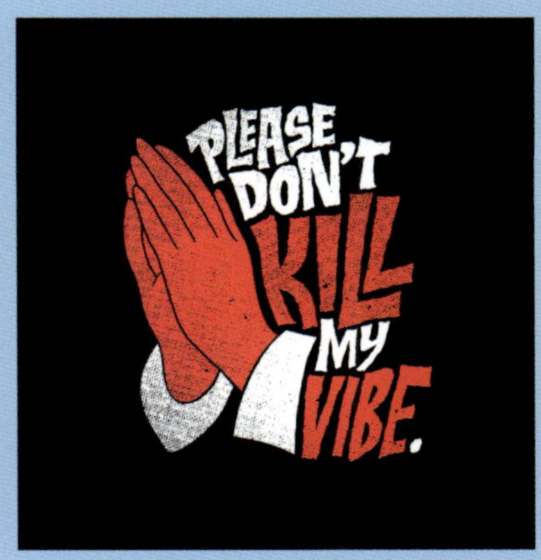

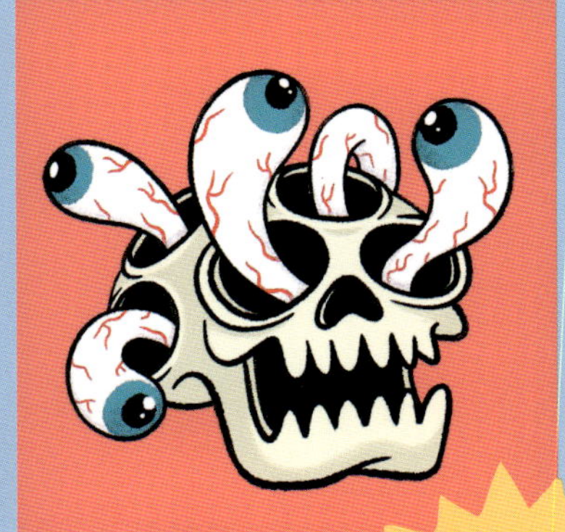

DAILY DRAWING PRACTICE SPOTLIGHT

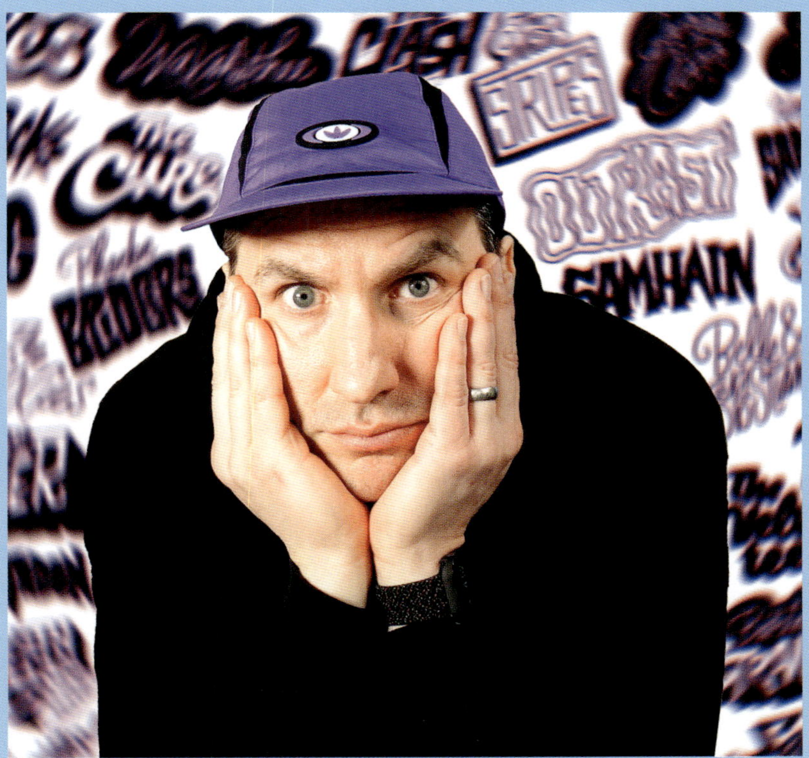

Chris Piascik

chrispiascik.com

Chris Piascik is an American illustrator and lettering artist from Connecticut. He has been doing daily drawings for over a decade and a half, which might make his one of the longest-running Daily Practices out there today. While his massive archive of work no longer lives online, he has created multiple printed books of his collections (a fantastic way to leverage new creative opportunities from your daily drawings). He continues to share his love of drawing to his 115k+ subscribers on YouTube.

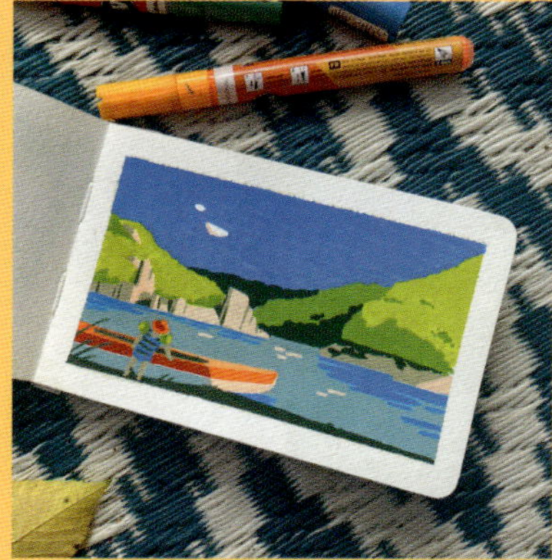
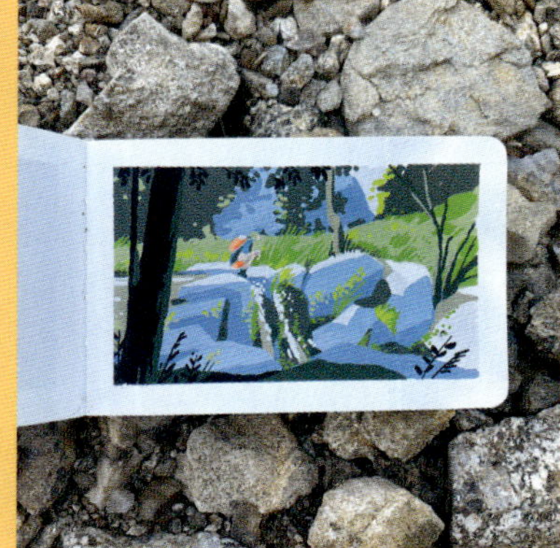
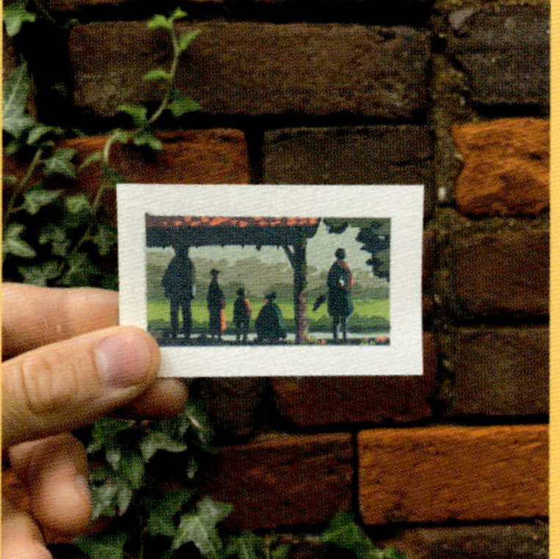
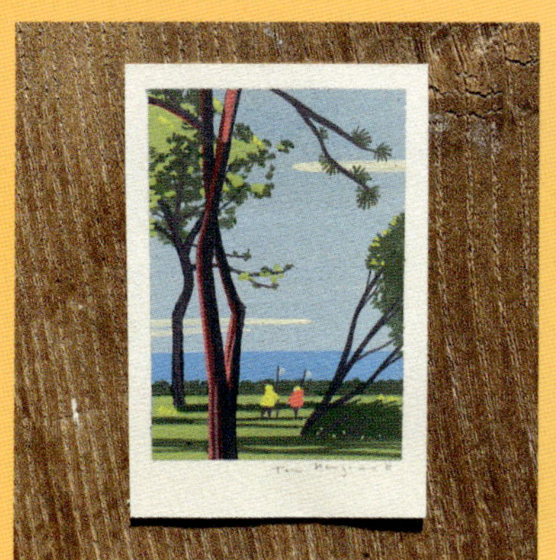
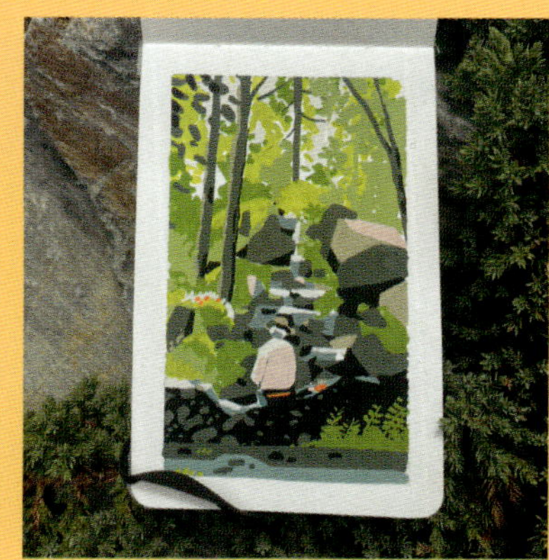
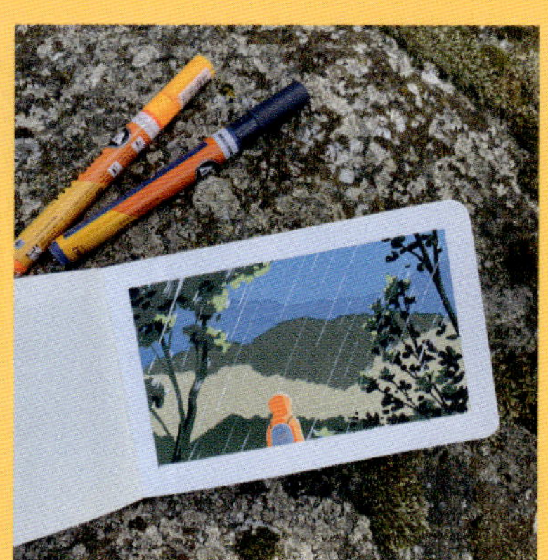

DAILY DRAWING PRACTICE SPOTLIGHT

Tom Haugomat

@tomhaugomat
Tom Haugomat is a world-renowned illustrator and animation director living in Paris, France. He's made work in publishing, advertising, and editorial for an impressive list of clients around the world. He regularly shares images from his sketchbook on his Instagram feed, peppered in between his more refined gallery work and client projects.

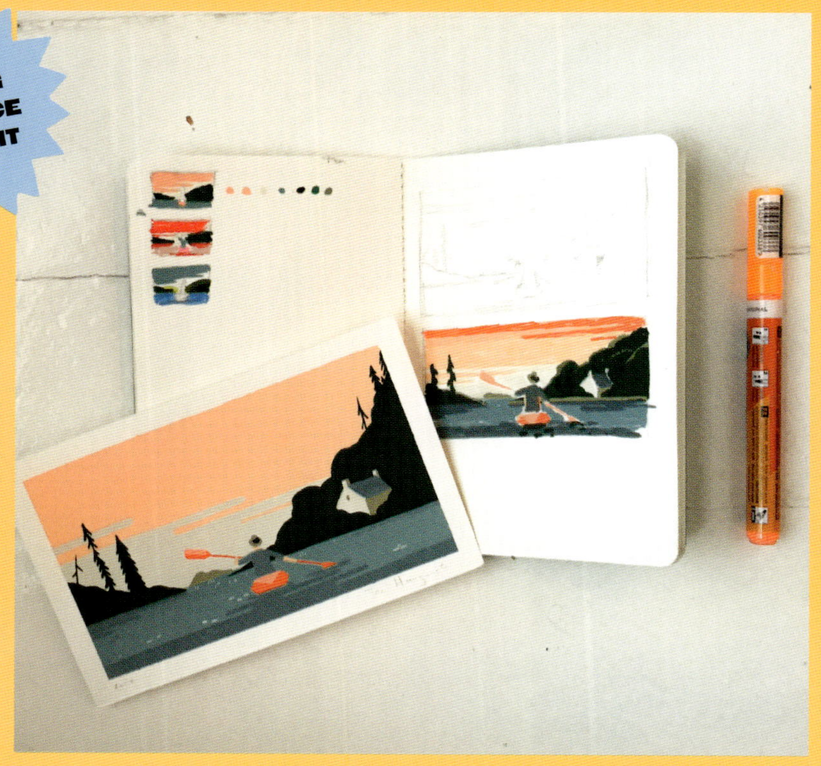

ACKNOWLEDGMENTS

For such a solitary endeavor, writing a book sure involves a lot of people! And while I'm the one doing the most work, it also requires the patience and contributions of those around me. Thank you to my wife, Amanda, for giving me space to write this book, in all the steps and years it took to get me here. And thanks for your unwavering support and love along the way. Thank you to my girls, Nina and Marie. You are my favorite daily projects!

Of course, I'm grateful to my editor, Jonathan Simcosky, who patiently coached me through this project—and one failed attempt previously—and who ultimately made me a published writer. Thank you for giving me a chance, and then giving me another one.

Thanks also to book designer Jolin Masson for your beautiful work (and for enduring my countless revisions), and to our art director, Kelly Desabrais—and to everyone else at Rockport who helped usher this book into the world.

Thank you to the artists and students who contributed their images for the spotlights and examples in this book. Thanks not only for letting me share your images but also for taking the time to dig them up, and for the inspiration you've provided over the years, from the very early days of art blogging all the way to now. I hope you all feel the love!

I've had the privilege of making pictures for books written by other authors. Now I am the author of my own book. (I'm actually getting weepy as this fact sinks in!) When my friend Rob's mom gave me a copy of *Drawing From the Right Side of the Brain* (shout-out to Mrs. Stehlik!), perhaps she saw a spark in me that I wasn't able to see in myself. But at that time, I would never have even dreamed of becoming an illustrator or especially writing a book—not in a million years.

Thanks of course to my mom and dad (memory eternal!). Dad, thank you for being so supportive of my creative career, from the day I quit my first career to go to art school, all the way to our last time together in 2009.

There are many I'm sure I've left out that deserve to be mentioned here. If this is you, please forgive me—but also, thank you!

Finally, I'm grateful to God for his many blessings, including the opportunity to share my passion for drawing with the world in this way.

—TF

ABOUT THE AUTHOR

Tom Froese is an award-winning illustrator, teacher, podcaster—and now, writer! His illustrations have been featured by clients around the world, including Airbnb, Yahoo!, and Canadian Tire. As a Top Teacher on Skillshare, Tom has helped over 120,000 students build confidence in their creative work through approachable, concept-driven classes. He believes that daily drawing is the most powerful tool for creative growth, and encourages artists to embrace imperfection and play in their own practice. Tom lives in British Columbia, Canada, with his wife and two kids, where he draws, teaches, and podcasts from his backyard studio.

You can find out more about his work and classes at tomfroese.com or follow him at @mrtomfroese.

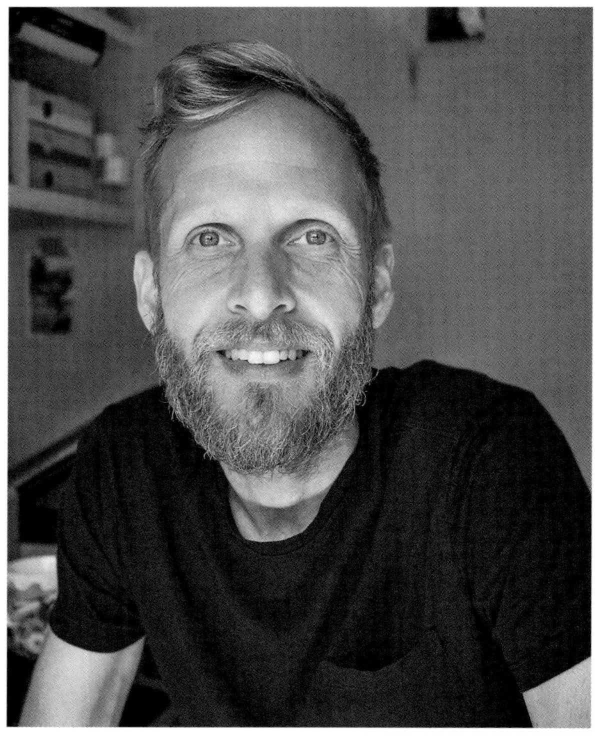

INDEX